To:

_____

From:

_____

Date:

_____

© 2010 Summerside Press™
Minneapolis 55438
www.summersidepress.com

Faith: Promises to Inspire the Heart
A *Pocket Inspirations* Book

ISBN 978-1-935416-95-1

Compiled by Barbara Farmer
Designed by Jeff and Lisa Franke

*Summerside Press™ is an inspirational publisher offering fresh,
irresistible books to uplift the heart and engage the mind.*

Printed in USA.

Faith

Promises to Inspire the Heart

Pi Pocket
INSPIRATIONS

summerside
PRESS

I Believe

Faith allows us to continually delight in life
since we have placed our needs in God's hands.

JANET WEAVER SMITH

I believe in the sun even if it isn't shining.
I believe in love even when I am alone.
I believe in God even when He is silent.

Faith is not shelter against difficulties,
but belief in the face of all contradictions.

PAUL TOURNIER

If it can be verified, we don't need faith....
Faith is for that which lies on the other side of reason.
Faith is what makes life bearable, with all its
tragedies and ambiguities and sudden, startling joys.

MADELEINE L'ENGLE

To believe in God starts with a conclusion about Him, develops into confidence in Him, and then matures into a conversation with Him.

STUART BRISCOE

Pure gold put in the fire comes out of it proved pure; genuine faith put through this suffering comes out proved genuine.... It's your faith, not your gold, that God will have on display as evidence of his victory.

1 PETER 1:6–7 MSG

I am convinced beyond a shadow of any doubt that the most valuable pursuit we can embark upon is to know God.

KAY ARTHUR

Faith is not belief without proof, but trust without reservations.

ELTON TRUEBLOOD

For Himself

Although it be good to think upon
the kindness of God, and to love Him and
worship Him for it; yet it is far better
to gaze upon the pure essence of Him and to
love Him and worship Him for Himself.

We desire many things,
and God offers us only one thing.
He can offer us only one thing—Himself.
He has nothing else to give.
There is nothing else to give.

PETER KREEFT

The reason for loving God is God Himself,
and the measure in which we should love Him
is to love Him without measure.

BERNARD OF CLAIRVAUX

There is an essential connection between
experiencing God, loving God, and trusting God.
You will trust God only as much as you love Him,
and you will love Him to the extent you have
touched Him, rather that He has touched you.

BRENNAN MANNING

You alone are the LORD.
You made the heavens...,
the earth and all that is on it,
the seas and all that is in them.
You give life to everything, and
the multitudes of heaven worship you.

NEHEMIAH 9:6 NIV

*It is in silence that God is known, and
through mysteries that He declares Himself.*

ROBERT H. BENSON

Faith Shines Through

As a countenance is made beautiful by
the soul's shining through it, so the world is
beautiful by the shining through it of God.

FREDRICH HEINRICH

*I see Heaven's glories shine,
and faith shines equal,
arming me from fear.*

EMILY BRONTË

Our feelings do not affect God's facts.
They may blow up, like clouds, and cover
the eternal things that we do most truly believe.
We may not see the shining of the promises—
but they still shine!

AMY CARMICHAEL

So keep a firm grip on the faith....
It won't be long before this generous God
who has great plans for us in Christ...will have you
put together and on your feet for good.

1 PETER 5:9–10 MSG

Begin today! No matter how feeble the light,
let it shine as best it may. The world may need
just that quality of light which you have.

HENRY C. BLINN

One taper lights a thousand,
Yet shines as it has shone;
And the humblest light may kindle
A brighter than its own.

HEZEKIAH BUTTERWORTH

You are a child of your heavenly Father.
Confide in Him. Your faith in His love and power
can never be bold enough.

BASILEA SCHLINK

This is my Father's world;
He shines in all that's fair.
In the rustling grass I hear Him pass;
He speaks to me everywhere.

MALTBIE D. BABCOCK

Providing All Our Needs

Each of us may be sure that if God sends us
on stony paths He will provide us with strong shoes,
and He will not send us out on any journey
for which He does not equip us well.

ALEXANDER MACLAREN

God provides resting places as well as
working places. Rest, then, and be thankful
when He brings you, wearied, to a wayside well.

L. B. COWMAN

Your ears shall hear a word behind you, saying,
"This is the way, walk in it," whenever you turn
to the right hand or whenever you turn to the left.

ISAIAH 30:21 NKJV

Where there is faith, there is love.
Where there is love, there is peace.
Where there is peace, there is God.
Where there is God, there is no need.

God cares for the world He created, from
the rising of a nation to the falling of the sparrow.
Everything in the world lies under the watchful
gaze of His providential eyes, from the numbering
of the days of our life to the numbering of the
hairs on our head. When we look at the world
from that perspective, it produces within us
a response of reverence.

KEN GIRE

If you have a special need today,
focus your full attention on the goodness
and greatness of your Father rather than
on the size of your need. Your need is
so small compared to His ability to meet it.

A new path lies before us;
we're not sure where it leads;
But God goes on before us,
providing all our needs.

LINDA MAURICE

Faith for the Future

God may be invisible, but He's in touch.
You may not be able to see Him, but He is in control.
And that includes you—your circumstances.
That includes what you've just lost.
That includes what you've just gained.
That includes all of life—past, present, future.

CHARLES SWINDOLL

Faith makes the uplook good,
the outlook bright, the inlook favorable,
and the future glorious.

V. RAMOND EDMAN

Joy comes from knowing God loves me
and knows who I am and where I'm going...
that my future is secure as I rest in Him.

JAMES DOBSON

Never be afraid to trust an unknown future
to an all-knowing God.

CORRIE TEN BOOM

No matter what our past may have held,
and no matter how many future days we have,
[God] stands beside us and loves us.

GARY SMALLEY AND JOHN TRENT

Great is the LORD and greatly to be praised; and His
greatness is unsearchable.... The LORD is good to all,
and His tender mercies are over all His works.

PSALM 145:3, 9 NKJV

How could I be anything but quite happy
if I believed always that all the past is forgiven,
and all the present furnished with power,
and all the future bright with hope.

JAMES SMETHAM

I don't know what the future holds,
but I know who holds the future.

E. STANLEY JONES

With Every Breath

God doesn't want us to just depend on Him as
a last resort.... He wants us to depend on Him
for every breath we take. And...that kind
of dependent life is not stifling. It's liberating!

STORMIE OMARTIAN

This is the real gift: we have been given
the breath of life, designed with a unique,
one-of-a-kind soul that exists forever—
whether we live it as a burden or a joy or with
indifference doesn't change the fact that we've
been given the gift of being now and forever.
Priceless in value, we are handcrafted by God,
who has a personal design and plan for each of us.

WENDY MOORE

We have come to know and have believed
the love which God has for us. God is love,
and the one who abides in love abides in God,
and God abides in him.

1 JOHN 4:16 NASB

There is nothing but God's grace. We walk upon it;
we breathe it; we live and die by it;
it makes the nails and axles of the universe.

ROBERT LOUIS STEVENSON

To be grateful is to recognize the Love of God
in everything He has given us—
and He has given us everything.
Every breath we draw is a gift of His love,
every moment of existence is a gift of grace.

THOMAS MERTON

On that day the LORD their God
will rescue his people,
just as a shepherd rescues his sheep.
They will sparkle in his land
like jewels in a crown.

ZECHARIAH 9:16 NLT

*God knows the rhythm of my spirit
and knows my heart thoughts.
He is as close as breathing.*

The Faith Within

No journey carries one far unless,
as it extends into the world around us,
it goes an equal distance into the world within.

LILLIAN SMITH

For the LORD searches every heart....
If you seek him, he will be found by you.

1 CHRONICLES 28:9 NIV

Within each of us there is an inner place
where the living God Himself longs to dwell,
our sacred center of belief.

Let us not set the standards of our conquest
to mean the maintenance of comfort but rather,
the development of an inner presence.

CHRISTOPHER DE VINCK

As you have received Christ Jesus the Lord,
so walk in Him, having been firmly rooted
and now being built up in Him and
established in your faith.

COLOSSIANS 2:6–7 NASB

The Lord's chief desire is to reveal Himself to you
and, in order for Him to do that, He gives you
abundant grace. The Lord gives you the experience
of enjoying His presence. He touches you,
and His touch is so delightful that, more than ever,
you are drawn inwardly to Him.

MADAME JEANNE GUYON

Our inner happiness depends not
on what we experience but on the degree of
our gratitude to God, whatever the experience.

ALBERT SCHWEITZER

Walk and talk and work and laugh with your friends,
but behind the scenes, keep up the life of
simple prayer and inward worship.

THOMAS R. KELLY

God waits for us in the
inner sanctuary of the soul.
He welcomes us there.

RICHARD J. FOSTER

Grow in Love

It is an extraordinary and beautiful thing
that God, in creation...works with the beauty
of matter; the reality of things; the discoveries of
the senses, all five of them; so that we, in turn,
may hear the grass growing; see a face
springing to life in love and laughter....
The offerings of creation...our glimpses of truth.

MADELEINE L'ENGLE

Love is a tender plant; when properly nourished,
It becomes sturdy and enduring.

H. B. BROWN

In the deepest heart of every human
God planted a longing for Himself,
as He is: a God of love.

EUGENIA PRICE

*I believe that life is given us
so we may grow in love.*

HELEN KELLER

God is the sunshine that warms us,
the rain that melts the frost and
waters the young plants.
The presence of God is a climate of
strong and bracing love, always there.

JOAN ARNOLD

Love allows us to live,
and through living we grow in loving.

EVELYN MANDEL

We ought always to thank God for you...
and rightly so, because your faith is growing
more and more, and the love every one of you
has for each other is increasing.

2 THESSALONIANS 1:3 NIV

Love is little deeds we show,
Love will make my spirit grow;
Grow in peace, grow in light
Love will do the thing that's right.

CHARLES DALMON

Through His Power

In difficulties, I can drink freely of God's power
and experience His touch of refreshment and blessing—
much like an invigorating early spring rain.

ANABEL GILLHAM

Should we feel at times disheartened and
discouraged, a simple movement of heart toward
God will renew our powers. Whatever He may
demand of us, He will give us at the moment
the strength and courage that we need.

FRANÇOIS FÉNELON

Look for the weak people in your life today,
and see if you can discover what makes them strong,
for then you will understand God's power.

CHRISTOPHER DE VINCK

Human love would never have the power it has
were it not rooted in an express image of God.

J. MOUROUX

This life is not all. It is an "unfinished symphony"...
with those who know that they are related to God
and have felt "the power of an endless life."

HENRY WARD BEECHER

O troubled heart, tho' thy foes unite,
let thy faith be strong and thy armor bright;
Thou shall overcome thro' His power and might,
and more than conqueror be.

FANNY CROSBY

In all these things we are more than conquerors
through him who loved us.

ROMANS 8:37 NIV

Prayer imparts the power to walk and not faint.

OSWALD CHAMBERS

In God's Hands

If we pray for anything according to the
will of God, we already have what we pray for
the moment we ask it. We do not know exactly
when it will arrive; but we...have learned to
leave this in His hands, and to live just as happily
whether the answer arrives immediately or later.

OLE HALLESBY

It is such a comfort to drop the tangles of life into
God's hands and leave them there.

L. B. COWMAN

God is able to make all grace abound to you,
so that in all things at all times, having all that
you need, you will abound in every good work.

2 CORINTHIANS 9:8 NIV

The devout soul is always safe in every state, if it
makes everything an occasion either of rising up,
or falling down into the hands of God, and
exercising faith, and trust, and resignation to Him.

WILLIAM LAW

God writes with a pen that never blots,
speaks with a tongue that never slips,
and acts with a hand that never fails.

HUBERT VAN ZELLER

Nothing happens to us that God
hasn't already handled before.

JANETTE OKE

*Until we meet again, may God
hold you in the palm of His hand.*

Beyond Expectations

One of the most wonderful things about
knowing God is that there's always so much
more to know, so much more to discover.
Just when we least expect it, He intrudes
into our neat and tidy notions about
who He is and how He works.

JONI EARECKSON TADA

Keep close to your rule, the Word of God,
and to your guide, the Spirit of God,
and never be afraid of expecting too much.

JOHN WESLEY

I asked God for all things that I might enjoy life.
He gave me life that I might enjoy all things.

*Faith expects from God
what is beyond all expectations.*

What have we to expect? Anything.
What have we to hope for? Everything.
What have we to fear? Nothing.

EDWARD B. PUSEY

God wants us to approach life,
full of expectancy that God is going to
be at work in every situation as we
release our faith in Him.

COLIN URQUHART

You pay God a compliment
by asking great things of Him.

TERESA OF AVILA

Divine guidance is promised to us,
and our faith must therefore
confidently look for and expect it.

HANNAH WHITALL SMITH

Truly, O God of Israel, our Savior,
you work in mysterious ways.

ISAIAH 45:15 NLT

God Will Make a Way

Part of our job is simply to be...always attentive to
what we are doing and what is going on inside us,
at the same time we listen and pay attention
to the people and events around us. Part of our job
is to expect that, if we are attentive and willing,
God will "give us prayer," will give us the things
we need, "our daily bread," to heal and grow in love.

ROBERTA BONDI

If we just give God the little that we have,
we can trust Him to make it go around.

GLORIA GAITHER

Know that wisdom is such to your soul;
if you find it, you will find a future,
and your hope will not be cut off.

PROVERBS 24:14 NRSV

Peace *with* God brings the peace *of* God.
It is a peace that settles our nerves, fills our mind,
floods our spirit, and in the midst of the uproar
around us, gives us the assurance
that everything is all right.

BOB MUMFORD

None of us knows what the next change is going to be,
what unexpected opportunity is just around the corner,
waiting to change all the tenor of our lives.

KATHLEEN NORRIS

God is with us, and His power is around us.

CHARLES H. SPURGEON

And the peace of God, which transcends all
understanding, will guard your hearts
and your minds in Christ Jesus.

PHILIPPIANS 4:7 NIV

Always There

God has put into each of our lives a void
that cannot be filled by the world.
We may leave God or put Him on hold,
but He is always there, patiently waiting
for us...to turn back to Him.

EMILIE BARNES

And I am convinced that nothing can ever separate
us from God's love. Neither death nor life,
neither angels nor demons, neither our fears for today
nor our worries about tomorrow.

ROMANS 8:38 NLT

We are always in the presence of God....
There is never a nonsacred moment!
His presence never diminishes. Our awareness
of His presence may falter, but the reality
of His presence never changes.

MAX LUCADO

Eating lunch with a friend. Trying to do
a decent day's work. Hearing the rain patter
against the window. There is no event so
commonplace but that God is present within it,
always hiddenly, always leaving you room to
recognize Him or not to recognize Him,
but all the more fascinatingly because of that,
all the more compellingly and hauntingly.

FREDERICK BUECHNER

Fear not tomorrow, God is already there.

Even when we cannot see the why and
wherefore of God's dealings, we know that
there is love in and behind them,
and so we can rejoice always.

J. I. PACKER

God's hand is always there; once you grasp it
you'll never want to let it go.

Proven Promises

God has not promised skies always blue,
flower-strewn pathways all our lives through;
God has not promised sun without rain,
joy without sorrow, peace without pain.
But God has promised strength for the day,
rest for the labor, light for the way,
grace for the trials, help from above,
unfailing sympathy, undying love.

ANNIE JOHNSON FLINT

The Lord doesn't always remove the sources of stress
in our lives...but He's always there and cares for us.
We can feel His arms around us on the darkest night.

JAMES DOBSON

We may...depend upon God's promises,
for...He will be as good as His word.
He is so kind that He cannot deceive us,
so true that He cannot break His promise.

MATTHEW HENRY

All that we have and are is one of the unique
and never-to-be repeated ways God has chosen
to express Himself in space and time.
Each of us, made in His image and likeness,
is yet another promise He has made to the universe
that He will continue to love it and care for it.

BRENNAN MANNING

The hope we have in Christ is an absolute certainty.
We can be sure that the place Christ is preparing
for us will be ready when we arrive, because
with Him nothing is left to chance.
Everything He promised He will deliver.

BILLY GRAHAM

*As for God, His way is perfect;
the word of the LORD is proven;
He is a shield to all who trust in Him.*

2 SAMUEL 22:31 NKJV

Continual Delight

Do you know why the mighty God of the
universe chooses to answer prayer? It is because
His children ask. God delights in our asking.
He is pleased at our asking. His heart
is warmed by our asking.

RICHARD J. FOSTER

I will answer them before they even call to Me.
While they are still talking about their needs,
I will go ahead and answer their prayers!

ISAIAH 65:24 NLT

God loves us, not because we are lovable
but because He is love, not because
He needs to receive but because
He delights to give.

C. S. LEWIS

All [God's] glory and beauty come from within,
and there He delights to dwell. His visits
there are frequent, His conversation sweet,
His comforts refreshing, His peace
passing all understanding.

THOMAS À KEMPIS

Joy is perfect acquiesce in God's will
because the soul delights itself in God Himself.

H. W. WEBB-PEPLOE

We have a Father in heaven who is almighty, who
loves His children as He loves His only-begotten Son,
and whose very joy and delight it is to...help them
at all times and under all circumstances.

GEORGE MUELLER

*Faith allows us to continually delight in life
since we have placed our needs in God's hands.*

JANET L. WEAVER SMITH

Live Fully

Live fully each moment of today.
Trust God to let you work through it.
He will give you all you need.
Don't skip over the painful...moment—
even it has its important and rightful place.

You will find as you look back upon your life,
that the moments when you have really lived
are the moments when you have
done things in the spirit of love.

HENRY DRUMMOND

Live your life while you have it.
Life is a splendid gift—
there is nothing small about it.

FLORENCE NIGHTINGALE

Go after God, who piles on all the riches
we could ever manage.

1 TIMOTHY 6:17 MSG

Into all our lives, in many simple, familiar,
homely ways, God infuses this element of joy
from the surprises of life, which unexpectedly
brighten our days, and fill our eyes with light.

SAMUEL LONGFELLOW

Don't just get older, get better. Live realistically.
Give generously. Adapt willingly.
Trust fearlessly. Rejoice daily.

CHARLES SWINDOLL

Each day is a little life. Live it to its fullest.

Be such a person, and live such a life,
that if every one were such as you,
and every life a life such as yours,
this earth would be God's paradise.

PHILLIPS BROOKS

Praise Follows Trust

They that trust the Lord
find many things to praise Him for.
Praise follows trust.

LILY MAY GOULD

There is an activity of the spirit, silent, unseen,
which must be the dynamic of any form of truly
creative, fruitful trust. When we commit a
predicament, a possibility, a person to God in
genuine confidence, we do not merely step aside
and tap our foot until God comes through.
We remain involved. We remain in
contact with God in gratitude and praise.

EUGENIA PRICE

I will praise you forever, O God,
for what you have done.
I will trust in your good name
in the presence of your faithful people.

PSALM 52:9 NLT

God came to us because God wanted to join us
on the road, to listen to our story, and to help us
realize that we are not walking in circles but
moving toward the house of peace and joy....
The God of love who gave us life sent us [the] only
Son to be with us at all times and in all places,
so that we never have to feel lost in our struggles
but always can trust that God walks with us.

HENRI J. M. NOUWEN

Praise Him for all that is past.
Trust Him for all that is to come.

JOSEPH HART

Trust God where you cannot trace Him.
Do not try to penetrate the cloud He brings
over you; rather look to the bow that is on it.
The mystery is God's; the promise is yours.

JOHN MACDUFF

Believing and Doing

You can no more show me your works apart from your faith than I can show you my faith apart from my works. Faith and works, works and faith, fit together hand in glove.

JAMES 2:18 MSG

Strive for excellence. Don't try to get by with less. Don't slough off. Don't ignore your responsibilities. One of the best ways to make your faith ring true... is by your commitment to excellence and honesty.

KEN DAVIS

A Christian should always remember that the value of his or her good works is not based on their number and excellence, but on the love of God which prompts one to do these things.

JUAN DE LA CRUZ

Work is my primary expression of faith
and praise to God, my service to the neighbors
He commands me to love, my responsible
stewardship of His gifts, and the most efficient
means of communicating the good news
of salvation to the world.

JUDITH ALLEN SHELLY

Great works do not always lie our way,
but every moment we may do little ones
excellently, that is, with great love.

FRANCIS DE SALES

All work that is worth anything is done in faith.

ALBERT SCHWEITZER

Eternity in Our Hearts

Let Jesus be in your heart,
Eternity in your spirit,
The world under your feet,
The will of God in your actions.
And let the love of God shine forth from you.

CATHERINE OF GENOA

We do not look at the things which are seen,
but at the things which are not seen.
For the things which are seen are temporary,
but the things which are not seen are eternal.

2 CORINTHIANS 4:18 NKJV

I thank You, O Lord, that You have so set
eternity within my heart that no earthly thing
can ever satisfy me wholly.

JOHN BAILLIE

Deep within us all there is an amazing inner sanctuary of the soul, a holy place...to which we may continuously return. Eternity is at our hearts, pressing upon our time-torn lives, warming us... calling us home unto Itself. Yielding to these persuasions...utterly and completely, to the Light within, is the beginning of true life.

THOMAS R. KELLY

Live near to God, and so all things will appear to you little in comparison with eternal realities.

ROBERT MURRAY M'CHEYNE

We have been in God's thought from all eternity, and in His creative love, His attention never leaves us.

MICHAEL QUOIST

The Light of Faith

Happy is the person who knows what to
remember of the past, what to enjoy in
the present, and what to plan for the future.

ARNOLD GLASOW

There is a past which is gone forever,
but there is a future which is still our own.

F. W. ROBERTSON

Trust the past to the mercy of God,
the present to His love, and
the future to His Providence.

AUGUSTINE

To believe in something not yet proved
and to underwrite it with our lives;
it is the only way we can leave the future open.

LILLIAN SMITH

You can never change the past. But by the grace of God, you can win the future. So remember those things which will help you forward, but forget those things which will only hold you back.

RICHARD C. WOODSOME

Forgetting what is behind and straining toward what is ahead, I press on toward the goal to win the prize for which God has called me heavenward.

PHILIPPIANS 3:13 NIV

The uncertainties of the present always give way to the enchanted possibilities of the future.

GELSEY KIRKLAND

Cease to inquire whatever the future has in store, and take as a gift whatever the day brings forth.

HORACE

The only light upon the future is faith.

THEODORE HOECKER

Tied to the Infinite

In comparison with this big world, the human heart
is only a small thing. Though the world is so large,
it is utterly unable to satisfy this tiny heart.
Our ever growing soul and its capacities can be
satisfied only in the infinite God. As water is
restless until it reaches its level, so the soul
has no peace until it rests in God.

SADHU SUNDAR SINGH

We need time to dream, time to remember,
and time to reach the infinite. Time to be.

GLADYS TABER

The Lord's loving kindnesses indeed never cease,
for His compassions never fail. They are new
every morning; great is Your faithfulness.

LAMENTATIONS 3:22–23 NASB

An infinite God can give all of Himself to each of His children. He does not distribute Himself that each may have a part, but to each one He gives all of Himself as fully as if there were no others.

A. W. TOZER

The Infinite has sowed His name in the heaven in burning stars, but on the earth He has sowed His name in tender flowers.

JEAN PAUL RICHTER

Faith is the subtle chain that binds us to the infinite.

ELIZABETH OAKES SMITH

You are in the Beloved...therefore infinitely dear to the Father, unspeakably precious to Him. You are never, not for one second, alone.

NORMAN DOWTY

A Step of Faith

Great faith isn't the ability to believe
long and far into the misty future.
It's simply taking God at His word
and taking the next step.

JONI EARECKSON TADA

For the very structures of earth are God's;
He has laid out His operations on a firm foundation.
He protectively cares for His faithful friends,
step by step.

1 SAMUEL 2:8–9 MSG

*I would rather walk with God in the dark
than go alone in the light.*

MARY GARDINER BRAINARD

I said to the man who stood at the gate of the year,
I said to a man who stood at the gate of the year,
"Give me a light that I may tread safely into
the unknown," And he replied, "Go out into the
darkness and put your hand in the hand of God.
That shall be to you better than a light
and safer than a known way."

M. LOUISE HASKINS

Hope does not necessarily take the form of
excessive confidence; rather, it involves
the simple willingness to take the next step.

STANLEY HAUERWAS

When you come to the edge of all the light you
have, and must take a step into the darkness of the
unknown, believe that one of two things will happen.
Either there will be something solid for you to
stand on—or you will be taught how to fly.

PATRICK OVERTON

Belonging to Him

If we really fully belong to God, then we must
be at His disposal and we must trust in Him.
We must never be preoccupied with the future.
There is no reason to be. God is there.

MOTHER TERESA

Those who know God have great contentment in God.
There is no peace like the peace of those whose
minds are possessed with full assurance that they
have known God, and God has known them, and that
this relationship guarantees God's favor to them
in life, through death and on forever.

J. I. PACKER

I have held many things in my hands and I have
lost them all; but whatever I have placed
in God's hands, that I still possess.

MARTIN LUTHER

Peace of conscience, liberty of heart,
the sweetness of abandoning ourselves in the
hands of God, the joy of always seeing the light
grow in our hearts, finally, freedom from the fears
and insatiable desires of the times, multiply a
hundredfold the happiness which the true
children of God possess in the midst
of their crosses, if they are faithful.

FRANÇOIS FÉNELON

Our God is so wonderfully good, and lovely,
and blessed in every way that the mere fact
of belonging to Him is enough for
an untellable fullness of joy!

HANNAH WHITALL SMITH

*Whom have I in heaven but You? And there
is none upon earth that I desire besides You.*

PSALM 73:25 NKJV

A Better Thing

If God, like a father, denies us what we want now,
it is in order to give us some far better thing later on.
The will of God, we can rest assured,
is invariably a better thing.

ELISABETH ELLIOT

God's kingdom isn't a matter of what you
put in your stomach, for goodness' sake.
It's what God does with your life as he sets it right,
puts it together, and completes it with joy.

ROMANS 14:17 MSG

The Creator thinks enough of you
to have sent Someone very special
so that you might have life—
abundantly, joyfully,
completely, and victoriously.

Give your heart's best treasure,
And the more you spend
From your little store,
With a double bounty,
God will give you more.

ADELAIDE ANN PROCTER

The God of the universe—the One who
created everything and holds it all in His hands—
created each of us in His image, to bear His likeness,
His imprint. It is only when Christ dwells within
our hearts, radiating the pure light of His love
through our humanity that we discover who we are
and what we were intended to be. There is no other
joy that reaches as deep or as wide or as high—
there is no other joy that is more complete.

WENDY MOORE

*Love is a circle...the more you give,
the more comes around.*

Enduring Faith

I abide in Christ and in doing so I find rest,
and the peace of God which passes all
understanding fills my heart and life.

JOHN HUNTER

Remain in me, and I will remain in you.
For a branch cannot produce fruit
if it is severed from the vine, and you
cannot be fruitful unless you remain in me.

JOHN 15:4 NLT

His justice is full and complete,
His mercy to us has no end;
the clouds are a path for His feet,
He comes on the wings of the wind.

CHRISTOPHER IDLE

Faith is what makes life bearable,
with all its tragedies and ambiguities
and sudden, startling joys.

MADELEINE L'ENGLE

A pure spirit is a sparkling stream,
full of clear thought, and continually
renewed in the crystal river of God's love.

JANET L. WEAVER SMITH

If one is joyful, it means that one is faithfully
living for God, and that nothing else counts; and
if one gives joy to others one is doing God's work.
With joy without and joy within, all is well.

JANET ERSKINE STUART

You have granted me life and loving kindness;
and *Your* care has preserved my spirit.

JOB 10:12 NASB

The Eyes of My Heart

Faith is the ability to let your light shine
even after your fuse is blown.
Faith is seeing light with the eyes of your heart,
when the eyes of your body see only darkness ahead.

BARBARA JOHNSON

If you have never heard the mountains singing,
or seen the trees of the field clapping their hands,
do not think because of that they don't.
Ask God to open your ears so you may hear it,
and your eyes so you may see it, because,
though few people ever know it,
they do, my friend, they do.

MCCANDLISH PHILLIPS

Open my eyes so I can see
what you show me of your miracle-wonders.

PSALM 119:18 MSG

Half the joy of life is in little things taken on the run.
Let us run if we must—even the sands do that—
but let us keep our hearts young and our eyes open
that nothing worth our while shall escape us.
And everything is worth its while
if we only grasp it and its significance.

VICTOR CHERBULIEZ

Open my eyes that I may see
Glimpses of truth Thou hast for me.
Place in my hands the wonderful key
That shall unclasp and set me free.

CLARA H. SCOTT

It is only with the heart that one can see rightly.
What is essential is invisible to the eye.

ANTOINE DE SAINT-EXUPÉRY

Nothing Is Impossible

Faith is the first factor in a life devoted to service.
Without faith, nothing is possible.
With it, nothing is impossible.

MARY MCLEOD BETHUNE

Christian hope, unlike most other kinds of hope,
is not mere optimism. It's not even a matter of
thinking positively: "Cheer up. Things will
work out." Christian hope is applied faith.
If God Himself is here with us in His Holy Spirit,
then all things are possible.

BRUCE LARSON

Only those who see the invisible
can do the impossible.

Know therefore that the Lord your God is God,
the faithful God who maintains covenant loyalty
with those who love him and keep
his commandments, to a thousand generations.

DEUTERONOMY 7:9 NRSV

If we will make use of prayer to call down upon ourselves and others those things which will glorify the name of God, then...we shall see such answers to prayer as we had never thought were possible.

OLE HALLESBY

If our faith is to have a firm foundation we must be convinced beyond any possible doubt that God is altogether worthy of our trust.

A. W. TOZER

The mind determines what's possible.
The soul surpasses it.

PILAR COOLINTA

Your steadfast love, O Lord,
extends to the heavens,
your faithfulness to the clouds.

PSALM 36:5 NRSV

Firm Foundation

God, your Father, is greater than your problems.
He can solve them all. Put your trust in
Him and you will experience this.

BASILEA SCHLINK

How firm a foundation, ye saints of the Lord,
Is laid for your faith in His excellent Word!
What more can He say than to you He hath said,
You, who unto Jesus for refuge have fled?...
Fear not, I am with thee, O be not dismayed,
For I am thy God and will still give thee aid;
I'll strengthen and help thee, and cause thee to stand
Upheld by My righteous, omnipotent hand.

R. KEEN

God's truth stands firm like a
foundation stone with this inscription:
"The Lord knows those who are his."

2 TIMOTHY 2:19 NLT

Faith in God is not blind. It is based on
His character and His promises.

Infinite and yet personal, personal and yet infinite,
God may be trusted because He is the True One.
He is true, He acts truly, and He speaks truly....
God's truthfulness is therefore foundational
for His trustworthiness.

OS GUINNESS

*Confidence is not based on wishful thinking,
but in knowing that God is in control.*

Everything in the heavens and on earth
is yours, O LORD.... Power and might
are in your hand, and at your discretion
people are made great and given strength.

1 CHRONICLES 29:11–12 NLT

The Gift of Faith

Lord...give me the gift of faith....
Teach me to live this moment only,
looking neither to the past with regret,
nor the future with apprehension.
Let love be my aim and my life a prayer.

ROSEANN ALEXANDER-ISHAM

God will do this, for he is faithful to do
what he says, and he has invited you into
partnership with his Son, Jesus Christ our Lord.

1 CORINTHIANS 1:9 NLT

Faith is given a glimpse of *something*,
however dimly. Men and women of faith know
they are strangers and exiles on the earth
because somehow and somewhere along the line
they have been given a glimpse of home.

FREDERICK BUECHNER

When faith is strong, troubles become trifles.
There can be comfort in sorrow because
in the midst of mourning, God gives a song.

BILLY GRAHAM

I took an inventory and looked into my little bag
to see what I had left over. I had one jewel
left in the bag, the brightest jewel of all.
I had the gift of faith.

LOLA FALANA

Trust in your Redeemer's strength...exercise what
faith you have, and by and by He shall rise
upon you with healing beneath His wings.
Go from faith to faith and you shall
receive blessing upon blessing.

CHARLES H. SPURGEON

*We have been greatly encouraged...because
you have remained strong in your faith.*

1 THESSALONIANS 3:7 NLT

A Certain Hope

Hope is definitely not the same thing as optimism.
It is not the conviction that something will
turn out well, but the certainty that something
makes sense, regardless of how it turns out.

VÁCLAV HAVEL

I never spoke with God
nor visited in Heaven,
Yet certain am I of the spot
as if the chart were given.

EMILY DICKINSON

There will always be the unknown.
There will always be the unprovable.
But faith confronts those frontiers
with a thrilling leap. Then life becomes
vibrant with adventure!

ROBERT SCHULLER

God guides us, despite our uncertainties and our vagueness, even through our failings and mistakes.... He leads us step by step, from event to event. Only afterwards, as we look back over the way we have come and reconsider certain important moments in our lives in the light of all that has followed them, or when we survey the whole progress of our lives, do we experience the feeling of having been led without knowing it, the feeling that God has mysteriously guided us.

PAUL TOURNIER

Faith is the assurance of things hoped for, the conviction of things not seen.

HEBREWS 11:1 NRSV

Faith is a living, daring confidence in God's grace, so sure and certain that a man could stake his life on it a thousand times.

MARTIN LUTHER

Dare to Believe

Love is there for us, love so great that it does
not turn its face away from us. That Love is Jesus.
We can dare to hope and believe again.

GLORIA GAITHER

Whatever your years, there is
in every being's heart the love of wonder,
the undaunted challenges of events,
the unfailing childlike appetite for what
comes next, and the joy of the game of life.
You are as young as your hope.

DOUGLAS MACARTHUR

You are never alone. In your heart of hearts,
in the place where no two people are ever alike,
Christ is waiting for you. And what you
never dared hope for springs to life.

BROTHER ROGER OF TAIZÉ

At the very heart and foundation of all
God's dealings with us, however...mysterious
they may be, we must dare to believe in
and assert the infinite, unmerited,
and unchanging love of God.

L. B. COWMAN

Love makes burdens lighter, because you
divide them. It makes joys more intense,
because you share them. It makes you stronger,
so that you can reach out and become involved
with life in ways you dared not risk alone.

Therefore, since we have a great high priest
who has gone through the heavens,
Jesus the Son of God, let us hold
firmly to the faith we profess.

HEBREWS 4:14 NIV

*Faith in God gives your life a center from which
you can reach out and dare to love the world.*

BARBARA FARMER

In God We Trust

With God our trust can be...utterly free.
In Him are no limitations, no flaws, no weaknesses.
His judgment is perfect, His knowledge of us is
perfect, His love is perfect. God alone is trustworthy.

EUGENIA PRICE

Love GOD, your God. Walk in his ways.
Keep his commandments, regulations, and
rules so that you will live, really live,
live exuberantly, blessed by God.

DEUTERONOMY 30:16 MSG

It is only a tiny rosebud—
A flower of God's design;
But I cannot unfold the petals
With these clumsy hands of mine.

For the pathway that lies before me
My Heavenly Father knows—
I'll trust Him to unfold the moments
Just as He unfolds the rose.

God's timing is rarely our timing.
But far better than we do,
He numbers our days and knows
our moments and our hours.
Our task is to trust.

OS GUINNESS

The highest pinnacle of the spiritual life is not
joy in unbroken sunshine, but absolute and
undoubting trust in the love of God.

A. W. THOROLD

So faith bounds forward to its goal in God,
and love can trust her Lord to lead her there;
upheld by Him my soul is following hard,
till God hath full fulfilled my deepest prayer.

FREDERICK BROOK

*Trust involves letting go
and knowing God will catch you.*

JAMES DOBSON

Always Near

Lord, grant me a quiet mind, that trusting Thee,
for Thou art kind, I may go on without a fear,
for Thou, my Lord, art always near.

AMY CARMICHAEL

It is good for me to draw near to God;
I have put my trust in the Lord GOD.

PSALM 73:28 NKJV

God still draws near to us in the ordinary,
commonplace, everyday experiences and places....
He comes in surprising ways.

HENRY GARIEPY

We need never shout across the spaces to an
absent God. He is nearer than our own soul,
closer than our most secret thoughts.

A. W. TOZER

We do not need to search for heaven,
over here or over there, in order to find
our eternal Father. In fact, we do not even
need to speak out loud, for though we speak in
the smallest whisper or the most fleeting thought,
He is close enough to hear us.

TERESA OF AVILA

*Draw near to God and
He will draw near to you.*

JAMES 4:8 NKJV

By putting the gift of yearning for God
into every human being's heart,
God at the same time draws all people
made in God's image to God's self
and into their own true selves.

ROBERTA BONDI

Faith Is Knowing

From the tiny birds of the air and from the
fragile lilies of the field we learn the same truth,
which is so important for those who desire
a life of simple faith: God takes care of His own.
He knows our needs. He anticipates our crises.
He is moved by our weaknesses. He stands
ready to come to our rescue. And at just the right
moment He steps in and proves Himself
as our faithful heavenly Father.

CHARLES SWINDOLL

Know by the light of faith that God is present,
and be content with directing all
your actions toward Him.

BROTHER LAWRENCE

*Faith is not believing that God can—
it's knowing that He will.*

Behold, I am with you and will keep you
wherever you go, and will bring you back
to this land; for I will not leave you
until I have done what I have promised you.

GENESIS 28:15 NASB

Faithful servants have a way of knowing
answered prayer when they see it, and
a way of not giving up when they don't.

MAX LUCADO

Living a life of faith means never knowing
where you are being led. But it does mean
loving and knowing the One who is leading.
It is literally a life of faith, not of
understanding and reason—a life of
knowing Him who calls us to go.

OSWALD CHAMBERS

Complete Trust

God does not allow us to continue to reduce
Him to a size and a shape we can manage.
He moves in our lives in ways that burst our
categories and overwhelm our finiteness.
When we realize He's bigger than
anything we can get our minds around,
we can begin to relax and enjoy Him.

PAULA RHINEHART

God wants us to feel that our way through life
is rough and perplexing, so that we may learn
thankfully to lean on Him. Therefore
He takes steps to drive us out of
self-confidence to trust in Himself—
for the secret of the godly life
is to "wait on the Lord."

J. I. PACKER

There is no unbelief;
Whoever plants a seed beneath the sod
And waits to see it push away the clod,
He trusts in God.

ELIZABETH YORK CASE

If you see that the job is too big for you, that it's
something only God can do, and you trust him
to do it...that trusting-him-to-do-it is what
gets you set right with God, by God.

ROMANS 4:4 MSG

God is looking for people who will come
in simple dependence upon His grace,
and rest in simple faith upon His greatness.
At this very moment, He's looking at you.

JACK HAYFORD

*The more we depend on God
the more dependable we find He is.*

CLIFF RICHARD

Faith Lights the Way

Faith, the spiritual strong searchlight,
illuminates the way, and although sinister doubts
may lurk..., I walk unafraid toward the
Enchanted Wood where...life and death are one
in the Presence of the Lord.

HELEN KELLER

Even though I walk through the darkest valley,
I fear no evil, for you are with me;
your rod and your staff—they comfort me.

PSALM 23:4 NRSV

It doesn't take a huge spotlight to draw attention
to how great our God is. All it takes is for one
committed person to so let their light shine before men,
that a world lost in darkness welcomes the light.

GARY SMALLEY AND JOHN TRENT

Let your faith in Christ, the omnipresent One,
be in the quiet confidence that He will every day
and every moment keep you as the apple of
His eye, keep you in perfect peace and in the
sure experience of all the light and the
strength you need in His service.

ANDREW MURRAY

Nothing can compare to the beauty and
greatness of the soul in which our King dwells
in His full majesty. No earthly fire can compare
with the light of its blazing love. No bastions
can compare with its ability to endure forever.

TERESA OF AVILA

*The shadows are behind you
if you walk toward the light.*

Time with Him

God loves to look at us, and loves it when we
will look back at Him. Even when we try to
run away from our troubles...God will find us,
bless us, even when we feel most alone, unsure....
God will find a way to let us know that
He is with us *in this place*, wherever we are.

KATHLEEN NORRIS

Open wide the windows of our spirits and fill us
full of light; open wide the door of our hearts
that we may receive and entertain You
with all the powers of our adoration.

CHRISTINA ROSSETTI

That is God's call to us—simply to be
people who are content to live close to Him
and to renew the kind of life in which the
closeness is felt and experienced.

THOMAS MERTON

There is a difference between living in Christ
and living for Christ.... He is more interested in
the time you spend with Him than with the
works you accomplish in His name.

CAROLYN LUNN

*Live carefree before God;
he is most careful with you.*

1 PETER 5:7 MSG

We need quiet time to examine our lives openly and
honestly.... Spending quiet time alone gives your mind
an opportunity to renew itself and create order.

SUSAN L. TAYLOR

I will give thanks, O LORD, with all my heart...
As soon as I pray, you answer me;
you encourage me by giving me strength.

PSALM 138:1, 3 NLT

A Living Faith

Finding acceptance with joy, whatever the
circumstances of life—whether they are
petty annoyances or fiery trials—
this is a living faith that grows.

MARY LOU STEIGLEDER

By grace we see what we see.
To have faith is to respond to what we see
by longing for it the rest of our days;
by trying to live up to it and toward it
through all the wonderful and terrible things;
by breathing it in like air and growing strong on it;
by looking to see it again and see it better.

FREDERICK BUECHNER

Be patient with yourself and others.
There are no shortcuts to spirituality.
Growing fruit takes time.

Don't lose a minute in building on what you've
been given, complementing your basic faith with
good character, spiritual understanding...and generous
love, each dimension fitting into and developing
the others. With these qualities active and growing
in your lives...no day will pass without its reward as
you mature in your experience of our Master Jesus.

2 PETER 1:5–8 MSG

In a special way, human beings...being made in
the image of God, only become real human beings,
are only able to grow and thrive as human beings
as they also yearn for God.

ROBERTA BONDI

*I want to help you to grow as beautiful as God
meant you to be when He thought of you first.*

GEORGE MACDONALD

Our Refuge

To build in darkness does require faith.
But one day the light returns and you discover
that you have become a fortress...;
you may even find yourself...sought by others
as a beacon in their dark.

OLGA ROSMANITH

Call upon Me in the day of trouble;
I shall rescue you, and you will honor Me.

PSALM 50:15 NASB

When God has become our shepherd,
our refuge, our fortress, then we can reach out
to Him in the midst of a broken world and
feel at home while still on the way.

HENRI J. M. NOUWEN

God is our merciful Father and the source
of all comfort. He comforts us in all our troubles
so that we can comfort others. When they are
troubled, we will be able to give them
the same comfort God has given us.

2 CORINTHIANS 1:3–4 NLT

When you accept the fact that sometimes seasons
are dry and times are hard and that God is in control
of both, you will discover a sense of divine refuge,
because the hope then is in God and not in yourself.

CHARLES SWINDOLL

*Let my soul take refuge...beneath the shadow
of Your wings; let my heart, this sea of
restless waves, find peace in You, O God.*

AUGUSTINE

Faith and Sight

Faith does more than give reality
to that which we do not see;
it makes us look differently at visible things.

JONI EARECKSON TADA

Now we see but a poor reflection as in a mirror;
then we shall see face to face. Now I know in part;
then I shall know fully, even as I am fully known.

1 CORINTHIANS 13:12 NIV

It is God's will that we believe that we see Him
continually, though it seems to us that the sight be
only partial; and through this belief He makes us
always to gain more grace, for God wishes to be seen,
and He wishes to be sought, and He wishes to be
expected, and He wishes to be trusted.

JULIAN OF NORWICH

I do not seek to understand that I may believe,
but I believe in order to understand.
For this I believe—that unless I believe,
I should not understand.

ANSELM OF CANTERBURY

When you magnify an object, you enlarge it so that
you can understand it. When we magnify God,
we do the same. We enlarge our awareness of Him
so we can understand Him more. This is exactly
what happens in the chapel of worship—
we take our mind off ourselves and set it on God.
The emphasis is on Him.

MAX LUCADO

*May God give you eyes to see beauty
only the heart can understand.*

God's Abundance

I think what we're longing for is not "the good life"
as it's been advertised to us in the American dream,
but life in its fullness, its richness, its abundance.
Living more reflectively helps us
enter into that fullness.

KEN GIRE

God is a rich and bountiful Father,
and He does not forget His children,
nor withhold from them anything which
it would be to their advantage to receive.

J. K. MACLEAN

He shall be like a tree planted by the rivers
of water, that brings forth its fruit in its season,
whose leaf also shall not wither;
and whatever he does shall prosper.

PSALM 1:3 NKJV

Faith is the bucket of power lowered by the rope of prayer into the well of God's abundance. What we bring up depends upon what we let down. We have every encouragement to use a big bucket.

VIRGINIA WHITMAN

The grace of our Lord was exceedingly abundant, with faith and love which are in Christ Jesus.

1 TIMOTHY 1:14 NKJV

His overflowing love delights to make us partakers of the bounties He graciously imparts.

HANNAH MORE

The resource from which [God] gives is boundless, measureless, unlimited, unending, abundant, almighty, and eternal.

JACK HAYFORD

Trust in His Leading

You can trust the Lord too little,
but you can never trust Him too much.

My flesh and my heart fail;
but God is the strength of my heart
and my portion forever.

PSALM 73:26 NKJV

I always told Him, "I trust You.
I don't know where to go or what to do,
but I expect You to lead me," and He always did.

HARRIET TUBMAN

Trust! The way will open, the right issue will come,
the end will be peace, the cloud will be lifted,
and the light of eternal noonday shall shine at last.

L. B. COWMAN

In your unfailing love
you will lead the people you have redeemed.
In your strength you will guide them
to your holy dwelling.

EXODUS 15:13 NIV

*The most effective...way to show
our love for God is to trust Him.*

EUGENIA PRICE

When we trust, the Lord works.
What is done is not done by us, but by Him.

HANNAH WHITALL SMITH

Through Christ you have come to trust in God.
And you have placed your faith and hope
in God because he raised Christ from the dead
and gave him great glory.

1 PETER 1:21 NLT

A Tapestry of Faith

Father, help me to see the dark threads too
as part of Your design. And so learn
to trust You in all things.

ELIZABETH SHERRILL

My life is but a weaving
Between my Lord and me,
I cannot choose the colors
He worketh steadily.
Oftimes He weaveth sorrow,
And I in foolish pride
Forget He sees the upper
And I, the underside.
The dark threads are as needful
In the Weaver's skillful hand
As the threads of gold and silver
In the pattern He has planned.

Neither height nor depth, nor anything else
in all creation, will be able to separate us from
the love of God that is in Christ Jesus our Lord.

ROMANS 8:39 NIV

Even when all we see are the tangled threads
on the backside of life's tapestry, we know that
God is good and is out to do us good always.

RICHARD J. FOSTER

*It's the little things that make up
the richest part of the tapestry of our lives.*

God will never, never, never let us down
if we have faith... in Him. He will always
look after us. So we must cleave to Jesus.
Our whole life must simply be woven into Jesus.

MOTHER TERESA

Wait on the Lord

So wait before the Lord. Wait in the stillness.
And in that stillness, assurance will come to you.
You will know that you are heard;
you will know that your Lord ponders
the voice of your humble desires; you will
hear quiet words spoken to you yourself,
perhaps to your grateful surprise and refreshment.

AMY CARMICHAEL

The LORD longs to be gracious to you;
he rises to show you compassion.
For the LORD is a God of justice.
Blessed are all who wait for him!

ISAIAH 30:18 NIV

The way may at times seem dark, but light will arise,
if you trust in the Lord, and wait patiently for Him.

ELIZABETH T. KING

Lead me in Your truth and teach me,
For You are the God of my salvation;
On You I wait all the day.

PSALM 25:5 NKJV

*God makes a promise— faith believes it,
hope anticipates it, patience quietly awaits it.*

In all ranks of life the human heart yearns
for the beautiful; and the beautiful things
that God makes are His gift to all alike.

HARRIET BEECHER STOWE

Day by day the LORD takes care
of the innocent, and they will receive
an inheritance that lasts forever.

PSALM 37:18 NLT

Sustaining Faith

Faith...has sustained me—faith in the God
of the Bible, a God, as someone once put it,
not small enough to be understood
but big enough to be worshipped.

ELISABETH ELLIOT

For the eyes of the LORD run
to and fro throughout the whole earth,
to show Himself strong on behalf
of those whose heart is loyal to Him.

2 CHRONICLES 16:9 NKJV

We walk without fear, full of hope and courage
and strength to do His will, waiting for the
endless good which He is always giving
as fast as He can get us able to take it in.

GEORGE MACDONALD

God speaks to the crowd, but His call comes to individuals, and through their personal obedience He acts. He does not promise them nothing but success, or even final victory in this life.... God does not promise that He will protect them from trials, from material cares, from sickness, from physical or moral suffering. He promises only that He will be with them in all these trials, and that He will sustain them if they remain faithful to Him.

PAUL TOURNIER

Whate'er the care which breaks thy rest,
Whate'er the wish that swells thy breast;
Spread before God that wish, that care,
And change anxiety to prayer.

There is hope in your future, says the LORD.

JEREMIAH 31:17 NKJV

Eternally His

Day-to-day living becomes a window
through which we get a glimpse of life eternal.
The eternal illuminates and gives focus to the daily.

JANICE RIGGLE HUIE

Jesus, our Savior. He broke the power of death
and illuminated the way to life and
immortality through the Good News.

2 TIMOTHY 1:10 NLT

I believe in the immortality of the soul
because I have within me immortal longings.

HELEN KELLER

*We are ever so secure
in the everlasting arms.*

Heaven will be the endless portion
of those who have heaven in their soul.

Nothing we can do will make the Father love us less;
nothing we do can make Him love us more.
He loves us unconditionally with an everlasting love.
All He asks of us is that we respond to Him
with the free will that He has given to us.

NANCIE CARMICHAEL

As we follow Him who is everlasting
we will touch the things that last forever.

God's love is like a river springing up in the
Divine Substance and flowing endlessly through
His creation, filling all things with life
and goodness and strength.

THOMAS MERTON

I am wholly His; I am peculiarly His;
I am universally His; I am eternally His.

THOMAS BENTON BROOKS

Ready to Receive

Live for today but hold your hands open
to tomorrow. Anticipate the future and its changes
with joy. There is a seed of God's love in every
event, every circumstance, every...situation
in which you may find yourself.

BARBARA JOHNSON

Many flowers open to the sun,
but only one follows him constantly.
Heart, be thou the sunflower,
not only open to receive God's blessing,
but constant in looking to Him.

JEAN PAUL RICHTER

Everything in life is most fundamentally a gift.
And you receive it best, and you live it best,
by holding it with very open hands.

LEO O'DONOVAN

GOD rewrote the text of my life when I opened
the book of my heart to His eyes.

PSALM 18:24 MSG

From God, great and small, rich and poor,
draw living water from a living spring,
and those who serve Him freely and gladly
will receive grace answering to grace.

THOMAS À KEMPIS

God gives His gifts where He finds
the vessel empty enough to receive them.

C. S. LEWIS

The soul should always stand ajar,
ready to welcome the ecstatic experience.

EMILY DICKINSON

*We have received so much,
because He has so freely given.*

Faith in Small Things

Faith in small things has repercussions
that ripple all the way out. In a huge, dark room
a little match can light up the place.

JONI EARECKSON TADA

If you have faith the size of a mustard seed,
you will say to this mountain, "Move from
here to there," and it will move;
and nothing will be impossible for you.

MATTHEW 17:20 NRSV

I am beginning to learn that it is the sweet, simple
things of life which are the real ones after all.

LAURA INGALLS WILDER

Just as angels are attracted to the light
of joy and kindness, so too are miracles
attracted to the lamp of faith and love.

MARY AUGUSTINE

Be faithful in little things, for in them
our strength lies. To the good God nothing is little,
because He is so great and we so small.

MOTHER TERESA

Is it so small a thing to have enjoyed the sun,
to have lived light in the spring, to have loved,
to have thought, to have done?

MATTHEW ARNOLD

Faith sees the invisible,
believes the incredible,
and receives the impossible.

*A little thing is a little thing, but
faithfulness in a little thing is a big thing.*

HUDSON TAYLOR

A Dose of Wonder

When I need a dose of wonder I wait for
a clear night and go look for the stars....
Often the wonder of the stars is enough
to return me to God's loving grace.

MADELEINE L'ENGLE

I still find each day too short for all
the thoughts I want to think, all the walks
I want to take, all the books I want to read,
and all the friends I want to see.
The longer I live, the more my mind dwells
upon the beauty and the wonder of the world.

JOHN BURROUGHS

As we grow in our capacities to see and enjoy
the joys that God has placed in our lives,
life becomes a glorious experience of
discovering His endless wonders.

There is not enough darkness in all the world
to put out the light of one small candle....
In moments of discouragement, defeat, or even
despair, there are always certain things to cling to.
Little things usually: remembered laughter,
the face of a sleeping child, a tree in the wind—
in fact, any reminder of something deeply felt
or dearly loved. No man is so poor
as not to have many of these small candles.
When they are lighted, darkness goes away
and a touch of wonder remains.

ARTHUR GORDON

*No eye has seen, no ear has heard,
and no mind has imagined what God
has prepared for those who love Him.*

1 CORINTHIANS 2:9 NLT

Classroom of Faith

With God, life is eternal—both in quality and length.
There is no joy comparable to the joy of discovering
something new from God, about God. If the continuing
life is a life of joy, we will go on discovering, learning.

EUGENIA PRICE

Your walk with God is essential. His heart
is not seen in an occasional chat or weekly visit.
We learn His will as we take up residence
in His house every single day.

MAX LUCADO

Every day we live is a priceless gift
of God, loaded with possibilities to learn
something new, to gain fresh insights.

DALE EVANS ROGERS

We can get a right start only by accepting God
as He is and learning to love Him for what He is.
As we go on to know Him better we shall find it a
source of unspeakable joy that God is just what He is.

A. W. TOZER

More about Jesus would I know,
More of His grace to others show;
More of His saving fulness see,
More of His love who died for me.

More about Jesus let me learn,
More of His holy will discern;
Spirit of God, my teacher be,
Showing the things of Christ to me.

ELIZA E. HEWITT

The instructions of the LORD are perfect,
reviving the soul. The decrees of the LORD
are trust worthy, making wise the simple.

PSALM 19:7 NLT

God Is in Control

What matters supremely is not the fact
that I know God, but the larger fact which
underlies it—the fact that He knows me.
I am graven on the palms of His hands.
I am never out of His mind. All my knowledge
of Him depends on His sustained initiative
in knowing me. I know Him because
He first knew me, and continues to know me.

J. I. PACKER

Confidence is not rooted in circumstances;
it is knowing that our times are in His hands.

Certainly God has heard; He has
given heed to the voice of my prayer.

PSALM 66:19 NASB

It's usually through our hard times, the unexpected
and not-according-to-plan times, that we experience
God in more intimate ways. We discover an
unquenchable longing to know Him more.
It's a passion that isn't concerned that life fall
within certain predictable lines, but a passion that
pursues God and knows He is relentless
in His pursuit of each one of us.

WENDY MOORE

*God gives the very best to those
who leave the choice to Him.*

"If you'll hold on to me for dear life,"
says GOD, "...I'll give you the best of care
if you'll only get to know and trust me."

PSALM 91:14–16 MSG

Rest in His Strength

Trust is giving up what little I have
in strength and power so I can confidently
relax in His power and strength.

GLORIA GAITHER

The LORD is my strength and my shield;
my heart trusts in him, and I am helped.
My heart leaps for joy and
I will give thanks to him in song.

PSALM 28:7 NIV

When God finds a soul that rests in Him and
is not easily moved, He operates within it in His
own manner. That soul allows God to do great
things within it. He gives to such a soul the key to
the treasures He has prepared for it so that it might
enjoy them. And to this same soul He gives the joy
of His presence which entirely absorbs such a soul.

CATHERINE OF GENOA

God does many things which we do not
understand.... A true faith must rest solidly
on [God's] character and His Word, not on our
particular conceptions of what He ought to do.

ELISABETH ELLIOT

In those times I can't seem to find God,
I rest in the assurance He knows how to find me.

NEVA COYLE

Strength, rest, guidance, grace, help,
sympathy, love—all from God to us!
What a list of blessings!

EVELYN STENBOCK

*God's peace is joy resting.
His joy is peace dancing.*

F. F. BRUCE

A Faithful Heart

Not everyone possesses...a conspicuous talent.
We are not equally blessed with great intellect
or physical beauty or emotional strength. But we
have all been given the same ability to be faithful.

GIGI GRAHAM TCHIVIDJIAN

Well done, my good and faithful servant.
You have been faithful in handling this
small amount, so now I will give you many
more responsibilities. Let's celebrate together!

MATTHEW 25:21 NLT

The greatest ability is dependability.

VANCE HAVNER

The important thing really is not the deed well done
or the medal that you possess, but the dedication
and dreams out of which they grow.

ROBERT H. BENSON

One hundred years from today your present income will be inconsequential. One hundred years from now it won't matter if you got that big break, took the trip to Europe, or finally traded up to a Mercedes.... It will matter that you knew God. It will greatly matter, one hundred years from now, that you made a commitment to Jesus Christ.

DAVID SHIBLEY

When you are inspired by a dream, God has hit the ball into your court. Now you have to hit it back with commitment.

ROBERT SCHULLER

Commit to hope. There's reason to! For the believer, hope is divinely assured things that aren't here yet! Our hope is grounded in unshakable promises.

JACK HAYFORD

Every Need Supplied

You can trust God right now to
supply all your needs for today.
And if your needs are more tomorrow,
His supply will be greater also.

Be still, and in the quiet moments,
listen to the voice of your heavenly Father.
His words can renew your spirit...
no one knows you and your needs like He does.

JANET L. WEAVER SMITH

God wants nothing from us except our needs,
and these furnish Him with room to display
His bounty when He supplies them freely....
Not what I have, but what I do not have, is the first
point of contact between my soul and God.

CHARLES H. SPURGEON

Jesus Christ has brought every need, every joy,
every gratitude, every hope of ours before God. He
accompanies us and brings us into the presence of God.

DIETRICH BONHOEFFER

The "air" which our souls need also envelops
all of us at all times and on all sides.
God is round about us...on every hand, with
many-sided and all-sufficient grace.

OLE HALLESBY

*My God will supply all your needs according
to His riches in glory in Christ Jesus.*

PHILIPPIANS 4:19 NASB

God is waiting for us to come to Him with our needs....
God's throne room is always open.

CHARLES STANLEY

The Unknown Curve

The simple fact of being...in the presence of
the Lord and of showing Him all that I think,
feel, sense, and experience, without trying to hide
anything, must please Him. Somehow, somewhere,
I know that He loves me, even though I do not
feel that love as I can feel a human embrace,
even though I do not hear a voice as I hear
human words of consolation.... God is greater than
my senses, greater than my thoughts, greater than
my heart. I do believe that He touches me
in places that are unknown even to myself.

HENRI J. M. NOUWEN

Faith and doubt: both are needed—
not as antagonists, but working side by side—
to take us around the unknown curve.

LILLIAN SMITH

Faith brings us on highways
that make our reasoning dizzy.

CORRIE TEN BOOM

The unknown is not so frightening when
we realize that our all-knowing God is in it.

STORMIE OMARTIAN

I proclaim to you new things from this time,
Even hidden things which you have not known.

ISAIAH 48:6 NASB

I know that God is faithful.
I know that He answers prayers,
many times in ways I may not understand.

SHEILA WALSH

If anyone loves God, he is known by Him.

1 CORINTHIANS 8:3 NASB

Draw Near to God

Whoso draws nigh to God,
one step through doubtings dim,
God will advance a mile
in blazing light to him.

We are of such value to God that He came
to live among us...and to guide us home.
He will go to any length to seek us, even to
being lifted high upon the cross to draw us
back to Himself. We can only respond
by loving God for His love.

CATHERINE OF SIENNA

God proves to be good to
the man who passionately waits,
to the woman who diligently seeks.
It's a good thing to quietly hope,
quietly hope for help from God.

LAMENTATIONS 3:25–26 MSG

A living, loving God can and does make
His presence felt, can and does speak to us
in the silence of our hearts, can and does
warm and caress us till we no longer doubt
that He is near, that He is here.

BRENNAN MANNING

I have sought Thy nearness;
With all my heart have I called Thee,
And going out to meet Thee
I found Thee coming toward me.

YEHUDA HALEVI

*Let us draw near to God.... Let us hold
unswervingly to the hope we profess,
for he who promised is faithful.*

HEBREWS 10:22–23 NIV

God's Living Word

For the word of God is living and active
and sharper than any two-edged sword, and
piercing as far as the division of soul and spirit,
of both joints and marrow, and able to judge
the thoughts and intentions of the heart.
And there is no creature hidden from His sight,
but all things are open and laid bare to the eyes
of Him with whom we have to do.

HEBREWS 4:12–13 NASB

When we give the Word of God
space to live in our heart,
the Spirit of God will use it to take root,
penetrating the earthiest recesses of our lives.

KEN GIRE

*Your word I have hidden in my heart,
That I might not sin against You.*

PSALM 119:11 NKJV

The Word of God is
light to the mind and fire to the will.
It enables us to know God and to love Him.

LAWRENCE OF BRINDISI

Every part of Scripture is God-breathed
and useful one way or another—
showing us truth, exposing our rebellion,
correcting our mistakes, training us
to live God's way. Through the Word
we are put together and shaped up
for the tasks God has for us.

2 TIMOTHY 3:16–17 MSG

Amid ancient lore the Word of God stands
unique and preeminent. Wonderful in its
construction, admirable in its adaptation,
it contains truths that a child may comprehend,
and mysteries into which angels desire to look.

FRANCES ELLEN WATKINS HARPER

Walk of Faith

My Lord God, I have no idea where
I am going. I do not see the road ahead
of me. I cannot know for certain where
it will end…. But I believe that the desire
to please You does in fact please You.
And I hope I have that desire in all that
I am doing. I hope that I will never do
anything apart from that desire.
And I know that if I do this, You will
lead me by the right road though
I may know nothing about it.

Therefore will I trust You always
though I may seem to be lost and
in the shadow of death. I will not fear,
for You are ever with me.
And You will never leave me
to face my perils alone.

THOMAS MERTON

Forbid that I should walk through
Thy beautiful world with unseeing eyes:
Forbid that the lure of the market-place
should ever entirely steal my heart away from
the love of the open acres and the green trees:
Forbid that under the low roof of workshop
or office or study I should ever forget
Thy great overarching sky.

JOHN BAILLIE

*Yet I am always with you;
you hold me by my right hand.*

PSALM 73:23 NIV

I will look with favor on the faithful in the land,
so that they may live with me; whoever walks
in the way that is blameless shall minister to me.

PSALM 101:6 NRSV

In His Light

Sunshine spills through autumn-colored leaves,
lighting up their brilliance like stained-glass
windows in a great cathedral, expressing the
wonder of God's love, declaring His glory.

Turn your eyes upon Jesus,
look full in His wonderful face,
and the things of earth will grow strangely dim,
by the light of His glory and grace.

HELEN LIMMEL

Let us fix our eyes on Jesus, the author and
perfecter of our faith, who for the joy set
before him endured the cross,...and sat down
at the right hand of the throne of God.

HEBREWS 12:2 NIV

From the world we see, hear, and touch, we behold
inspired visions that reveal God's glory. In the
sun's light, we catch warm rays of grace and glimpse
His eternal design. In the birds' song, we hear
His voice and it reawakens our need of Him.
At the wind's touch, we feel His Spirit
and sense our eternal existence.

WENDY MOORE

You have set Your glory above the heavens.
Thy glory flames from sun and star:
Center and soul of every sphere,
Yet to each loving heart how near.

OLIVER WENDELL HOLMES

*Our fulfillment comes in knowing God's glory,
loving Him for it, and rejoicing in it.*

ROBERT COLEMAN

Believing Is Seeing

By faith, we see the world called into
existence by God's word, what we see
created by what we don't see.

HEBREWS 11:3 MSG

I would rather live in a world where my life
is surrounded by mystery than live in a world
so small that my mind could comprehend it.

HARRY EMERSON FOSDICK

I am still confident of this:
I will see the goodness of the LORD
in the land of the living.
Wait for the LORD;
be strong and take heart
and wait for the LORD.

PSALM 27:13–14 NIV

Open your mouth and taste, open your
eyes and see—how good GOD is.
Blessed are you who run to him.
Worship GOD if you want the best;
worship opens doors to all his goodness.

PSALM 34:8–9 MSG

When faithfulness is most difficult,
it can be most rewarding.

If we are children of God, we have a
tremendous treasure in nature and will realize
that it is holy and sacred. We will see God
reaching out to us in every wind that blows,
every sunrise and sunset, every cloud in the sky,
every flower that blooms, and every leaf that fades.

OSWALD CHAMBERS

Some things have to be believed to be seen.

LYNN YEAKEL

Simply Trust

God is here. I have joyously discovered that
He is always "up to something" in my life,
and I am learning to quit second-guessing Him
and simply trust the process.

GLORIA GAITHER

He who dwells in the shelter of the Most High
will abide in the shadow of the Almighty.
I will say to the LORD, "My refuge and my fortress,
My God, in whom I trust!"

PSALM 91:1–2 NASB

God, who has led you safely on so far,
will lead you on to the end. Be altogether at rest
in the loving holy confidence which you ought
to have in His heavenly Providence.

FRANCIS DE SALES

Scripture reassures us, "No one who trusts God
like this—heart and soul—will ever regret it."
It's exactly the same no matter what....
The same God for all of us, acting the
same incredibly generous way.

ROMANS 10:11-12 THE MESSAGE

Heaven often seems distant and unknown,
but if He who made the road...is our guide,
we need not fear to lose the way.

HENRY VAN DYKE

*Have confidence in God's mercy, for when
you think He is a long way from you,
He is often quite near.*

THOMAS À KEMPIS

"For I know the plans that I have for you,"
declares the LORD, "plans for welfare and
not for calamity to give you a future and a hope."

JEREMIAH 29:11 NASB

Blessings from Above

Lift up your eyes. Your heavenly Father
waits to bless you—in inconceivable ways to make
your life what you never dreamed it could be.

ANNE ORTLUND

O Lord, you are a great and awesome God!
You always fulfill your covenant and
keep your promises of unfailing love to those
who love you and obey your commands.

DANIEL 9:4 NLT

I wish you love, and strength, and faith, and wisdom,
Goods, gold enough to help some needy one.
I wish you songs, but also blessed silence,
And God's sweet peace when every day is done.

DOROTHY NELL MCDONALD

The heavenly Father welcomes us with open arms
and imparts to us blessing upon blessing—
not because we are upright but because
Jesus Christ has clothed us with His own virtue.

*God puts each fresh morning,
each new chance of life, into our hands
as a gift to see what we will do with it.*

May the LORD, the God of your fathers, increase you
a thousand-fold more than you are and bless you,
just as He has promised you!

DEUTERONOMY 1:11 NASB

Be on the lookout for mercies. The more we
look for them, the more of them we will see.
Blessings brighten when we count them.

MALTBIE D. BABCOCK

Perfect Peace

Do not let your heart be troubled;
believe in God, believe also in Me.
In My Father's house are many dwelling places;
if it were not so, I would have told you;
for I go to prepare a place for you.
If I go and prepare a place for you,
I will come again and receive you to Myself,
that where I am, there you may be also....
I will not leave you as orphans;
I will come to you.... Peace I leave with you;
My peace I give to you; not as
the world gives do I give to you.
Do not let your heart be troubled,
nor let it be fearful.

JOHN 14:1–3, 18, 27 NASB

The God of peace gives perfect peace to those
whose hearts are stayed upon Him.

CHARLES H. SPURGEON

Joy is not happiness so much as gladness;
it is the ecstasy of eternity in a soul that has made
peace with God and is ready to do His will.

You will keep in perfect peace
him whose mind is steadfast,
because he trusts in you.

Isaiah 26:3 niv

Have courage for the great sorrows of life,
and patience for the small ones; and when
you have...accomplished your daily task,
go to sleep in peace. God is awake.

Victor Hugo

*Only God gives true peace—a quiet gift
He sets within us just when we think
we've exhausted our search for it.*

Everything Is Possible

Faith is not an effort, a striving, a ceaseless
seeking, as so many earnest souls suppose,
but rather a letting go, an abandonment,
an abiding rest in God that nothing, not even
the soul's shortcomings, can disturb.

As the beloved of God, under the shadow of
His wings—and as the apple of God's eye—
the seeds of great faith live within us.

GARY SMALLEY AND JOHN TRENT

Faith is not a sense, not sight, not reason,
but a taking God at His Word.

EVANS

*With men it is impossible, but not with God;
for with God all things are possible.*

MARK 10:27 NKJV

The soul is a temple, and God is silently
building it by night and by day. Precious thoughts
are building it, unselfish love is building it;
all-penetrating faith is building it.

HENRY WARD BEECHER

Abandon yourself utterly for the love of God,
and in this way you will become truly happy.

HENRY SUSO

Isn't it a wonderful morning?
The world looks like something God
had just imagined for His own pleasure.

LUCY MAUD MONTGOMERY

Hope is the anchor of the soul,
the stimulus to action, and
the incentive to achievement.

God's Power at Work

I pray that you, being rooted and
established in love, may have power,
together with all the saints, to grasp
how wide and long and high and
deep is the love of Christ, and to know
this love that surpasses knowledge—
that you may be filled to the measure of
all the fullness of God. Now to him who
is able to do immeasurably more than
all we ask or imagine, according to
his power that is at work within us,
to him be glory in the church and in
Christ Jesus throughout all generations,
for ever and ever! Amen.

EPHESIANS 3:17–21 NIV

God has not given us a spirit of fear and timidity,
but of power, love, and self-discipline.

2 TIMOTHY 1:7 NLT

God longs to give favor—that is,
spiritual strength and health—to those
who seek Him, and Him alone.
He grants spiritual favors and victories,
not because the one who seeks Him
is holier than anyone else, but in order to
make His holy beauty and His great
redeeming power known.... For it is through
the living witness of others that we are
drawn to God at all. It is because of His
creatures, and His work in them,
that we come to praise Him.

TERESA OF AVILA

The light of God surrounds me;
The love of God enfolds me;
The power of God protects me;
The presence of God watches over me.
Wherever I am, God is.

Enfolded in His Peace

Calm me, O Lord, as You stilled the storm,
Still me, O Lord, keep me from harm.
Let all the tumult within me cease,
Enfold me, Lord, in Your peace.

CELTIC TRADITIONAL

Don't fret or worry. Instead of
worrying, pray. Let petitions and praises
shape your worries into prayers,
letting God know your concerns.
Before you know it, a sense of
God's wholeness, everything coming
together for good, will come and
settle you down. It's wonderful
what happens when Christ displaces
worry at the center of your life.

PHILIPPIANS 4:6–7 MSG

Nothing in all creation
is so like God as stillness.

MEISTER ECKHART

O this full and perfect peace,
O this transport all divine—
In a love which cannot cease,
I am His, and He is mine.

GEORGE WADE ROBINSON

The peace of God is that eternal calm
which lies far too deep down to be reached
by any external trouble or disturbance.

A. T. PIERSON

*If peace be in the heart
the wildest winter storm
is full of solemn beauty.*

C. F. RICHARDSON

God cannot give us a happiness and peace
apart from Himself, because it is not there.
There is no such thing.

C. S. LEWIS

Renewing Promises

Each time a rainbow appears, stretching
from one end of the sky to the other,
it's God renewing His promise.
Each shade of color, each facet of light
displays the radiant spectrum of God's love—
a promise that life can be new for each one of us.

The joyful birds prolong the strain,
their song with every spring renewed;
the air we breathe, and falling rain,
each softly whispers: God is good.

JOHN HAMPDEN GURNEY

May God give you eyes to see beauty
only the heart can understand.

All the world is an utterance of the Almighty.
Its countless beauties, its exquisite adaptations,
all speak to you of Him.

PHILLIPS BROOKS

Not every day of our lives is overflowing
with joy and celebration. But there are moments
when our hearts nearly burst within us for the
sheer joy of being alive. The first sight of
our newborn babies, the warmth of love
in another's eyes, the fresh scent of rain
on a hot summer's eve—moments like these
renew in us a heartfelt appreciation for life.

GWEN ELLIS

*Oh, worship the LORD
in the beauty of holiness!*

PSALM 96:9 NKJV

Our Creator would never have made
such lovely days, and given us the deep hearts
to enjoy them, above and beyond all thought,
unless we were meant to be immortal.

NATHANIEL HAWTHORNE

Encountering God

God is with us in the midst of our daily,
routine lives. In the middle of cleaning the
house or driving somewhere in the pickup....
Often it's in the middle of the most mundane
task that He lets us know He is there with us.
We realize, then, that there can be no "ordinary"
moments for people who live their lives with Jesus.

MICHAEL CARD

Much of what is sacred is hidden in the
ordinary, everyday moments of our lives.
To see something of the sacred in those
moments takes slowing down so we can
live our lives more reflectively.

KEN GIRE

The direct experience of God is grace indeed,
and basically there is no one to whom it is refused.

IGNATIUS OF LOYOLA

We encounter God in the ordinariness of life,
not in the search for spiritual highs and
extraordinary, mystical experiences,
but in our simple presence in life.

BRENNAN MANNING

If each moment is sacred—
a time and place where we
encounter God—life itself is sacred.

JEAN M. BLOMQUIST

It is through one's encounter with God
that one reaches his or her highest destiny.

CAROL GISH

This is how we experience his deep and abiding
presence in us: by the Spirit he gave us.

1 JOHN 3:24 MSG

Faithful in Prayer

Prayer is such an ordinary, everyday,
mundane thing. Certainly, people who pray
are no more saints than the rest of us.
Rather, they are people who want to share
a life with God, to love and be loved,
to speak and to listen, to work and to be
at rest in the presence of God.

ROBERTA BONDI

The privilege of prayer to me is one of
the most cherished possessions, because
faith and experience alike convince me
that God Himself sees and answers.

SIR WILFRED GRENFELL

Nothing in your daily life is so insignificant
and so inconsequential that God will not
help you by answering your prayer.

OLE HALLESBY

Sometimes remembering the day of our
salvation or remembering answered prayer
is the last knot on the end of our rope to cling to.
When we're struggling with doubts, looking back
at the foundation of our faith is a positive activity.

VIRGINIA THOMAS

*Prayer should be the key of the day
and the lock of the night.*

Can we find a friend so faithful,
Who will all our sorrows share?
Jesus knows our every weakness:
Take it to the Lord in prayer.

GEORGE SCRIVEN

Give your burdens to the LORD,
and he will take care of you.

PSALM 55:22 NLT

Leave It to God

Because God is responsible for our welfare,
we are told to cast all our care upon Him, for
He cares for us. God says, "I'll take the burden—
don't give it a thought—leave it to Me."
God is keenly aware that we are dependent
upon Him for life's necessities.

BILLY GRAHAM

Prayer...is bona fide letting go, but it is a release
with hope. We have no fatalist resignation. We are
buoyed up by a confident trust in the character of God.

RICHARD J. FOSTER

If you are at a place in your life where you
feel like you can't take one step without
the Lord's help, be glad.
He has you where He wants you.

STORMIE OMARTIAN

Contentment comes as the infallible result of
great acceptances, great humilities—of not
trying to make ourselves this or that, but
of surrendering ourselves to the fullness of life—
of letting life flow through us.

DAVID GRAYSON

*I pray hard, work hard,
and leave the rest to God.*

FLORENCE GRIFFITH JOYNER

Those who know Your name
will put their trust in You,
for You, O LORD, have not forsaken
those who seek You.

PSALM 9:10 NASB

I believe the promises of God enough to venture an eternity on them.

G. CAMPBELL MORGAN

Edward Bellamy (1850–98) was admitted to the bar in 1871, but that same year he abandoned his practice to become associate editor of the *Springfield Union* (Massachusetts), but his main interest lay in the field of literature. He wrote several short stories and three novels, including *Dr. Heidenhoff's Process* (1880), before he married Emma Sanderson in 1882. Forced by ill health to give up his editorial career, Bellamy devoted himself to writing. His novel *Miss Ludington's Sister* was published in 1884. The young author's intense awareness of injustices in the economic and social systems, as well as his desire for reforms, impelled him to write *Looking Backward* in 1888. "Bellamy Clubs" sprang up across the nation and the novelist embarked on a series of lecture tours and speaking engagements. In 1891, he founded the *New Nation*, a Boston newspaper, as an organ for his views, but increasing illness forced him to suspend publication. He continued, however, to work on the sequel to *Looking Backward*. It was published under the title *Equality* (1897).

Walter James Miller—poet, playwright, critic, translator—has authored, coauthored, or edited sixty-four books, scores of scholarly articles, and hundreds of television and radio programs. Professor of English at New York University, he has won a writing fellowship from the New York Foundation for the Arts/Ruttenberg Foundation.

Eliot Fintushel writes novels and short stories in and around the genre of science fiction and is a contributing editor to *Tricycle* magazine. Away from the word processor, he is also a busker and a traveling showman, a two-time winner of the National Endowment's Fellowship for Solo Performance Artists.

Edward Bellamy

LOOKING BACKWARD

2000–1887

With an Introduction by
Walter James Miller

and a New Afterword by
Eliot Fintushel

SIGNET CLASSICS

SIGNET CLASSICS
Published by New American Library, a division of
Penguin Group (USA) Inc., 375 Hudson Street,
New York, New York 10014, USA
Penguin Group (Canada), 90 Eglinton Avenue East, Suite 700, Toronto,
Ontario M4P 2Y3, Canada (a division of Pearson Penguin Canada Inc.)
Penguin Books Ltd., 80 Strand, London WC2R 0RL, England
Penguin Ireland, 25 St. Stephen's Green, Dublin 2,
Ireland (a division of Penguin Books Ltd.)
Penguin Group (Australia), 250 Camberwell Road, Camberwell, Victoria 3124,
Australia (a division of Pearson Australia Group Pty. Ltd.)
Penguin Books India Pvt. Ltd., 11 Community Centre, Panchsheel Park,
New Delhi - 110 017, India
Penguin Group (NZ), 67 Apollo Drive, Rosedale, North Shore 0632,
New Zealand (a division of Pearson New Zealand Ltd.)
Penguin Books (South Africa) (Pty.) Ltd., 24 Sturdee Avenue,
Rosebank, Johannesburg 2196, South Africa

Penguin Books Ltd., Registered Offices:
80 Strand, London WC2R 0RL, England

Published by Signet Classics, an imprint of New American Library,
a division of Penguin Group (USA) Inc.

First Signet Classics Printing, May 2000
First Signet Classics Printing (Fintushel Afterword), January 2009
10 9 8 7 6 5

Introduction copyright © Walter James Miller, 2000
Afterword copyright © Eliot Fintushel, 2009
All rights reserved

 REGISTERED TRADEMARK—MARCA REGISTRADA

CONTENTS

THE FUTURE OF FUTURISM

An Introduction to Looking Backward

Edward Bellamy's *Looking Backward* ranks as one of those rare fictions that explode in the political arena and then become literary classics. Obviously this requires more than just shocking new ideas. It takes too a unique blend of literary skills.

Ivan Turgenev's heart-wrenching *A Sportsman's Notebook* (1852) helped shame the Tsar into freeing the serfs. Harriet Beecher Stowe's sensational *Uncle Tom's Cabin* (1852) stirred President Lincoln himself to comment on fiction's political power. "So this," he greeted the best-selling author, "is the little lady who started this war." Read: the Civil War that freed America's black slaves. And Upton Sinclair's muckraking *The Jungle* (1906) gave President Theodore Roosevelt the leverage to force Congress to pass pure-food laws.

Bellamy shared some aims with these three authors but his were more comprehensive and fundamental. He wanted not only to show that a viciously competitive economic system is wasteful, unjust, and degrading to all concerned, rich and poor alike; he also prophesied that it could evolve into a cooperative society with more dignity and self-fulfillment for everyone.

Like Joseph Heller's *Catch-22* (1961), another novel of incalculable political impact, Bellamy's book got off to a slow start. But soon it sold in the millions, and it went global in more than twenty translations. Historians credit it with inspiring some forty or more other Utopian works, some—like William Morris's—in direct answer to Bellamy's. Enthusiastic readers organized more than 162 Bellamy Clubs in the States alone. These clubs were dedicated to transferring Bellamy's Utopia from fiction to fact. They listed as members some of the most celebrated names of the day.

A tiny sampling: William Dean Howells, leading novelist, editor, virtually America's literary dictator, who was inspired by Bellamy's success to write his own Utopian novel; Laurence Grunwold, who had already published one but hailed Bellamy's as far better; the Rev. Everett Edward Hale, author of *Man Without a Country,* later the Chaplain of the Senate; Julia Ward Howe, writer of "The Battle Hymn of the Republic"; Anne Whitney the sculptor; Hamlin Garland the fiction writer; leaders of the Women's Christian Temperance Union, like Abby Morton Diaz, and of the Theosophical movement, like Helen Blavatsky.

Clearly some of the most influential minds suspected that the competitive system was not the best of all possible systems, moral or economic. But conspicuously missing from the Bellamy Clubs were leaders of labor and farm organizations also on the march against the Establishment. Bellamy's movement was "not *of* the proletariat but *for* the proletariat," biographer Sylvia Bowman says. Bellamyites "put the silk hat on socialism."

These middle-class Clubbers organized the Nationalist Party and two magazines, *The Nationalist* and *The New Nation.* ("Nationalism" was understood to connote nationalization of industry.) At least fifty other periodicals declared themselves pro-Nationalist. Other dissident groups, like the People's (Populist) Party and the Theosophical Society, often allied themselves wholeheartedly with Bellamy's movement. In 1892, with Nationalist aid, Populists polled more than one million votes for president and elected three governors and several state legislators. And in dozens of cities, Nationalists won the right to take "public" utilities away from private companies.

We can see a good example of Bellamy's direct influence on national politics in the way William Jennings Bryan campaigned for president. At the 1896 Democratic convention, speaking for his "free silver" policies, he challenged his opponents with an electrifying slogan: "Thou shalt not crucify mankind on a cross of gold." This slogan won him the presidential nomination. He had counted on his audience to catch his allusion to

Looking Backward. Near the end of that novel, Julian West flings out his famous plea to the Boston aristocrats: "I have seen Humanity hanging on a cross."

The Nationalist Party as such faded only when the major parties learned Bismarck's trick of stealing popular ideas from smaller, radical parties. Reading Bellamy, history buffs readily recognize Nationalist principles in twentieth-century social legislation. One typical instance of a Bellamy principle that bore fruit: He had urged the government to set up federal corporations to discover whether nonprofit industries could serve humanity better than private companies did. Along these lines the New Deal created the Tennessee Valley Authority. One of its functions was to serve as a "yardstick," to measure actual costs of generating electricity against the prices charged by utilities run for profit. It's no coincidence that the first major biography of Edward Bellamy was written, lovingly, by Arthur Morgan, who was TVA chairman from 1933 to 1938.

For at least six generations the Bellamy family was groping its way toward a major work like *Looking Backward*. Around 1720, Samuel Bellamy, a Robin Hood–type pirate captain, described laws as made by "rich men for their own security. . . . They rob the poor under cover of the law." Then in 1762, the novelist's great-great-grandfather, the Rev. Joseph Bellamy, enjoined the General Assembly of Connecticut to imagine a society without competition and poverty, enjoying cooperation and economic security. Many other Bellamys used the pulpit to preach radical views. The Rev. Rufus Bellamy, Edward's father, refused to threaten people with eternal damnation and was ousted from his church by the wealthiest families in town. Mrs. Maria Putnam Bellamy, Rufus's wife and herself a clergyman's daughter, preached to her three sons the need for activist altruism. Charles, Edward's older brother, wrote the novel *The Breton Mill* (1879), in which a character declares that mill workers are still "men . . . in spite of all the degradation the rich and powerful" lavish on them. From this background emerged the man who was to write America's greatest Utopian novel.

Born in 1850 in Chicopee Falls, Massachusetts, Edward grew up in a family accustomed to spirited intellectual debate at mealtime; as a child he kept notebooks of his own observations. The Bellamys lived in the beautiful residential section near the factory owners whom Edward dubbed "feudal barons." They ran the town, even to hiring and firing the clergymen. But walking just a few streets away he could see the drab, crowded tenements from which stunted, joyless children went off to their ten-hour workdays in the mills. Young Edward denounced industrialists who made fortunes on child labor as "worse than Napoleons."

Along with this social awareness he thrilled at the thought of military glory, because he was growing up while the Union Army was fighting its great ideological war. At seventeen he applied for West Point but failed the physical. Still his admiration for the way a well-trained army can get things done would influence his notion of the "industrial army" in his Utopia. At Union College he was again the nonconformist, not attending classes but studying privately. Briefly in Germany, he disapproved of the Socialists there as insufficiently concerned with humanity's *non*materialist needs. Back home, he passed the bar exams, took on his first case—that of a widow evicted for nonpayment of rent—then quit the bar, convinced that lawyers are there to uphold plutocracy.

For six years, he wrote editorials and reviews for leading New York and Massachusetts papers. He said in print, for example, that we needed a Society for the Prevention of Cruelty to Children (1,000,000 American kids were working long hours for low pay); that a rise in prices was rarely followed by a raise in wages; that workers and maybe even the middle class would soon be forced into serfdom.

By 1878 he was also publishing fiction in magazines. Of his many sensitive stories, one especially concerns us. *The Duke of Stockbridge,* serialized in 1879, is set in western Massachusetts during Shays Rebellion (1786–87). The novel features Revolutionary War veterans who feel they have exchanged rule by a king for rule by the rich. While Shays's 2000-odd men had been away fighting for liberty, Boston bankers did not hesitate to foreclose soldiers' farms and imprison their relatives for debt. *It's important to note that in* Stockbridge, *as in* Looking Backward, *Bellamy forgives the rich because they too are "victims" of the system!*

In 1882, Emma Sanderson, who had confessed her love for Edward only to hear he was against marriage, became engaged to another man. Bellamy was suddenly inspired to marry her. They had two children; relating to his family, he said, completed his growth as a human being.

But since the Panic of 1873, the country at large had stewed in economic depression. Violence flared as labor faced gunfire from militias and from private detectives. Fearing a repetition of Shays Rebellion, Bellamy wondered how a writer could create a better world.

He started by creating this framework for *Looking Backward: 2000–1887*: In 1887, a rich young Bostonian, Julian West, an insomniac, hires a hypnotist to give him a good night's sleep. But through unforeseeable circumstances, he wakes up 113 years later in the household of a Doctor Leete in a radically different Boston. This new society appoints West a professor to teach the history of the period in which he lived his first thirty years. But he finds that Bostonians in 2000 just can't believe what life was like back in old capitalist America. So he writes an autobiographical novel, *Looking Backward,* to help them understand the full contrast, to appreciate how much better off they are than Americans were in the past.

Now these are the conditions under which West's postcapitalist readers are living in *Bellamy's* 2000:

> *All persons have the right to equal education, to discover and develop their own full potential, to do gainful*

work related to their individual talents. All persons doing their best are equal to all others doing their best and so all are entitled to equal pay. That pay comes not in money but in a credit-card account. All citizens have the right to use their credit according to their individual tastes. The credit card expires at the end of the year; unused credit reverts to the public treasury.

Society runs not by competition but by collaboration. Everybody works in the "industrial army" or in allied corps. No one lives on the work of others. No one works after forty-five except people who aspire to executive posts.

Technology is directed to serve the public and not to enrich the few. Marriage is for love because no one need marry to gain financial support. No one is dependent on any other person. Children are supported not by their parents but by the public treasury. There is little crime because there are no poor persons needing to rob others.

We must assume that these conditions help explain the novel's perennial popularity.

Of course it's West's *fictional* readers who do the "looking backward." But Bellamy's *real* original readers, even while identifying with West's readers, were also "looking forward." For them the contrast worked in the opposite direction: It was between their world of the 1880s and the future world Bellamy said would *evolve* from their own nineteenth-century industrial society. That is, American corporations of the 1880s would merge again and again into, at last, One Big Corporation which finally, out of its good sense and sheer humanity, would yield its universal power to public control. This evolution would be complete well before 2000.

For us readers today the contrasts are even more complex. We read with different questions and special ironies: How much of Bellamy's analysis of our system still obtains? Could the evolution that he foresaw still work out that way in the twenty-first century? Or would that

One Big Corporation simply *become* the government? Are we, in spite of ourselves, still essentially living à la 1887, or *Moving Backward* to it?

For us, even more than for Bellamy's original readers, he has identified developments to watch (out for) and maybe try to direct or redirect.

Bellamy's ingenious plot and these multiple points of view are two reasons the novel appeals to us as *art*. Another is his magnificent use of involved metaphors, like his famous "coach parable" and "umbrella symbol." Religious allusions, many subliminal, reinforce his message that his socialism is actually Judeo-Christian Messianism, realized at last. Another artistic attraction is Bellamy's sensitive treatment of the psychological shocks Julian must survive, of the understanding that Edith Leete shows in easing his transition, of his development from the "guilt-ridden rich boy" to the egalitarian working historian.

Bellamy's flexible dialogue ranges from sweet love talk—as Edith wonders how to woo a man from a culture with primitive sexual mores!—to philosophical talks between the Leetes and Julian that rival Plato's dialogues. Bellamy's most celebrated ploy is his reversal of the traditional dream device. Often in fiction the hero awakes to discover that his fantastic adventures have just been a dream. Bellamy's twist on this classical formula provides us with one of the most thrilling catharses in world literature.

After 1888, Bellamy worked tirelessly, at podium and desk, answering questions and criticisms. For example, he had taken a giant step in guaranteeing women unconditional economic independence. But he aroused justifiable annoyance among feminists when he put women in a separate industrial army. He even made the classical male-chauvinist error of sanctifying women, and making them maternal figures for men who were supposed to be striving for equal mates.

Another complaint was that *Looking Backward* had

not given readers enough details of *how* the transition from old capitalism to new socialism had been accomplished. Doctor Leete simply assures Julian it was a nonviolent revolution. Astute science fiction critics like H. Bruce Franklin could later see Bellamy's *Nationalism* and middle-class *Socialism* developing willy-nilly into Hitlerian *National Socialism*.

In interviews Bellamy always had one of his parables ready for this *how* question. You don't tell a young man about the agonies of courtship and marriage. Rather you introduce him to an attractive woman and the *how* works itself out. Bellamy felt he had pictured such an attractive society that humanity would surely figure out how to woo and win it.

His speeches and articles in response to such questions finally developed into a sequel, *Equality* (1897). Some readers agree with Bernard Shaw that this second novel is superfluous, that *Looking Backward* is self-explanatory. But many readers of the original Utopia want to go on to such surprises as meeting the real Reverend Barton, who in *Looking Backward* is just heard in a sermon by radiotelephone.

Science fiction aficionados claim Bellamy as one of their great futurists. He accurately predicted substitution of credit cards for money, rapid consolidation of corporations, globalization of capitalism, revolutionary effects of technology on everything from how we shop, eat, launder, and practice religion to how we listen to music and enjoy leisure.

Mary Shelley had so warned us, in 1818, about "science run amok" that in 2000 (Bellamy's very year!) Europeans, alarmed at genetically altered food, were calling it "Frankenstein food" (later shortened to "frankenfood"). And Verne's Captain Nemo predicted, in 1865, that electricity could be generated by stretching wires from low, cold strata of water to hot surface strata; and now in the twenty-first century precisely that technique is being developed in the Caribbean.

So, if Shelley, Verne, and Bellamy, each working

alone, could so spot future developments, why don't governments make systematic, large-scale *team* efforts to predict and prepare for them? For example, for decades competitive technologies could foresee but ignored certain computer disasters that *could* have hit the world in the first second of (Bellamy's!) 2000. Said the *New York Times* on that New Year's Day: the disasters were largely averted only because "governments and corporations *eventually* listened to the dire warnings of the year 2000 readiness advocates" and then had to invest "more than $250 billion worldwide in finding and fixing the problem" (italics ours). Why hadn't they listened earlier to the "readiness" futurists? Edward Bellamy would see this as the kind of waste engendered by the wrong kind of economic system.

For similar reasons, as early as the 1960s Ferdinand Lundberg had asked why we don't appoint, to the cabinet of every prime minister and president, a secretary of prognostics.

One of our big twenty-first-century concerns, then, is still the future of futurism. And because Bellamy always reliably provokes new readers to think more clearly about where we're going, we owe him our permanent gratitude.

Minutes before he died—of tuberculosis at forty-eight—the realistic, philosophical Bellamy explained to Emma: "I'm just going into the next room." It was a typical Bellamy metaphor for both his economic and his spiritual expectations.

—Walter James Miller
Professor of English
School of Continuing and
Professional Studies
New York University

PREFACE

HISTORICAL SECTION, SHAWMUT COLLEGE,
BOSTON, DECEMBER 26, 2000.

LIVING AS we do in the closing year of the twentieth century, enjoying the blessings of a social order at once so simple and logical that it seems but the triumph of common sense, it is no doubt difficult for those whose studies have not been largely historical to realize that the present organization of society is, in its completeness, less than a century old. No historical fact is, however, better established than that till nearly the end of the nineteenth century it was the general belief that the ancient industrialized system, with all its shocking social consequences, was destined to last, with possibly a little patching, to the end of time. How strange and well-nigh incredible does it seem that so prodigious a moral and material transformation as has taken place since then could have been accomplished in so brief an interval! The readiness with which men accustom themselves, as matters of course, to improvements in their condition, which, when anticipated, seemed to leave nothing more to be desired, could not be more strikingly illustrated. What reflection could be better calculated to moderate the enthusiasm of reformers who count for their reward on the lively gratitude of future ages!

The object of this volume is to assist persons who, while desiring to gain a more definite idea of the social contrasts between the nineteenth and twentieth centuries, are daunted by the formal aspect of the histories which treat the subject. Warned by a teacher's experience that learning is accounted a weariness to flesh, the author has sought to alleviate the instructive quality of the book by casting it in the form of a romantic narrative, which he would be glad to fancy not wholly devoid of interest on its own account.

The reader, to whom modern social institutions and their underlying principles are matters of course, may at times find Doctor Leete's explanations of them rather trite—but it must be remembered that to Doctor Leete's guest they were not matters of course, and that this book is written for the express purpose of inducing the reader to forget for the nonce that they are so to him. One word more. The almost universal theme of the writers and orators who have celebrated this bimillennial epoch has been the future rather than the past, not the advance that has been made, but the progress that shall be made, ever onward and upward, till the race shall achieve its ineffable destiny. This is well, wholly well, but it seems to me that nowhere can we find more solid ground for daring anticipations of human development during the next one thousand years, than by "Looking Backward" upon the progress of the last one hundred.

That this volume may be so fortunate as to find readers whose interest in the subject shall incline them to overlook the deficiencies of the treatment is the hope in which the author steps aside and leaves Mr. Julian West to speak for himself.

LOOKING BACKWARD

2000–1887

· I ·

I FIRST SAW THE LIGHT IN THE CITY OF BOSTON IN THE YEAR 1857. "What!" you say. "Eighteen fifty-seven? That is an odd slip. He means nineteen fifty-seven, of course." I beg your pardon, but there is no mistake. It was about four in the afternoon of December the 26th, one day after Christmas, in the year 1857, not 1957, that I first breathed the east wind of Boston, which, I assure the reader, was at that remote period marked by the same penetrating quality characterizing it in the present year of grace, 2000.

These statements seem so absurd on their face, especially when I add that I am a young man apparently of about thirty years of age, that no person can be blamed for refusing to read another word of what promises to be a mere imposition upon his credulity. Nevertheless I earnestly assure the reader that no imposition is intended, and will undertake, if he shall follow me a few pages, to entirely convince him of this. If I may, then, provisionally assume, with the pledge of justifying the assumption, that I know better than the reader when I was born, I will go on with my narrative. As every schoolboy knows, in the latter part of the nineteenth century the civilization of today, or anything like it, did not exist, although elements which were to develop it were already in ferment. Nothing had, however, occurred to modify the immemorial division of society into the four classes, or nations, as they may be more fitly called, since the differences between them were far greater than those between any nations nowadays, of the rich and the poor, the educated and the ignorant. I my-

5

self was rich and also educated, and possessed, therefore, all the elements of happiness enjoyed by the most fortunate in that age. Living in luxury, and occupied only with the pursuit of pleasures and refinements of life, I derived the means of my support from the labor of others, rendering no sort of service in return. My parents and grandparents had lived in the same way, and I expected that my descendants, if I had any, would enjoy a like easy existence.

But how could I live without service to the world? you ask. Why should the world have supported in utter idleness one who was able to render service? The answer is that my great-grandfather had accumulated a sum of money on which his descendants had ever since lived. The sum, you will naturally infer, must have been very large not to have been exhausted in supporting three generations of idleness. This, however, was not the fact. The sum had been originally by no means large. It was, in fact, much larger now that three generations had been supported on it in idleness, than it was at first. This mystery of use without consumption, of warmth without combustion, seems like magic, but was merely an ingenious application of the art now happily lost but carried to great perfection by your ancestors, of shifting the burden of one's support on the shoulders of others. The man who had accomplished this, and it was the end all sought, was said to live on the income of his investments. To explain at this point how the ancient methods of industry made this possible would delay us too much. I shall only stop now to say that interest on investments was a species of tax in perpetuity upon the product of those engaged in industry which a person possessing or inheriting money was able to levy. It must not be supposed that an arrangement which seems so unnatural and preposterous according to modern notions was never criticized by your ancestors. It had been the effort of lawgivers and prophets from the earliest ages to abolish interest, or at least to limit it to the smallest possible rate. All these efforts had, however, failed, as they necessarily must so long as the ancient social organizations prevailed. At the time of which I write, the latter part of the nineteenth century, governments had generally given up trying to regulate the subject at all.

By way of attempting to give the reader some general impression of the way people lived together in those days, and especially of the relations of the rich and poor to one another, perhaps I cannot do better than to compare society as it then was to a prodigious coach which the masses of humanity were harnessed to and dragged toilsomely along a very hilly and sandy road. The driver was hunger, and permitted no lagging, though the pace was necessarily very slow. Despite the difficulty of drawing the coach at all along so hard a road, the top was covered with passengers who never got down, even at the steepest ascents. These seats at the top were very breezy and comfortable. Well up out of the dust, their occupants could enjoy the scenery at their leisure, or critically discuss the merits of the straining team. Naturally such places were in great demand and the competition for them was keen, every one seeking as the first end in life to secure a seat on the coach for himself and to leave it to his child after him. By the rule of the coach a man could leave his seat to whom he wished, but on the other hand there were so many accidents by which it might at any time be wholly lost. For all that they were so easy, the seats were very insecure, and at every sudden jolt of the coach persons were slipping out of them and falling to the ground, where they were instantly compelled to take hold of the rope and help to drag the coach on which they had before ridden so pleasantly. It was naturally regarded as a terrible misfortune to lose one's seat, and the apprehension that this might happen to them or their friends was a constant cloud upon the happiness of those who rode.

But did they think only of themselves? you ask. Was not their very luxury rendered intolerable to them by comparison with the lot of their brothers and sisters in the harness, and the knowledge that their own weight added to the toil? Had they no compassion for fellow beings from whom fortune only distinguished them? Oh, yes, commiseration was frequently expressed by those who rode for those who had to pull the coach, especially when the vehicle came to a bad place in the road, as it was constantly doing, or to a particularly steep hill. At such times, the desperate straining of the team, their agonized leaping and plunging under the pitiless lashes of hunger, the many who fainted at the rope and were trampled in the mire, made a very distressing spectacle, which often called forth highly creditable displays of feeling on the top of the coach. At such times the passengers would call down encouragingly to the toilers of the rope, exhorting them to patience, and holding out hopes of possible compensation in another world for the hardness of their lot, while others contributed to buy salves and liniments for the crippled and injured. It was agreed that it was a great pity that the coach should be so hard to pull, and there was a sense of general relief when the specially bad piece of road was gotten over. This relief was not, indeed, wholly on account of the team, for there was always some danger at these bad places of a general overturn in which all would lose their seats.

It must in truth be admitted that the main effect of the spectacle of the misery of the toilers at the rope was to enhance the passengers' sense of value of their seats upon the coach, and to cause them to hold on to them more desperately than before. If the passengers could only have felt assured that neither they nor their friends would ever fall from the top, it is probable that, beyond contributing to the funds for liniments and bandages, they would have troubled themselves extremely little about those who dragged the coach.

I am well aware that this will appear to the men and women of the twentieth century an incredible inhumanity, but there are two facts, both very curious, which partly explain it. In the first place, it was firmly and sincerely believed that there was no other way in which Society could get along, except when the many pulled at the rope and the few rode, and not only this, but that no very radical improvement even was possible, either in the harness, the coach, the roadway, or the distribution of the toil. It had always been as it was, and it always would be so. It was a pity, but it could not be helped, and philosophy forbade wasting compassion on what was beyond remedy.

The other fact is yet more curious, consisting in a singular hallucination which those on top of the coach generally shared, that they were not exactly like their brothers and sisters who pulled at the rope, but of finer clay, in some way belonging to a higher order of beings who might just expect to be drawn. This seems unaccountable, but, as I once rode on this very coach and shared that very hallucination, I ought to be believed. The strangest thing about the hallucination was that those who had but just climbed up from the ground, before they had outgrown the marks of the rope upon their hands, began to fall under its influence. As for those whose parents and grandparents before them had been so fortunate as to keep their seats on the top, the conviction they cherished of the essential difference between their sort of humanity and the common article was absolute. The effect of such a delusion in moderating fellow feeling for the sufferings of the mass of men into a distant and philosophical compassion is obvious. To it I refer as the only extenuation I can offer for the indifference which, at the period I write of, marked my own attitude toward the misery of my brothers.

In 1887 I came into my thirtieth year. Although still unmarried, I was engaged to wed Edith Bartlett. She, like myself, rode on the top of the coach. That is to say, not to encumber ourselves further with an illustration which has, I hope, served its purpose of giving the reader some general impression of how we lived then, her family was wealthy. In that age, when money alone commanded all that was agreeable and refined in life, it was enough for a woman to be rich to have suitors, but Edith Bartlett was beautiful and graceful also.

My lady readers, I am aware, will protest at this. "Handsome she might have been," I hear them saying, "but graceful never, in the costumes which were the fashion at that period, when the head covering was a dizzy structure a foot tall, and the almost incredible extension of the skirt behind by means of artificial contrivances more thoroughly dehumanized the form than any former device of dressmakers. Fancy anyone graceful in such a costume!" The point is certainly well taken, and I can only reply that while the ladies of the twentieth century are lovely demonstrations of the effect of appropriate drapery in accenting feminine graces, my recollection of their great-grandmothers enables me to maintain that no deformity of costume can wholly disguise them.

Our marriage only waited on the completion of the house which I was building for our occupancy in one of the most desirable parts of the city, that is to say, a part chiefly inhabited by the rich. For it must be understood that the comparative desirability of different parts of Boston for residence depended then, not on natural features, but on the character of the neighboring population. Each class or nation lived by itself, in quarters of its own. A rich man living among the poor, an educated man among the uneducated, was like one living in isolation among a jealous and alien race. When the house had been begun, its completion by the winter of 1886 had been expected. The spring of the following year found it, however, yet incomplete, and my marriage still a thing of the future. The cause of a delay calculated to be particularly exasperating to an ardent lover was a series of strikes, that is to say, concerted refusals to work on the part of the bricklayers, masons, carpenters, painters, plumbers, and other trades concerned in housebuilding. What the specific causes of these strikes were I do not remember. Strikes had become so common at that period that people had ceased to inquire into their particular grounds. In one department of industry or another, they had been nearly incessant ever since the great business crisis of 1873. In fact, it had come to be the exceptional thing to see any class of laborers pursue their avocation steadily for more than a few months at a time.

The reader who observes the dates alluded to will of

course recognize in these disturbances of industry the first and incoherent phase of the great movement which ended in the establishment of the modern industrial system with all its social consequences. This is all so plain in the retrospect that a child can understand it, but not being prophets, we of that day had no clear idea what was happening to us. What we did see was that industrially the country was in a very queer way. The relationship between the workingman and the employer, between labor and capital, appeared in some unaccountable manner to have become dislocated. The working classes had quite suddenly and very generally become infected with a profound discontent with their condition, and an idea that it could be greatly bettered if they only knew how to go about it. On every side, with one accord, they preferred demands for higher pay, shorter hours, better dwellings, better educational advantages, and a share in the refinements and luxuries of life, demands which it was impossible to see the way to granting unless the world were to become a great deal richer than it then was. Though they knew something of what they wanted, they knew nothing of how to accomplish it, and the eager enthusiasm with which they thronged about anyone who seemed likely to give them any light on the subject lent sudden reputation to many would-be leaders, some of whom had little enough light to give. However chimerical the aspirations of the laboring classes might be deemed, the devotion with which they supported one another in the strikes, which were their chief weapon, and the sacrifices which they underwent to carry them out lent no doubt of their dead earnestness.

As to the final outcome of the labor troubles, which was the phrase by which the movement I have described was most commonly referred to, the opinions of the people of my class differed according to individual temperament. The sanguine argued very forcibly that it was in the very nature of things impossible that the new hopes of the workingmen could be satisfied, simply because the world had not the wherewithal to satisfy them. It was only because the masses worked very hard and lived on short commons that the race did not starve outright, and no considerable improvement in their condition was possible while the world, as a whole, remained so poor. It was not the capitalists whom the laboring men were contending with, these maintained, but the ironbound environment of humanity, and it was merely a question of the thickness of their skulls when they would discover the fact and make up their minds to endure what they could not cure.

The less sanguine admitted all this. Of course the workingmen's aspirations were impossible of fulfillment for natural reasons, but there were grounds to fear that they would not discover this fact until they had made a sad mess of society. They had the votes and the power to do so if they pleased, and their leaders meant they should. Some of these desponding observers went so far as to predict an impending social cataclysm. Humanity, they argued, having climbed to the top round of the ladder of civilization, was about to take a header into chaos, after which it would doubtless pick itself up, turn round, and begin to climb again. Repeated experiences of this sort in historic and prehistoric times possibly accounted for the puzzling bumps on the human cranium. Human history, like all great movements, was cyclical, and returned to the point of beginning. The idea of indefinite progress in a right line was a chimera of the imagination, with no analogue in nature. The parabola of a comet was perhaps a yet better illustration of the career of humanity. Tending upward and sunward from the aphelion of barbarism, the race attained the perihelion of civilization only to plunge downward once more to its nether goal in the regions of chaos.

This, of course, was an extreme opinion, but I remember serious men among my acquaintances who, in discussing the signs of the times, adopted a very similar tone. It was no doubt the common opinion of thoughtful men that society was approaching a critical period which might result in great changes. The labor troubles, their causes, course, and cure, took lead of all other topics in the public prints, and in serious conversation.

The nervous tension of the public mind could not have been more strikingly illustrated than it was by the alarm resulting from the talk of a small band of men who called themselves anarchists, and proposed to terrify the American people into adopting their ideas by threats of violence, as if a mighty nation which had but just put down a rebellion of half its own numbers, in order to maintain its political system, were likely to adopt a new social system out of fear.

As one of the wealthy, with a large stake in the existing order of things, I naturally shared the apprehensions of my class. The particular grievance I had against the working classes at the time of which I write, on account of the effect of their strikes in postponing my wedded bliss, no doubt lent a special animosity to my feeling toward them.

· II ·

THE THIRTIETH DAY OF MAY, 1887, FELL ON A MONDAY. IT was one of the annual holidays of the nation in the latter third of the nineteenth century, being set apart under the name of Decoration Day, for doing honor to the memory of the soldiers of the North who took part in the war for the preservation of the union of the states. The survivors of the war, escorted by military and civic processions and bands of music, were wont on this occasion to visit the cemeteries and lay wreaths of flowers upon the graves of their dead comrades, the ceremony being a very solemn and touching one. The oldest brother of Edith Bartlett had fallen in the war, and on Decoration Day the family was in the habit of making a visit to Mount Auburn, where he lay.

I had asked permission to make one of the party, and, on our return to the city at nightfall, remained to dine with the family of my betrothed. In the drawing room, after dinner, I picked up the evening paper and read of a fresh strike in the building trades, which would probably still further delay the completion of my unlucky house. I remember distinctly how exasperated I was at this, and the objurations, as forcible as the presence of the ladies permitted, which I lavished upon workmen in general, and these strikers in particular. I had abundant sympathy from those about me, and the remarks made in the desultory conversation which followed, upon the unprincipled conduct of the labor agitators, were calculated to make those gentlemen's ears tingle. It was agreed that affairs were going from bad to worse very fast, and that there was no telling what we should come to soon. "The worst of it," I remember Mrs. Bartlett's saying, "is that the working classes all over the world seem to be going crazy at once. In Europe it is far worse even than here. I'm sure I should not dare to live there at all. I asked Mr. Bartlett the other day where we should emigrate to if all the terrible things took place which those socialists threaten. He said he did not know any place now where society could be called stable except Greenland, Patagonia, and the Chinese Empire." "Those Chinamen knew what they were about," somebody added, "when they refused to let in our Western civilization. They knew what it would lead to better than we did. They saw it was nothing but dynamite in disguise."

After this, I remember drawing Edith apart and trying to persuade her that it would be better to be married at once without waiting for the completion of the house, spending the time to travel till our home was ready for us. She was remarkably handsome that evening, the mourning costume that she wore in recognition of the day setting off to great advantage the purity of her complexion. I can see her even now with my mind's eye just as she looked that night. When I took my leave she followed me into the hall and I kissed her goodby as usual. There was no circumstance out of the common to distinguish this parting from previous occasions when we had bade each other goodby for a night or a day. There was absolutely no premonition in my mind, or I am sure in hers, that this was more than an ordinary separation.

Ah, well!

The hour at which I had left my betrothed was a rather early one for a lover, but the fact was no reflection on my devotion. I was a confirmed sufferer from insomnia, and, although otherwise perfectly well, had been completely fagged out that day, from having slept scarcely at all the two previous nights. Edith knew this and had insisted on sending me home by nine o'clock, with strict orders to go to bed at once.

The house in which I lived had been occupied by three generations of the family in which I was the only living representative in the direct line. It was a large, ancient wooden mansion, very elegant in an old-fashioned way within, but situated in a quarter that had long since become undesirable for residence from its invasion by tenement houses and manufactories. It was not a house to which I could think of bringing a bride, much less so dainty a one as Edith Bartlett. I had advertised it for sale, and meanwhile merely used it for sleeping purposes, dining at my club. One servant, a faithful colored man by the name of Sawyer, lived with me and attended to my few wants. One feature of the house I expected to miss greatly when I should leave it, and this was the sleeping chamber which I had built under the foundations. I could not have slept in the city at all, with its never-ceasing nightly noises, if I had been obliged to use an upstairs chamber. But in this subterranean room no murmur from the upper world ever penetrated. When I had entered it and closed the door, I was surrounded by the silence of the tomb. In order to prevent the dampness of the subsoil from penetrating the chamber the walls had been laid in hydraulic cement and were very thick, and the floor was likewise protected. In order that the room might serve also as a vault, equally proof against violence and flames, for the storage of valuables, I had roofed it with stone slabs hermetically sealed, and the outer door was of iron with a thick coating of asbestos. A small pipe, communicating with a windmill on the top of the house, insured the renewal of air.

It might seem that the tenant of such a chamber ought

to be able to command slumber, but it was rare that I slept well, even there, two nights in succession. So accustomed was I to wakefulness that I minded little the loss of one night's rest. A second night, however, spent in my reading chair instead of my bed, tired me out, and I never allowed myself to go longer than that without slumber, from fear of nervous disorder. From this statement it will be inferred that I had at my command some artificial means of inducing sleep in the last resort, and so in fact I had. If after two sleepless nights I found myself on the approach of the third without sensations of drowsiness, I called in Doctor Pillsbury.

He was a doctor by courtesy only, what was called in those days an "irregular" or "quack" doctor. He called himself a "Professor of Animal Magnetism." I had come across him in the course of some amateur investigations into the phenomena of animal magnetism. I don't think he knew anything about medicine, but he was certainly a remarkable mesmerist. It was for the purpose of being put to sleep by his manipulations that I used to send for him when I found a third night of sleeplessness impending. Let my nervous excitement or mental preoccupation be however great, Doctor Pillsbury never failed, after a short time, to leave me in a deep slumber, which continued till I was aroused by a reversal of the mesmerizing process. The process for awaking a sleeper was much simpler than that for putting him to sleep, and for convenience I had made Doctor Pillsbury teach Sawyer how to do it.

My faithful servant alone knew for what purpose Doctor Pillsbury visited me, or that he did so at all. Of course, when Edith became my wife I should have to tell her my secrets. I had not hitherto told her this, because there was unquestionably a slight risk in the mesmeric sleep, and I knew she would set her face against my practice. The risk, of course, was that it might become too profound and pass into a trance beyond the mesmerizer's power to break, ending in death. Repeated experiments had fully convinced me that the risk was next to nothing if reasonable precautions were exercised,

and of this I hoped, though doubtingly, to
Edith. I went directly home after leaving her,
once sent Sawyer to fetch Doctor Pillsbury. Mean
I sought my subterranean sleeping chamber, and
changing my costume for a comfortable dressing gown,
sat down to read the letters by the evening mail which
Sawyer had laid on my reading table.

One of them was from the builder of my new house,
and confirmed what I had inferred from the newspaper
item. The new strikes, he said, had postponed indefinitely the completion of the contract, as neither masters
nor workmen would concede the point at issue without
a long struggle. Caligula wished that the Roman people
had but one neck that he might cut it off, and as I read
this letter I am afraid that for a moment I was capable
of wishing the same thing concerning the laboring classes
of America. The return of Sawyer with the doctor interrupted my gloomy meditations.

It appeared that he had with difficulty been able to
secure his services, as he was preparing to leave the city
that very night. The doctor explained that since he had
seen me last he had learned of a very fine professional
opening in a distant city, and decided to take prompt
advantage of it. On my asking, in some panic, what I
was to do for someone to put me to sleep, he gave me
the names of several mesmerizers in Boston who, he
averred, had quite as great powers as he.

Somewhat relieved on this point, I instructed Sawyer
to rouse me at nine o'clock next morning, and, lying
down on the bed in my dressing gown, assumed a comfortable attitude, and surrendered myself to the manipulations of the mesmerizer. Owing, perhaps, to my
unusually nervous state, I was slower than common in
losing consciousness, but at length a delicious drowsiness
stole over me.

"HE IS GOING TO OPEN HIS EYES. HE HAD BETTER SEE BUT one of us at first."

"Promise me, then, that you will not tell him."

The first voice was a man's, the second a woman's, and both spoke in whispers.

"I will see how he seems," replied the man.

"No, no, promise me," persisted the other.

"Let her have her way," whispered a third voice, also a woman.

"Well, well, I promise, then," answered the man. "Quick, go! He is coming out of it."

There was a rustle of garments and I opened my eyes. A fine-looking man of perhaps sixty was bending over me, an expression of much benevolence mingled with great curiosity upon his features. He was an utter stranger. I raised myself on an elbow and looked around. The room was empty. I certainly had never been in it before, or one furnished like it. I looked back at my companion. He smiled.

"How do you feel?' he inquired.

"Where am I?" I demanded.

"You are in my house," was the reply.

"How came I here?"

"We will talk about that when you are stronger. Meanwhile, I beg you will feel no anxiety. You are among friends and in good hands. How do you feel?"

"A bit queerly," I replied, "but I am well, I suppose. Will you tell me how I came to be indebted to your hospitality? What has happened to me? How came I here? It was in my own house that I went to sleep."

"There will be time enough for explanations later," my unknown host replied, with a reassuring smile. "It will be better to avoid agitating talk until you are a little more yourself. Will you oblige me by taking a couple of swallows of this mixture? It will do you good. I am a physician."

I repelled the glass with my hand and sat up on the couch, although with an effort, for my head was strangely light.

"I insist upon knowing at once where I am and what you have been doing with me," I said.

"My dear sir," responded my companion, "let me beg that you will not agitate yourself. I would rather you did not insist upon explanations so soon, but if you do, I will try to satisfy you, provided that you will take this draught, which will strengthen you somewhat."

I thereupon drank what he offered me. Then he said, "It is not so simple a matter as you evidently suppose to tell you how you came here. You can tell me quite as much on that point as I can tell you. You have just been roused from a deep sleep, or, more properly, trance. So much I can tell you. You say you were in your own house when you fell into that sleep. May I ask you when that was?"

"When?" I replied. "When? Why, last evening, of course, at about ten o'clock. I left my man Sawyer orders to call me at nine o'clock. What has become of Sawyer?"

"I can't precisely tell you that," replied my companion, regarding me with a curious expression, "but I am sure that he is excusable for not being here. And now can you tell me a little more explicitly when it was that you fell into that sleep, the date, I mean?"

"Why, last night, of course. I said so, didn't I? That is, unless I have overslept an entire day. Great heavens! That cannot be possible, and yet I have an odd sensation of having slept a long time. It was Decoration Day that I went to sleep."

"Decoration Day?"

"Yes, Monday the 30th."

"Pardon me, the 30th of what?"

"Why, of this month, of course, unless I have slept into June, but that can't be."

"This month is September."

"September! You don't mean I've slept since May! God in heaven! Why, it is incredible."

"We shall see," replied my companion. "You say that it was May 30th when you went to sleep?"

"Yes."

"May I ask of what year?"

I stared blankly at him, incapable of speech, for some moments.

"Of what year?" I feebly echoed at last.

"Yes, of what year, if you please? After you have told me that, I shall be able to tell you how long you have slept."

"It was the year 1887," I said.

My companion insisted that I should take another draught from the glass, and felt my pulse.

"My dear sir," he said, "your manner indicates that you are a man of culture, which I am aware was by no means the matter of course in your day it now is. No doubt, then, you have yourself made the observation that nothing in this world can be truly said to be more wonderful than anything else. The causes of all phenomena are equally adequate, and the results equally matters of course. That you should be startled by what I shall tell you is to be expected; but I am confident that you will not permit it to affect your equanimity unduly. Your appearance is that of a young man of barely thirty, and your bodily condition seems not greatly different from that of one just roused from a somewhat too long and profound sleep, and yet this is the tenth day of September in the year 2000, and you have slept exactly one hundred and thirteen years, three months, and eleven days."

Feeling partially dazed, I drank a cup of some sweet broth at my companion's suggestion, and, immediately afterward becoming very drowsy, went off into a deep sleep.

When I awoke it was broad daylight in the room, which had been lighted artificially when I was awake before. My mysterious host was sitting near. He was not looking at me when I opened my eyes, and I had a good opportunity to study him and meditate upon my extraordinary situation, before he observed that I was awake. My giddiness was all gone, and my mind perfectly clear. The story that I had been asleep one hundred and thirteen years, which, in my former weak and bewildered condition, I had accepted without question, recurred to me now only to be rejected as a preposterous attempt at an imposture, the motive of which it was impossible remotely to surmise.

Something extraordinary had certainly happened to account for my waking in this strange house with this unknown companion, but my fancy was utterly impotent to suggest more than the wildest guess as to what that something might have been. Could it be that I was the victim of some sort of conspiracy? It looked so, certainly, and yet, if human lineaments ever gave true evidence, it was certain that this man by my side, with a face so refined and ingenuous, was no party to any scheme of crime or outrage. Then it occurred to me to question if I might not be the butt of some elaborate practical joke on the part of my friends who had somehow learned the secret of my underground chamber and taken this means of impressing me with the peril of mesmeric experiments. There were great difficulties in the way of this theory; Sawyer would never have betrayed me, nor had I any friends at all likely to undertake such an enterprise; nevertheless the supposition that I was the victim of a practical joke seemed on the whole the only one tenable. Half expecting to catch a glimpse of some familiar face grinning from behind a chair or curtain, I looked carefully about the room. When my eyes rested on my companion, he was looking at me.

"You have had a fine nap of twelve hours," he said briskly, "and I can see that it has done you good. You look much better. Your color is good and your eyes are bright. How do you feel?"

"I never felt better," I said, sitting up.

"You remember your first waking, no doubt," he pursued, "and your surprise when I told you how long you had been asleep?"

"You said, I believe, that I had slept one hundred and thirteen years."

"Exactly."

"You will admit," I said, with an ironical smile, "that the story was rather an improbable one."

"Extraordinary, I admit," he responded, "but given the proper conditions, not improbable nor inconsistent with what we know of the trance state. When complete, as in your case, the vital functions are absolutely suspended, and there is no waste of the tissues. No limit can be set to the possible duration of a trance when the external conditions protect the body from physical injury. This trance of yours is indeed the longest of which there is any positive record, but there is no known reason wherefore, had you not been discovered and had the chamber in which we found you continued intact, you might not have remained in a state of suspended animation till, at the end of indefinite ages, the gradual refrigeration of the earth had destroyed the bodily tissue and set the spirit free."

I had to admit that, if I were indeed the victim of a practical joke, its authors had chosen an admirable agent for carrying out their imposition. The impressive and even eloquent manner of this man would have lent dignity to an argument that the moon was made of cheese. The smile with which I had regarded him as he advanced his trance hypothesis did not appear to confuse him in the slightest degree.

"Perhaps," I said, "you will go on and favor me with some particulars as to the circumstances under which you discovered this chamber of which you speak, and its contents. I enjoy good fiction."

"In this case," was the grave reply, "no fiction could be so strange as the truth. You must know that these many years I have been cherishing the idea of building a laboratory in the large garden beside this house, for the purpose of chemical experiments for which I have a taste. Last Thursday the excavation for the cellar was at last begun. It was completed by that night, and Friday the masons were to have come. Thursday night we had a tremendous deluge of rain, and Friday morning I found my cellar a frog pond and the walls quite washed down. My daughter, who had come out to view the disaster with me, called my attention to a corner of masonry laid bare by the crumbling away of one of the walls. I cleared a little earth from it, and, finding that it seemed part of a large mass, determined to investigate it. The workmen I sent for unearthed an oblong vault some eight feet below the surface, and set in the corner of what evidently had been the foundation walls of an ancient house. A layer of ashes and charcoal on the top of the vault showed that the house above had perished by fire. The vault itself was perfectly intact, the cement being as good as when first applied. It had a door, but this we could not force, and found entrance by removing one of the flagstones which formed the roof. The air which came up was stagnant but pure, dry and not cold. Descending with a lantern, I found myself in an apartment fitted up as a bedroom in the style of the nineteenth century. On the bed lay a young man. That he was dead and must have been dead a century was of course to be taken for granted; but the extraordinary state of preservation of the body struck me and the medical colleagues whom I had summoned with amazement. That the art of such embalming as this had ever been known we should not have believed, yet here seemed conclusive testimony that our immediate ancestors had possessed it. My medical colleagues, whose curiosity was highly excited, were at once for undertaking experiments to test the nature of the process employed, but I withheld them. My motive in doing, at least the only motive I now need speak of, was the recollection of something I once had read about the extent to which your contemporaries had cultivated the subject of animal magnetism. It had occurred to me as just conceivable that you might be in a trance, and that the secret of your bodily integrity after so long a time was not the craft of an embalmer, but life. So extremely fanciful did this idea seem, even to me, that I did not risk the ridicule of my fellow physicians by mentioning it, but gave some other reason

23

for postponing their experiments. No sooner, however, had they left me, than I set on foot a systematic attempt at resuscitation, of which you know the result."

Had its theme been yet more incredible, the circumstantiality of this narrative, as well as the impressive manner and personality of the narrator, might have staggered a listener, and I had begun to feel very strange, when, as he closed, I chanced to catch a glimpse of my reflection in a mirror hanging on the wall of the room. I rose and went up to it. The face I saw was the face to a hair and a line and not a day older than the one I had looked at as I tied my cravat before going to Edith that Decoration Day, which, as this man would have me believe, was celebrated one hundred and thirteen years before. At this, the colossal character of the fraud which was being attempted on me came over me afresh. Indignation mastered my mind as I realized the outrageous liberty that had been taken.

"You are probably surprised," said my companion, "to see that, although you are a century older than when you lay down to sleep in that underground chamber, your appearance is unchanged. That should not amaze you. It is by virtue of the total arrest of the vital functions that you have survived this great period of time. If your body could have undergone any change during your trance, it would long ago have suffered dissolution."

"Sir," I replied, turning to him, "what your motive can be in reciting to me with a serious face this remarkable farrago, I am utterly unable to guess, but you are surely yourself too intelligent to suppose that anybody but an imbecile could be deceived by it. Spare me any more of this elaborate nonsense and once for all tell me whether you refuse to give me an intelligible account of where I am now and how I came here. If so, I shall proceed to ascertain my whereabouts for myself, whoever may hinder."

"You do not, then, believe that this is the year 2000?"

"Do you really think it necessary to ask me that?" I returned.

"Very well," replied my extraordinary host. "Since I

cannot convince you, you shall convince yourself. Are you strong enough to follow me upstairs?"

"I am as strong as I ever was," I replied angrily, "as I may have to prove if this jest is carried much further."

"I beg, sir," was my companion's response, "that you will not allow yourself to be too fully persuaded that you are the victim of a trick, lest the reaction, when you are convinced of the truth of my statements, should be too great."

The tone of concern, mingled with commiseration, with which he said this, and the entire absence of any sign of resentment of my hot words, strangely daunted me, and I followed him from the room with an extraordinary mixture of emotions. He led the way up two flights of stairs and then up a shorter one, which landed us upon a belvedere on the housetop. "Be pleased to look around you," he said, as we reached the platform, "and tell me if this is the Boston of the nineteenth century."

At my feet lay a great city. Miles of broad streets, shaded by trees and lined with fine buildings, for the most part not in continuous blocks but set in larger or smaller enclosures, stretched in every direction. Every quarter contained large open squares filled with trees, along which statues glistened and fountains flashed in the late-afternoon sun. Public buildings of a colossal size and architectural grandeur unparalleled in my day raised their stately piles on every side. Surely I had never seen this city nor one comparable to it before. Raising my eyes at last toward the horizon, I looked westward. That blue ribbon winding away to the sunset—was it not the sinuous Charles? I looked east—Boston harbor stretched before me within its headlands, not one of its green islets missing.

I knew then that I had been told the truth concerning the prodigious thing which had befallen me.

· IV ·

I DID NOT FAINT, BUT THE EFFORT TO REALIZE MY POSITION made me very giddy, and I remember that my companion had to give me a strong arm as he conducted me from the roof to a roomy apartment on the upper floor of the house, where he insisted on my drinking a glass or two of good wine and partaking of a light repast.

"I think you are going to be all right now," he said cheerily. "I should not have taken so abrupt a means to convince you of your position if your course, while perfectly excusable under the circumstances, had not rather obliged me to do so. I confess," he added, laughing, "I was a little apprehensive at one time that I should undergo what I believe you used to call a knockdown in the nineteenth century, if I did not act rather promptly. I remembered that the Bostonians of your day were famous pugilists, and thought best to lose no time. I take it you are now ready to acquit me of the charge of hoaxing you."

"If you had told me," I replied, profoundly awed, "that a thousand years instead of a hundred had elapsed since I last looked on this city, I should now believe you."

"Only a century has passed," he answered, "but many a millennium in the world's history has seen changes less extraordinary.

"And now," he added, extending his hand with an air of irresistible cordiality, "let me give you a hearty welcome to the Boston of the twentieth century and to this house. My name is Leete, Doctor Leete they call me."

"My name," I said as I shook his hand, "is Julian West."

"I am most happy to make your acquaintance, Mr. West," he responded. "Seeing that this house is built on the site of your own, I hope you will find it easy to make yourself at home in it."

After my refreshment Doctor Leete offered me a bath and a change of clothing, of which I gladly availed myself.

It did not appear that any very startling revolution in men's attire had been among the great changes my host had spoken of, for, barring a few details, my new habiliments did not puzzle me at all.

Physically, I was now myself again. But mentally, how it was with me, the reader will doubtless wonder. What were my intellectual sensations, he may wish to know, on finding myself so suddenly dropped as it were into a new world. In reply let me ask him to suppose himself suddenly, in the twinkling of an eye, transported from earth, say, to Paradise or Hades. What does he fancy would be his own experience? Would his thoughts return at once to the earth he had just left, or would he, after the first shock, well-nigh forget his former life for a while, albeit to be remembered later, in the interest excited by his new surroundings? All I can say is, that if his experience were at all like mine in the transition I am describing, the latter hypothesis would prove the correct one. The impressions of amazement and curiosity which my new surroundings produced occupied my mind, after the first shock, to the exclusion of all other thoughts. For the time the memory of my former life was, as it were, in abeyance.

No sooner did I find myself physically rehabilitated through the kind offices of my host, than I became eager to return to the housetop; and presently we were comfortably established there in easy chairs, with the city beneath and around us. After Doctor Leete had responded to numerous questions on my part, as to the ancient landmarks I missed and the new ones which had replaced them, he asked me what point of the contrast between the new and old city struck me most forcibly.

"To speak of small things before great," I responded, "I really think that the complete absence of chimneys and their smoke is the detail that first impressed me."

"Ah!" ejaculated my companion with an air of much interest. "I had forgotten the chimneys, it is so long ago since they went out of use. It is nearly a century since the crude method of combustion on which you depended for heat became obsolete."

"In general," I said, "what impresses me most about the city is the material prosperity on the part of the people which its magnificence implies."

"I would give a great deal for just one glimpse of the Boston of your day," replied Doctor Leete. "No doubt, as you imply, the cities of that period were rather shabby affairs. If you had the taste to make them splendid, which I would not be so rude as to question, the general poverty resulting from your extraordinary industrial system would not have given you the means. Moreover, the excessive individualism which then prevailed was inconsistent with much public spirit. What little wealth you had seems almost wholly to have been lavished in private luxury. Nowadays, on the contrary, there is no destination of the surplus wealth so popular as the adornment of the city, which all enjoy in equal degree."

The sun had been setting as we returned to the housetop, and as we talked night descended upon the city.

"It is growing dark," said Doctor Leete. "Let us descend into the house. I want to introduce my wife and daughter to you."

His words recalled to me the feminine voices which I had heard whispering about me as I was coming back to conscious life; and, most curious to learn what the ladies of the year 2000 were like, I assented with alacrity to the proposition. The apartment in which we found the wife and daughter of my host, as well as the entire interior of the house, was filled with a mellow light, which I knew must be artificial, although I could not discover the source from which it was diffused. Mrs. Leete was an exceptionally fine-looking and well-preserved woman of about her husband's age, while the daughter, who was in the first blush of womanhood, was the most beautiful girl I had ever seen. Her face was as bewitching as deep-blue eyes, delicately tinted complexion, and perfect features could make it, but even had her countenance lacked special charms, the faultless luxuriance of her figure would have given her place as a beauty among the women of the nineteenth century. Feminine softness and delicacy were in this lovely creature combined with an appearance of health and abounding physical vitality too often lacking in the maidens with whom alone I could compare her. It was a coincidence trifling in the comparison with the general strangeness of the situation, but still striking, that her name should be Edith.

The evening that followed was certainly unique in the history of social intercourse, but to suppose that our conversation was peculiarly strained or difficult would be a great mistake. I believe indeed that it is under what may be called unnatural, in the sense of extraordinary, circumstances that people behave most naturally, for the reason, no doubt, that such circumstances banish artificiality. I know at any rate that my intercourse that evening with these representatives of another age and world was marked by an ingenuous sincerity and frankness such as but rarely crown long acquaintance. No doubt the exquisite tact of my entertainers had much to do with this. Of course there was nothing we could talk of but the strange experience by virtue of which I was there, but they talked of it with an interest so naive and direct in its expression as to relieve the subject to a great degree of the element of the weird and the uncanny which might so easily have been overpowering. One would have supposed that they were quite in the habit of entertaining waifs from another century, so perfect was their tact.

For my own part, never do I remember the operations of my mind to have been more alert and more acute than that evening, or my intellectual sensibilities more keen. Of course I do not mean that the consciousness of my amazing situation was for a moment out of my mind, but its chief effect thus far was to produce a feverish elation, a sort of mental intoxication.*

* In accounting for this state of mind it must be remembered that, except for the topic of our conversations, there was in my surroundings next to nothing to suggest what had befallen me. Within a block of my home in the old Boston I could have found social circles vastly more foreign to me. The speech of the Bosto-

29

Edith Leete took little part in the conversation, but when several times the magnetism of her beauty drew my glance to her face, I found her eyes fixed on me with an absorbed intensity, almost like fascination. It was evident that I had excited her interest to an extraordinary degree, as was not astonishing, supposing her to be a girl of imagination. Though I supposed curiosity was the chief motive of her interest, it could but affect me as it would not have done if she had been less beautiful.

Doctor Leete, as well as the ladies, seemed greatly interested in my account of the circumstances under which I had gone to sleep in the underground chamber. All had suggestions to offer to account for my having been forgotten there, and the theory which we finally agreed on offers at least a plausible explanation, although whether it be in its details the true one, nobody, of course, will ever know. The layer of ashes found above the chamber indicated that the house had been burned down. Let it be supposed that the conflagration had taken place the night I fell asleep. It only remains to assume that Sawyer lost his life in the fire or by some accident connected with it, and the rest follows naturally enough. No one but he and Doctor Pillsbury either knew of the existence of the chamber and that I was in it, and Doctor Pillsbury, who had gone that night to New Orleans, had probably never heard of the fire at all. The conclusion of my friends, and of the public, must have been that I had perished in the flames. An excavation of the ruins, unless thorough, would not have disclosed the recess in the foundation walls connecting with my chamber. To be sure, if the site had been again built upon, at least immediately, such an excavation would have been necessary, but the troublous times and the undesirable character of the locality might well have pre-

nians of the twentieth century differs even less from that of their cultural ancestors of the nineteenth than did that of the latter from the language of Washington and Franklin, while the differences between the style of dress and furniture of the two epochs were not more marked than I have known fashion to make in the time of one generation.

vented rebuilding. The size of the trees in the garden now occupying the site indicated, Doctor Leete said, that for more than half a century, at least, it had been open ground.

· V ·

WHEN, IN THE COURSE OF THE EVENING, THE LADIES RE-tired, leaving Doctor Leete and myself alone, he sounded me as to my disposition for sleep, saying that if I felt like it my bed was ready for me; but if I was inclined to wakefulness nothing would please him better than to bear me company. "I am a late bird, myself," he said, "and, without suspicion of flattery, I may say that a companion more interesting than yourself could scarcely be imagined. It is decidedly not often that one has a chance to converse with a man of the nineteenth century."

Now I had been looking forward all evening with some dread to the time when I should be alone, on retir-ing for the night. Surrounded by these most friendly strangers, stimulated and supported by their sympathetic interest, I had been able to keep my mental balance. Even then, however, in pauses of the conversation I had had glimpses, vivid as lightning flashes, of the horror of strangeness that was waiting to be faced when I could no longer command diversion. I knew I could not sleep that night, and as for lying awake and thinking, it argues no cowardice, I am sure, to confess that I was afraid of it. When, in reply to my host's question, I frankly told him this, he replied that it would be strange if I did not feel just so, but that I need have no anxiety about sleep-ing; whenever I wanted to go to bed, he would give me a dose which would insure me a sound night's sleep with-out fail. Next morning, no doubt, I would awake with the feeling of an old citizen.

"Before I acquire that," I replied, "I must know a little more about the sort of Boston I have come back

31

to. You told me when we were upon the housetop that though a century only had elapsed since I fell asleep, it had been marked by greater changes in the conditions of humanity than many a previous millennium. With the city before me I could well believe that, but I am very curious to know what some of the changes have been. To make a beginning somewhere, for the subject is doubtless a large one, what solution, if any, have you found for the labor question? It was the Sphinx's riddle of the nineteenth century, and when I dropped out the Sphinx was threatening to devour society, because the answer was not forthcoming. It is well worth sleeping a hundred years to learn what the right answer was, if, indeed, you have found it yet."

"As no such thing as the labor question is known nowadays," replied Doctor Leete, "and there is no way in which it could arise, I suppose we may claim to have solved it. Society would indeed have fully deserved being devoured if it had failed to answer a riddle so entirely simple. In fact, to speak by the book, it was not necessary for society to solve the riddle at all. It may be said to have solved itself. The solution came as the result of a process of industrial evolution which could not have terminated otherwise. All that society had to do was to recognize and cooperate with that evolution, when its tendency had become unmistakable."

"I can only say," I answered, "that at the time I fell asleep no such evolution had been recognized."

"It was in 1887 that you fell into this sleep, I think you said."

"Yes, May 30, 1887."

My companion regarded me musingly for some moments. Then he observed, "And you tell me that even then there was no general recognition of the nature of the crisis which society was nearing? Of course, I fully credit your statement. The singular blindness of your contemporaries to the signs of the times is a phenomenon commented on by many of our historians, but few facts of history are more difficult for us to realize, so obvious and unmistakable as we look back seem the indications, which must also have come under your eyes, of the transformation about to come to pass. I should be interested, Mr. West, if you would give me a little more definite idea of the view which you and men of your grade of intellect took to the state and prospects of society in 1887. You must, at least, have realized that the widespread industrial and social troubles, and the underlying dissatisfaction of all classes with the inequalities of society, and the general misery of mankind, were portents of great changes of some sort."

"We did, indeed, fully realize that," I replied. "We felt that society was dragging anchor and in danger of going adrift. Whither it would drift nobody could say, but all feared the rocks."

"Nevertheless," said Doctor Leete, "the set of the current was perfectly perceptible if you had but taken pains to observe it, and it was not toward the rocks, but toward a deeper channel."

"We had a popular proverb," I replied, "that 'hindsight is better than foresight,' the force of which I shall now, no doubt, appreciate more fully than ever. All I can say is, that the prospect was such when I went into that long sleep that I should not have been surprised had I looked down from your housetop today on a heap of charred and moss-grown ruins instead of this glorious city."

Doctor Leete had listened to me with close attention and nodded thoughtfully as I finished speaking. "What you have said," he observed, "will be regarded as a most valuable vindication of Storiot, whose account of your era has been generally thought exaggerated in its picture of the gloom and confusion of men's minds. That a period of transition like that should be full of excitement and agitation was indeed to be looked for; but seeing how plain was the tendency of the forces in operation, it was natural to believe that hope rather than fear would have been the prevailing temper of the popular mind."

"You have not yet told me what was the answer to the riddle which you found," I said. "I am impatient to know by what contradiction of natural sequence the peace and prosperity which you now seem to enjoy could have been the outcome of an era like my own."

"Excuse me," replied my host, "but do you smoke?" It was not till our cigars were lighted and drawing well that he resumed. "Since you are in the humor to talk rather than sleep, as I certainly am, perhaps I cannot do better than to try to give you enough idea of our modern industrial system to dissipate at least the impression that there is any mystery about the process of its evolution. The Bostonians of your day had the reputation of being great askers of questions, and I am going to show you my descent by asking you one to begin with. What should you name as the most prominent feature of the labor troubles of your day?"

"Why, the strikes, of course," I replied.

"Exactly. But what made the strikes so formidable?"

"The great labor organizations."

"And what was the motive of these great organizations?"

"The workmen claimed they had to organize to get their rights from the big corporations," I replied.

"That is just it," said Doctor Leete. "The organization of labor and the strikes were an effect, merely, of the concentration of capital in greater masses than had ever been known before. Before this concentration began, while as yet commerce and industry were conducted by innumerable petty concerns with small capital, instead of a small number of great concerns with vast capital, the individual workman was relatively important and independent in his relations with the employer. Moreover, when a little capital or a new idea was enough to start a man in business for himself, workingmen were constantly becoming employers and there was no hard and fast line between the two classes. Labor unions were needless then, and general strikes were out of the question. But when the era of small concerns with small capital was succeeded by that of the great aggregations of capital, all this was changed. The individual laborer, who had been relatively important to the small employer, was reduced to insignificance and powerlessness over against

34

the great corporation, while at the same time the way upward to the grade of employer was closed to him. Self-defense drove him to union with his fellows.

"The records of the period show that the outcry against the concentration of capital was furious. Men believed that it threatened society with a form of tyranny more abhorrent than it had ever endured. They believed that the great corporations were preparing for them the yoke of a baser servitude than had ever been imposed on the race, servitude not to men but to soulless machines incapable of any motive but insatiable greed. Looking back, we cannot wonder at their desperation, for certainly humanity was never confronted with a fate more sordid and hideous than would have been the era of corporate tyranny which they anticipated.

"Meanwhile, without being in the smallest degree checked by the clamor against it, the absorption of business by ever-larger monopolies continued. In the United States there was not, after the beginning of the last quarter of the century, any opportunity whatever for individual enterprise in any important field of industry, unless backed by a great capital. During the last decade of the century, such small businesses as still remained were fast-failing survivals of a past epoch, or mere parasites on the great corporations, or else existed in fields too small to attract the great capitalists. Small businesses, as far as they still remained, were reduced to the condition of rats and mice, living in holes and corners, and counting on evading notice for the enjoyment of existence. The railroads had gone on combining till a few great syndicates controlled every rail in the land. In manufactories, every important staple was controlled by a syndicate. These syndicates, pools, trusts, or whatever their name, fixed prices and crushed all competition except when combinations as vast as themselves arose. Then a struggle, resulting in a still greater consolidation, ensued. The great city bazaar crushed its country rivals with branch stores, and in the city itself absorbed its smaller rivals till the business of a whole quarter was concentrated under one roof, with a hundred former proprietors of shops serving as clerks. Having no business of his own to put his money in, the small capitalist, at the same time that he took service under the corporation, found no other investment for his money but its stocks and bonds, thus becoming doubly dependent upon it.

"The fact that the desperate popular opposition to the consolidation of business in a few powerful hands had no effect to check it proves that there must have been a strong economical reason for it. The small capitalists, with their innumerable petty concerns, had in fact yielded the field to the great aggregations of capital, because they belonged to a day of small things and were totally incompetent to the demands of an age of steam and telegraphs and the gigantic scale of its enterprises. To restore the former order of things, even if possible, would have involved returning to the day of stage-coaches. Oppressive and intolerable as was the regime of the great consolidations of capital, even its victims, while they cursed it, were forced to admit the prodigious increase of efficiency which had been imparted to the national industries, the vast economies effected by concentration of management and unity of organization, and to confess that since the new system had taken the place of the old the wealth of the world had increased at a rate before undreamed of. To be sure this vast increase had gone chiefly to make the rich richer, increasing the gap between them and the poor; but the fact remained that, as a means of producing wealth, capital had been proved efficient in proportion to its consolidation. The restoration of the old system with the subdivision of capital, if it were possible, might indeed bring back a greater equality of conditions, with more individual dignity and freedom, but it would be at the price of general poverty and the arrest of material progress.

"Was there, then, no way of commanding the services of the mighty wealth-producing principle of consolidated capital without bowing down to a plutocracy like that of Carthage? As soon as men began to ask themselves these questions, they found the answer ready for them. The movement toward the conduct of business by larger and larger aggregations of capital, the tendency toward monopolies, which had been so desperately and vainly resisted, was recognized at last, in its true significance, as a process which only needed to complete its logical evolution to open a golden future to humanity.

"Early in the last century the evolution was completed by the final consolidation of the entire capital of the nation. The industry and commerce of the country, ceasing to be conducted by a set of irresponsible corporations and syndicates of private persons at their caprice and for their profit, were entrusted to a single syndicate representing the people, to be conducted in the common interest for the common profit. The nation, that is to say, organized as the one great business corporation in which all other corporations were absorbed; it became the only capitalist in the place of all other capitalists, the sole employer, the final monopoly in which all previous and lesser monopolies were swallowed up, a monopoly in the profits and economics of which all citizens shared. The epoch of trusts had ended in The Great Trust. In a word, the people of the United States concluded to assume the conduct of their own business, just as one hundred-odd years before they had assumed the conduct of their own government, organizing now for industrial purposes on precisely the same grounds that they had organized for political purposes. At last, strangely late in the world's history, the obvious fact was perceived that no business is so essentially the public business as the industry and commerce on which the people's livelihood depends, and that to entrust it to private persons to be managed for private profit is a folly similar in kind, though vastly greater in magnitude, to that of surrendering the functions of political government to kings and nobles to be conducted for their personal glorification."

"Such a stupendous change as you describe," said I, "did not, of course, take place without great bloodshed and terrible convulsions."

"On the contrary," replied Doctor Leete, "there was absolutely no violence. The change had been long foreseen. Public opinion had become fully ripe for it, and the whole mass of the people was behind it. There was no more possibility of opposing it by force than by argument. On the other hand the popular sentiment toward the great corporations and those identified with them had ceased to be one of bitterness, as they came to realize the necessity as a link, a transition phase, in the evolution of the true industrial system. The most violent foes of the great private monopolies were now forced to recognize how invaluable and indispensable had been their office in educating the people up to the point of assuming control of their own business. Fifty years before, the consolidation of the industries of the country under national control would have seemed a very daring experiment to the most sanguine. But by a series of object lessons, seen and studied by all men, the great corporations had taught the people an entirely new set of ideas on this subject. They had seen for many years syndicates handling revenues greater than those of states, and directing the labors of hundreds of thousands of men with an efficiency and economy unattainable in smaller operations. It had come to be recognized as an axiom that the larger the business the simpler the principles that can be applied to it; that, as the machine is truer than the hand, so the system, which in a great concern does the work of the master's eye in a small business, turns out more accurate results. Thus it came about that, thanks to the corporations themselves, when it was proposed that the nation should assume their functions, the suggestion implied nothing which seemed impracticable even to the timid. To be sure, it was a step beyond any yet taken, a broader generalization, but the very fact that the nation would be the sole corporation in the field would, it was seen, relieve the undertaking of many difficulties with which the partial monopolies had contended."

DOCTOR LEETE CEASED SPEAKING, AND I REMAINED SI-
lent, endeavoring to form some general conception of
the changes in the arrangements of society implied in
the tremendous revolution which he had described.

Finally I said, "The idea of such an extension of the
functions of government is, to say the least, rather
overwhelming."

"Extension!" he repeated. "Where is the extension?"

"In my day," I replied, "it was considered that the
proper functions of government, strictly speaking, were
limited to keeping the peace and defending the people
against the public enemy, that is, to the military and
police powers."

"And, in heaven's name, who are the public enemies?" exclaimed Doctor Leete. "Are they France, England, Germany, or hunger, cold, and nakedness? In
your day governments were accustomed, on the slightest
international misunderstanding, to seize upon the bodies
of citizens and deliver them over by hundreds and thousands to death and mutilation, wasting their treasures
the while like water; and all this oftenest for no imaginable profit to the victims. We have no wars now, and
our governments no war power, but in order to protect
every citizen against hunger, cold, and nakedness, and
provide for all his physical and mental needs, the function is assumed of directing his industry for a term of
years. No, Mr. West, I am sure on reflection you will
perceive that it was in your age, not in ours, that the
extension of the functions of governments was extraordinary. Not even for the best ends would men now allow
their governments such powers as were then used for
the most maleficent."

"Leaving comparisons aside," I said, "the demagoguery and corruption of our public men would have been
considered, in my day, insuperable objections to any as-

sumption by government of the charge of the national industries. We should have thought that no arrangement could be worse than to entrust the politicians with control of the wealth-producing machinery of the country. Its material interests were quite too much the football of parties as it was."

"No doubt you were right," rejoined Doctor Leete, "but all that is changed now. We have no parties or politicians, and as for demagoguery and corruption, they are words having only an historical significance."

"Human nature itself must have changed very much," I said.

"Not at all," was Doctor Leete's reply, "but the conditions of human life have changed, and with them the motives of human action. The organization of society with you was such that officials were under a constant temptation to misuse their power for the private profit of themselves or others. Under such circumstances it seems almost strange that you dared entrust them with any of your affairs. Nowadays, on the contrary, society is so constituted that there is absolutely no way in which an official, however ill-disposed, could possibly make any profit for himself or any one else by a misuse of his power. Let him be as bad an official as you please, he cannot be a corrupt one. There is no motive to be. The social system no longer offers a premium on dishonesty. But these are matters which you can only understand as you come, with time, to know us better."

"But you have not yet told me how you have settled the labor problem. It is the problem of capital which we have been discussing," I said. "After the nation had assumed conduct of the mills, machinery, railroads, farms, mines, and capital in general of the country, the labor question still remained. In assuming the responsibilities of capital the nation had assumed the difficulties of the capitalist's position."

"The moment the nation assumed the responsibilities of capital those difficulties vanished," replied Doctor Leete. "The national organization of labor under one direction was the complete solution of what was, in your day and under your system, justly regarded as the insoluble labor problem. When the nation became the sole employer, all the citizens, by virtue of their citizenship, became employees, to be distributed according to the needs of industry."

"That is," I suggested, "you have simply applied the principle of universal military service, as it was understood in our day, to the labor question."

"Yes," said Doctor Leete, "that was something which followed as a matter of course as soon as the nation had become the sole capitalist. The people were already accustomed to the idea that the obligation of every citizen, not physically disabled, to contribute his military services to the defense of the nation was equal and absolute. That it was equally the duty of every citizen to contribute his quota of industrial or intellectual services to the maintenance of the nation was equally evident, though it was not until the nation became the employer of labor that citizens were able to render this sort of service with any pretense either of universality or equity. No organization of labor was possible when the employing power was divided among hundreds or thousands of individuals and corporations, between which concert of any kind was neither desired, nor indeed feasible. It constantly happened then that vast numbers who desired to labor could find no opportunity, and on the other hand, those who desired to evade a part or all of their debt could easily do so."

"Service, now, I suppose, is compulsory upon all," I suggested.

"It is rather a matter of course than compulsion," replied Doctor Leete. "It is regarded as so absolutely natural and reasonable that the idea of its being compulsory has ceased to be thought of. He would be thought to be an incredibly contemptible person who should need compulsion in such a case. Nevertheless, to speak of service being compulsory would be a weak way to state its absolute inevitableness. Our entire social order is so wholly based upon and deduced from it that if it were conceivable that a man could escape it, he would be left with no possible way to provide for his existence. He would have excluded himself from the world, cut himself off from his kind, in a word, committed suicide."

"Is the term of service in this industry army for life?"

"Oh, no; it both begins later and ends earlier than the average working period in your day. Your workshops were filled with children and old men, but we hold the period of youth sacred to education, and the period of maturity, when the physical forces begin to flag, equally sacred to ease and agreeable relaxation. The period of industrial service is twenty-four years, beginning at the close of the course of education at twenty-one and terminating at forty-five. After forty-five, while discharged from labor, the citizen still remains liable to special calls, in case of emergencies causing a sudden great increase in the demand for labor, till he reaches the age of fifty-five, but such calls are rarely, in fact almost never, made. The fifteenth day of October of every year is what we call Muster Day, because those who have reached the age of twenty-one are then mustered into the industrial service, and at the same time those who, after twenty-four years' service, have reached the age of forty-five are honorably mustered out. It is the great day of the year with us, whence we reckon all other events, our Olympiad, save that it is annual."

· VII ·

"IT IS AFTER YOU HAVE MUSTERED YOUR INDUSTRIAL army into service," I said, "that I should expect the difficulty to arise, for there its analogy with a military army must cease. Soldiers have all the same thing, and a very simple thing, to do, namely, to practice the manual of arms, to march and stand guard. But the industrial army must learn and follow two or three hundred diverse trades and avocations. What administrative talent can be equal to determine wisely what trade or business every individual in a great nation shall pursue?"

"The administration has nothing to do with determining that point."

"Who does determine it, then?" I asked.

"Every man for himself in accordance with his natural aptitude, the utmost pains being taken to enable him to find out what his natural aptitude really is. The principle on which our industrial army is organized is that a man's natural endowments, mental and physical, determine what he can work at most profitably to the nation and most satisfactorily to himself. While the obligation of service in some form is not to be evaded, voluntary election, subject only to necessary regulation, is depended on to determine the particular sort of service every man is to render. As an individual's satisfaction during his term of service depends on his having an occupation to his taste, parents and teachers watch from early years for indications of special aptitudes in children. A thorough study of the national industrial system, with the history and rudiments of all the great trades, is an essential part of our education system. While manual training is not allowed to encroach on the general intellectual culture to which our schools are devoted, it is carried far enough to give our youth, in addition to their theoretical knowledge of the national industries, mechanical and agricultural, a certain familiarity with their tools and methods. Our schools are constantly visiting our workshops, and often are taken on long excursions to inspect particular industrial enterprises. In your day a man was not ashamed to be grossly ignorant of all trades except his own, but such ignorance would not be consistent with our idea of placing every one in a position to select intelligently the occupation for which he has most taste. Usually long before he is mustered into service a young man has found out the pursuit he wants to follow, has acquired a great deal of knowledge about it, and is waiting impatiently the time when he can enlist in its ranks."

"Surely," I said, "it can hardly be that the number of volunteers for any trade is exactly the number needed in that trade. It must be generally either under or over in demand."

"The supply of volunteers is always expected to fully equal the demand," replied Doctor Leete. "It is the business of the administration to see that this is the case. The rate of volunteering for each trade is closely watched. If there be a noticeably greater excess of volunteers over men needed in any trade, it is inferred that the trade offers greater attractions than others. On the other hand, if the number of volunteers for a trade tends to drop below the demand, it is inferred that it is thought more arduous. It is the business of the administration to seek constantly to equalize the attractions of either of the trades, so far as the conditions of labor in them are concerned, so that all trades shall be equally attractive to persons having natural tastes for them. This is done by making the hours of labor in different trades to differ according to their arduousness. The lighter trades, prosecuted under the most agreeable circumstances, have in this way the longest hours, while an arduous trade, such as mining, has very short hours. There is no theory, no a priori rule, by which the respective attractiveness of industries is determined. The administration, in taking burdens off one class of workers and adding them to other classes, simply follows the fluctuations of opinion among the workers themselves as indicated by the rate of volunteering. The principle is that no man's work ought to be, on the whole, harder for him than any other man's for him, the workers themselves to be the judges. There are no limits to the application of this rule. If any particular occupation is in itself so arduous or so oppressive that, in order to induce volunteers, the day's work in it had to be reduced to ten minutes, it would be done. If, even then, no man was willing to do it, it would remain undone. But of course, in point of fact, a moderate reduction in the hours of labor, or addition of other privileges, suffices to secure all needed volunteers for any occupation necessary to men. If, indeed, the unavoidable difficulties and dangers of such a necessary pursuit were so great that no inducement of compensating advantages would overcome men's repugnance to it, the administration would only need to take it out of the common order of occupations by declaring it 'extra hazardous,' and those who pursued it especially worthy of national gratitude, to be overrun with volunteers. Our young men are very greedy of honor, and do not let slip such opportunities. Of course you will see that dependence on the purely voluntary choice of avocations involves the abolition in all of anything like unhygienic conditions or special peril to life and limb. Health and safety are conditions common to all industries. The nation does not maim and slaughter its workmen by thousands, as did the private capitalists and corporations of your day."

"When there are more who want to enter a particular trade than there is room for, how do you decide between the applicants?" I inquired.

"Preference is given to those who have acquired the most knowledge of the trade they wish to follow. No man, however, who through successive years remains persistent in his desire to show what he can do at any particular trade, is in the end denied an opportunity. Meanwhile, if a man cannot at first win entrance into the business he prefers, he has usually one or more alternative preferences, pursuits for which he has some degree of aptitude, although not the highest. Everyone, indeed, is expected to study his aptitudes so as to have not only a first choice as to occupation, but a second or third, so that if, either at the outset of his career or subsequently, owing to the progress of invention or changes in demand, he is unable to follow his first vocation, he can still find reasonably congenial employment. This principle of secondary choices as to occupation is quite important in our system. I should add, in reference to the counter-possibility of some sudden failure of volunteers in a particular trade, or some sudden necessity of an increased force, that the administration, while depending on the voluntary system for filling up the trades as a rule, holds always in reserve the power to call for special volunteers, or draft any force needed from any quarter. Generally, however, all needs of this sort can be met by details from the class of unskilled or common laborers."

"How is this class of common laborers recruited?" I asked. "Surely nobody voluntarily enters that."

"It is the grade to which all new recruits belong for the first three years of their service. It is not till after this period, during which he is assignable to do any work at the discretion of his superiors, that the young man is allowed to elect a special avocation. These three years of stringent discipline none are exempt from, and very glad our young men are to pass from this severe school into the comparative liberty of the trades. If a man were so stupid as to have no choice as to occupation, he would simply remain a common laborer; but such cases, as you may suppose, are not common."

"Having once elected and entered on a trade or occupation," I remarked, "I suppose he has to stick to it the rest of his life."

"Not necessarily," replied Doctor Leete. "While frequent and merely capricious changes of occupation are not encouraged or even permitted, every worker is allowed, of course, under certain regulations and in accordance with the exigencies of the service, to volunteer for another industry which he thinks would suit him better than his first choice. In this case his application would be received just as if he were volunteering for the first time, and on the same terms. Not only this, but a worker may likewise, under suitable regulations and not too frequently, obtain a transfer to an establishment of the same industry in another part of the country which for any reason he may prefer. Under your system a discontented man could indeed leave his work at will, but he left his means of support at the same time, and took his chances as to future livelihood. We find that the number of men who wish to abandon an accustomed occupation for a new one, and old friends and associations for strange ones, is small. It is only the poorer sort of workmen who desire to change even as frequently as our regulations permit. Of course transfers or discharges, when health demands them, are always given."

"As an industrial system, I should think this might be extremely efficient," I said, "but I don't see that it makes any provision for the professional classes, the men who serve the nation with brains instead of hands. Of course you can't get along without the brain workers. How, then, are they selected from those who are to serve as farmers and mechanics? That must require a very delicate sort of sifting process, I should say."

"So it does," replied Doctor Leete. "The most delicate possible test is needed here, and so we leave the question whether a man shall be a brain or hand worker entirely to him to settle. At the end of the term of three years as a common laborer, which every man must serve, it is for him to choose, in accordance to his natural tastes, whether he will fit himself for an art or profession, or be a farmer or mechanic. If he feels that he can do better work with his brains than his muscles, he finds every facility for testing the reality of his supposed bent, of cultivating it, and, if fit, of pursuing it as his avocation. The schools of technology, of medicine, of art, of music, of histrionics, and of higher liberal learning are always open to aspirants without condition."

"Are not the schools flooded with young men whose only motive is to avoid work?"

Doctor Leete smiled a little grimly.

"No one is at all likely to enter the professional schools for the purpose of avoiding work, I assure you," he said. "They are intended for those with special aptitude for the branches they teach, and anyone without it would find it easier to do double hours at his trade than try to keep up with the classes. Of course many honestly mistake their vocation, and, finding themselves unequal to the requirements of the schools, drop out and return to industrial service; no discredit attaches to such persons, for the public policy is to encourage all to develop suspected talents which only actual tests can prove the reality of. The professional and scientific schools of your day depended on the patronage of their pupils for support, and the practice appears to have been common for giving diplomas to unfit persons, who afterward found their way into the professions. Our schools are national institutions, and to have passed their tests is a proof of special abilities not to be questioned.

"This opportunity for a professional training," the doctor continued, "remains open to every man till the age of thirty is reached, after which students are not received, as there would remain too brief a period before the age of discharge in which to serve the nation in their professions. In your day young men had to choose their professions very young, and therefore, in a large proportion of instances, wholly mistook their vocations. It is recognized nowadays that the natural aptitudes of some are later than those of others in developing, and therefore, while the choice of profession may be made as early as twenty-four, it remains open for six years longer."

A question which had a dozen times before been on my lips now found utterance, a question which touched upon what, in my time, had been regarded the most vital difficulty in the way of any final settlement of the industrial problem. "It is an extraordinary thing," I said, "that you should not yet have said a word about the method of adjusting wages. Since the nation is the sole employer, the government must fix the rate of wages and determine just how much everybody shall earn, from the doctors to the diggers. All I can say is, that this plan would never have worked with us, and I don't see how it can now unless human nature has changed. In my day, nobody was satisfied with his wages or salary. Even if he felt he received enough, he was sure his neighbor had too much, which was as bad. If the universal discontent on this subject, instead of being dissipated in curses and strikes directed against innumerable employers, could have been concentrated upon one, and that the government, the strongest ever devised would not have seen two pay days."

Doctor Leete laughed heartily.

"Very true, very true," he said, "a general strike would most probably have followed the first pay day, and a strike directed against the government is a revolution."

"How, then, do you avoid a revolution every pay day?" I demanded. "Has some prodigious philosopher devised a new system of calculus satisfactory to all for determining the exact and comparative value of all sorts of service, whether by brawn or brain, by hand or voice, by ear or eye? Or has human nature itself changed, so that no man looks upon his own thing but 'every man on the things of his neighbor'? One or the other of these events must be the explanation."

"Neither one nor the other, however, is," was my host's laughing response. "And now, Mr. West," he continued, "you must remember that you are my patient as well as my guest, and permit me to prescribe sleep for you before we have any more conversation. It is after three o'clock."

"The prescription is, no doubt, a wise one," I said. "I only hope it can be filled."

"I will see to that," the doctor replied, and he did, for he gave me a wineglass of something or other which sent me to sleep as soon as my head touched the pillow.

· VIII ·

WHEN I AWOKE I FELT GREATLY REFRESHED, AND LAY A considerable time in a dozing state, enjoying the sensation of bodily comfort. The experiences of the day previous, my waking to find myself in the year 2000, the sight of the new Boston, my host and his family, and the wonderful things I had heard, were a blank in my memory. I thought I was in my bedchamber at home, and the half-dreaming, half-waking fancies which passed before my mind related to the incidents and experiences of my former life. Dreamily I reviewed the incidents of Decoration Day, my trip in company with Edith and her parents to Mount Auburn, and my dining with them on our return to the city. I recalled how extremely well Edith had looked, and from that fell to thinking of our marriage; but scarcely had my imagination begun to develop this delightful theme than my waking dream was cut short by the recollection of the letter I had received the night before from the builder announcing that the new strikes might postpone indefinitely the completion of the new house. The chagrin which this recollection brought with it effectually roused me. I remembered that I had an appointment with the builder at eleven o'clock, to discuss the strike, and opening my eyes, looked up at the clock at the foot of my bed to see what time it was. But no clock met my glance, and what was more, I instantly perceived that I was not in my room. Starting up on my couch, I stared wildly round the strange apartment.

I think it must have been many seconds that I sat up thus in bed staring about, without being able to regain the clew to my personal identity. I was no more able to distinguish myself from pure being during those moments than we may suppose a soul in the rough to be before it has received the earmarks, the individualizing touches which make it a person. Strange that the sense of this inability should be such anguish! but so we are constituted. There are no words for the mental torture I endured during this helpless, eyeless groping for myself in a boundless void. No other experience of the mind gives probably anything like the sense of absolute intellectual arrest from the loss of a mental fulcrum, a starting point of thought, which comes during such a momentary obscuration of the sense of one's identity. I trust I may never know what it is again.

I do not know how long this condition had lasted—it seemed an interminable time—when, like a flash, the recollection of everything came back to me. I remembered who and where I was, and how I had come here, and that these scenes as of the life of yesterday which had been passing before my mind concerned a generation long, long ago moldered to dust. Leaping from bed, I stood in the middle of the room clasping my temples with all my might between my hands to keep them from bursting. Then I fell prone on the couch, and, burying my face in the pillow, lay without motion. The reaction which was inevitable, from the mental elation, the fever of the intellect that had been the first effect of my tremendous experience, had arrived. The emotional crisis which had awaited the full realization of my actual position, and all that it implied, was upon me, and with set teeth and laboring chest, gripping the bedstead with frenzied strength, I lay there and fought for my sanity. In my mind, all had broken loose, habits of feeling, associations of thought, ideas of persons and things, all had dissolved and lost coherence and were seething together in apparently irretrievable chaos. There were no rallying points, nothing was left stable. There only remained the will, and was any human will strong enough to say to such a weltering sea, "Peace, be still"? I dared not think. Every effort to reason upon what had befallen me, and realize what it implied, set up an intolerable swimming of the brain. The idea that I was two persons, that my identity was double, began to fascinate me with its simple solution of my experience.

I knew that I was on the verge of losing my mental balance. If I lay there thinking, I was doomed. Diversion of some sort I must have, at least the diversion of physical exertion. I sprang up, and hastily dressing, opened the door of my room and went downstairs. The hour was very early, it being not yet fairly light, and I found no one in the lower part of the house. There was a hat in the hall, and, opening the front door, which was fastened with a slightness indicating that burglary was not among the perils of the modern Boston, I found myself on the street. For two hours I walked or ran through the streets of the city, visiting most quarters of the peninsular part of the town. None but an antiquarian who knows something of the contrast which the Boston of today offers to the Boston of the nineteenth century can begin to appreciate what a series of bewildering surprises I underwent during that time. Viewed from the housetop the day before, the city had indeed appeared strange to me, but that was only in its general aspect. How complete the change had been I first realized now that I walked the streets. The few old landmarks which still remained only intensified this effect, for without them I might have imagined myself in a foreign town. A man may leave his native city in childhood, and return fifty years later, perhaps, to find it transformed in many features. He is astonished, but he is not bewildered. He is aware of a great lapse of time, and of changes likewise occurring in himself meanwhile. He but dimly recalls the city as he knew it when a child. But remember that there was no sense of any lapse of time with me. So far as my consciousness was concerned, it was but yesterday, but a few hours, since I had walked these streets in which scarcely a feature had escaped a complete metamorphosis. The mental image of the old city was so fresh and strong that it did not yield to the impression of the actual city, but contended with it, so that it was first one and then the other which seemed the more unreal. There was nothing I saw which was not blurred in this way, like the faces of a composite photograph.

Finally, I stood again at the door of the house from which I had come out. My feet must have instinctively brought me back to the site of my old home, for I had no clear idea of returning thither. It was no more home-like to me than any other spot in this city of a strange generation, nor were its inmates less utterly and necessarily strangers than all the other men and women now on the earth. Had the door of the house been locked, I should have been reminded by its resistance that I had no object in entering, and turned away, but it yielded to my hand, and advancing with uncertain steps through the hall, I entered one of the apartments opening from it. Throwing myself into a chair, I covered my burning eyeballs with my hands to shut out the horror of strangeness. My mental confusion was so intense as to produce actual nausea. The anguish of those moments, during which my brain seemed melting, or the abjectness of my sense of helplessness, how can I describe? In my despair I groaned aloud. I began to feel that unless some help should come I was about to lose my mind. And just then it did come. I heard the rustle of drapery, and looked up. Edith Leete was standing before me. Her beautiful face was full of the most poignant sympathy.

"Oh, what is the matter, Mr. West?" she said. "I was here when you came in. I saw how dreadfully distressed you looked, and when I heard you groan, I could not keep silent. What has happened to you? Where have you been? Can't I do something for you?"

Perhaps she involuntarily held out her hands in a gesture of compassion as she spoke. At any rate I had caught them in my own and was clinging to them with an impulse as instinctive as that which prompts the drowning man to seize upon and cling to the rope which is thrown him as he sinks for the last time. As I looked up into her compassionate face and her eyes moist with pity, my brain ceased to whirl. The tender human sympathy which thrilled in the soft pressure of her fingers had brought me the support I needed. Its effect to calm and soothe was like that of some wonder-working elixir.

"God bless you," I said, after a few moments. "He must have sent you to me just now. I think I was in danger of going crazy if you had not come." At this the tears came into her eyes.

"Oh, Mr. West!" she cried. "How heartless you must have thought us! How could we leave you to yourself so long! But it is over now, is it not? You are better, surely."

"Yes," I said, "thanks to you. If you will not go away quite yet, I shall be myself soon."

"Indeed I will not go away," she said, with a little quiver of her face, more expressive of her sympathy than a volume of words. "You must not think us so heartless as we seemed in leaving you so by yourself. I scarcely slept last night, for thinking how strange your waking would be this morning; but Father said you would sleep till late. He said that it would be better not to show too much sympathy with you at first, but to try to divert your thoughts and make you feel that you were among friends."

"You have indeed made me feel that," I answered.

"But you see it is a good deal of a jolt to drop a hundred years, and although I did not seem to feel it so much last night, I have had very odd sensations this morning." While I held her hands and kept my eyes on her face, I could already even jest a little at my plight.

"No one thought of such a thing as your going out in the city alone so early in the morning," she went on. "Oh, Mr. West, where have you been?"

Then I told her of my morning's experience, from my first waking till the moment I had looked up to see her before me, just as I have told it here. She was overcome by distressful pity during the recital, and, though I had released one of her hands, did not try to take from me the other, seeing, no doubt, how much good it did me to hold it. "I can think a little what this feeling must have been like," she said. "It must have been terrible. And to think you were left alone to struggle with it! Can you ever forgive us?"

"But it is gone now. You have driven it quite away for the present," I said.

"You will not let it return again?" she queried anxiously.

"I can't quite say that," I replied. "It might be too early to say that, considering how strange everything will still be to me."

"But you will not try to contend with it alone again, at least," she persisted. "Promise that you will come to us, and let us sympathize with you, and try to help you. Perhaps we can't do much, but it will surely be better than to try to bear such feelings alone."

"I will come to you if you will let me," I said.

"Oh yes, yes, I beg you will," she said eagerly. "I would do anything to help you that I could."

"All you need do is to be sorry for me, as you seem to be now," I replied.

"It is understood, then," she said, smiling with wet eyes, "that you are to come and tell me next time, and not run all over Boston among strangers."

This assumption that we were not strangers seemed

scarcely strange, so near within these few minutes had my trouble and her sympathetic tears brought us.

"I will promise, when you come to me," she added, with an expression of charming archness, passing, as she continued, into one of enthusiasm, "to seem as sorry for you as you wish, but you must not for a moment suppose that I am really sorry for you at all, or that I think you will long be sorry for yourself. I know, as well as I know that the world now is heaven compared with what it was in your day, that the only feeling you will have after a little while will be one of thankfulness to God that your life in that age was so strangely cut off, to be returned to you in this."

· IX ·

DOCTOR AND MRS. LEETE WERE EVIDENTLY NOT A LITTLE startled to learn, when they presently appeared, that I had been all over the city alone that morning, and it was apparent that they were agreeably surprised to see that I seemed so little agitated after the experience.

"Your stroll could scarcely have failed to be a very interesting one," said Mrs. Leete, as we sat down to table soon after. "You must have seen a good many new things."

"I saw very little that was not new," I replied. "But I think what surprised me as much as anything was not to find any stores on Washington Street, or any banks on State. What have you done with the merchants and bankers? Hung them all, perhaps, as the anarchists wanted to do in my day?"

"Not so bad as that," replied Doctor Leete. "We have simply dispensed with them. Their functions are obsolete in the modern world."

"Who sells you things when you want to buy them?" I inquired.

"There is neither selling nor buying nowadays; the distribution of goods is effected in another way. As to the bankers, having no money we have no use for those gentry."

"Miss Leete," said I, turning to Edith, "I am afraid that your father is making sport of me. I don't blame him, for the temptation my innocence offers must be extraordinary. But, really, there are limits to my credulity as to possible alterations in the social system."

"Father has no idea of jesting, I am sure," she replied, with a reassuring smile.

The conversation took another turn then, the point of ladies' fashions in the nineteenth century being raised, if I remember rightly, by Mrs. Leete, and it was not till after breakfast, when the doctor had invited me up to the housetop, which appeared to be a favorite resort of his, that he recurred to the subject.

"You were surprised," he said, "at my saying that we got along without money or trade, but a moment's reflection will show that trade existed and money was needed in your day simply because the business of production was left in private hands, and that, consequently, they are superfluous now."

"I do not at once see how that follows," I replied.

"It is very simple," said Doctor Leete. "When innumerable different and independent persons produced the various things needful to life and comfort, endless exchanges between individuals were requisite in order that they might supply themselves with what they desired. These exchanges constituted trade, and money was essential as their medium. But as soon as the nation became the sole producer of all sorts of commodities, there was no need of exchanges between individuals that they might get what they required. Everything was procurable from one source, and nothing could be procured anywhere else. A system of direct distribution from the national storehouses took the place of trade, and for this money was unnecessary."

"How is the distribution managed?" I asked.

"On the simplest possible plan," replied Doctor Leete. "A credit corresponding to his share of the annual product of the nation is given to every citizen on the public books at the beginning of each year, and a credit card issued him with which he procures at the public storehouses, found in every community, whatever he desires whenever he desires it. This arrangement, you will see, totally obviates the necessity for business transactions of any sort between individuals and consumers. Perhaps you would like to see what our credit cards are like.

"You observe," he pursued as I was curiously examining the piece of pasteboard he gave me, "that this card is issued for a certain number of dollars. We have kept the old word, but not the substance. The term, as we use it, answers to no real thing, but merely serves as an algebraical symbol for comparing the values of products with one another. For this purpose they are all priced in dollars and cents, just as in your day. The value of what I procure on this card is checked off by the clerk, who pricks out of these tiers of squares the price of what I order."

"If you wanted to buy something of your neighbor, could you transfer part of your credit to him as consideration?" I inquired.

"In the first place," replied Doctor Leete, "our neighbors have nothing to sell us, but in any event our credit would not be transferable, being strictly personal. Before the nation could even think of honoring any such transfer as you speak of, it would be bound to inquire into all the circumstances of the transaction, so as to be able to guarantee its absolute equity. It would have been reason enough, had there been no other, for abolishing money, that its possession was no indication of rightful title to it. In the hands of the man who had stolen it or murdered for it, it was as good as in those which had earned it by industry. People nowadays interchange gifts and favors out of friendship, but buying and selling is considered absolutely inconsistent with the mutual benevolence and disinterestedness which should prevail between citizens and the sense of community of interest which supports our social system. According to our ideas, buying and selling is essentially antisocial in all its tendencies. It is an education in self-seeking at the expense of others, and no society whose citizens are trained in such a school can possibly rise above a very low grade of civilization."

"What if you have to spend more than your card in any one year?" I asked.

"The provision is so ample that we are more likely not to spend it all," replied Doctor Leete. "But if extraordinary expenses should exhaust it, we can obtain a limited advance on the next year's credit, though this practice is not encouraged, and a heavy discount is charged to check it. Of course if a man showed himself a reckless spendthrift he would receive his allowance monthly or weekly instead of yearly, or if necessary not be permitted to handle it at all."

"If you don't spend your allowance, I suppose it accumulates?"

"That is also permitted to a certain extent when a special outlay is anticipated. But unless notice to the contrary is given, it is presumed that the citizen who does not fully expend his credit did not have occasion to do so, and the balance is turned into the general surplus."

"Such a system does not encourage saving habits on the part of citizens," I said.

"It is not intended to," was the reply. "The nation is rich, and does not wish the people to deprive themselves of any good thing. In your day, men were bound to lay up goods and money against coming failure of the means of support and for their children. This necessity made parsimony a virtue. But now it would have no such laudable object, and, having lost its utility, it has ceased to be regarded as a virtue. No man any more has any care for the morrow, either for himself or his children, for the nation guarantees the nurture, education, and comfortable maintenance of every citizen from the cradle to the grave."

"That is a sweeping guarantee!" I said. "What certainty can there be that the value of a man's labor will recompense the nation for its outlay on him? On the whole, society may be able to support all its members, but some must earn less than enough for their support, and others more; and that brings us back once more to the wages question, on which you have hitherto said nothing. It was at just this point, if you remember, that our talk ended last evening; and I say again, as I did then, that here I should suppose a national industrial system like yours would find its main difficulty. How, I ask once more, can you adjust satisfactorily the comparative wages or remuneration of the multitude of avocations, so unlike and so incommensurable, which are necessary for the service of society? In our day the market rate determined the price of labor of all sorts, as well as of goods. The employer paid as little as he could, and the worker got as much. It was not a pretty system ethically, I admit; but it did, at least, furnish us a rough-and-ready formula for settling a question which must be settled ten thousand times a day if the world was ever going to get forward. There seemed to us no other practicable way of doing it."

"Yes," replied Doctor Leete, "it was the only practicable way under a system which made the interests of every individual antagonistic to those of every other; but it would have been a pity if humanity could never have devised a better plan, for yours was simply the application to the mutual relations of men of the devil's maxim, 'Your necessity is my opportunity.' The reward of any service depended not upon its difficulty, danger, or hardship, for throughout the world it seems that the most perilous, severe, and repulsive labor was done by the worst-paid classes, but solely upon the straits of those who needed the service."

"All that is conceded," I said. "But, with all its defects, the plan of settling prices by the market rate was a practical plan; and I cannot conceive what satisfactory substitute you can have devised for it. The government being the only possible employer, there is of course no labor market or market rate. Wages of all sorts must be arbitrarily fixed by the government. I cannot imagine a more complex and delicate function than that must be, or one, however performed, more certain to breed universal dissatisfaction."

"I beg your pardon," replied Doctor Leete, "but I think you exaggerate the difficulty. Suppose a board of fairly sensible men were charged with settling the wages for all sorts of trades under a system which, like ours, guaranteed employment to all, while permitting the choice of avocations. Don't you see that, however unsatisfactory the first adjustment might be, the mistakes would soon correct themselves? The favored trades would have too many volunteers, and those discriminated against would lack them till the errors were set right. But this is aside from the purpose, for, though this plan would, I fancy, be practicable enough, it is no part of our system."

"How, then, do you regulate wages?" I once more asked.

Doctor Leete did not reply till after several moments of meditative silence. "I know, of course," he finally said, "enough of the old order of things to understand just what you mean by that question; and yet the present order is so utterly different at this point that I am a little at a loss how to answer you best. You ask me how we regulate wages; I can only reply that there is no idea in the modern social economy which at all corresponds with what was meant by wages in your day."

"I suppose you mean that you have no money to pay wages in," said I. "But the credit given the worker at the government storehouse answers to his wages with us. How is the amount of the credit given respectively to the workers in different lines determined? By what title does the individual claim his particular share? What is the basis of allotment?"

"His title," replied Doctor Leete, "is his humanity. The basis of his claim is the fact that he is a man."

"The fact that he is a man!" I repeated, incredulously. "Do you possibly mean that all have the same share?"

"Most assuredly."

The readers of this book never having practically known any other arrangement, or perhaps very carefully considered the historical accounts of former epochs in which a very different system prevailed, cannot be expected to appreciate the stupor of amazement into which Doctor Leete's simple statement plunged me.

"You see," he said, smiling, "that it is not merely that we have no money to pay wages in, but, as I said, we have nothing at all answering to your idea of wages."

By this time I had pulled myself together sufficiently to voice some of the criticisms which, man of the nineteenth century as I was, came uppermost in my mind, upon this, to me, astounding arrangement. "Some men do twice the work of others!" I exclaimed. "Are the clever workmen content with a plan that ranks them with the indifferent?"

"We leave no possible ground for any complaint of injustice," replied Doctor Leete, "by requiring precisely the same measure of service from all."

"How can you do that, I should like to know, when no two men's powers are the same?"

"Nothing could be simpler," was Doctor Leete's reply. "We require of each that he shall make the same effort; that is, we demand of him the best service it is in his power to give."

"And supposing all do the best they can," I answered, "the amount of the product resulting is twice greater from one man than from another."

"Very true," replied Doctor Leete, "but the amount of the resulting product has nothing whatever to do with the question, which is one of desert. Desert is a moral question, and the amount of the product a material quantity. It would be an extraordinary sort of logic which should try to determine a moral question by a material standard. The amount of the effort alone is pertinent to the question of desert. All men who do their best, do the same. A man's endowments, however god-like, merely fix the measure of his duty. The man of great endowments who does not do all he might, though he may do more than a man of small endowments who does his best, is deemed a less deserving worker than the latter, and dies a debtor to his fellows. The Creator

61

sets men's tasks for them by the faculties he gives them; we simply exact their fulfillment."

"No doubt that is very fine philosophy," I said. "Nevertheless it seems hard that the man who produces twice as much as another, even if both do their best, should have only the same share."

"Does it, indeed, seem so to you?" responded Doctor Leete. "Now, do you know, that seems very curious to me? The way it strikes people nowadays is, that a man who can produce twice as much as another with the same effort, instead of being rewarded for doing so, ought to be punished if he does not do so. In the nineteenth century, when a horse pulled a heavier load than a goat, I suppose you rewarded him. Now, we should have whipped him soundly if he had not, on the ground that, being much stronger, he ought to. It is singular how ethical standards change." The doctor said this with such a twinkle in his eye that I was obliged to laugh.

"I suppose," I said, "that the real reason that we rewarded men for their endowments, while we considered those of horses and goats merely as fixing the service to be severally required of them, was that the animals, not being reasoning beings, naturally did the best they could, whereas men could only be induced to do so by rewarding them according to the amount of their product. That brings me to ask why, unless human nature has mightily changed in a hundred years, you are not under the same necessity."

"We are," replied Doctor Leete. "I don't think there has been any change in human nature in that respect since your day. It is so constituted still that special incentives in the form of prizes, and advantages to be gained, are requisite to call out the best endeavors of the average man in any direction."

"But what inducement," I asked, "can a man have to put forth his best endeavors when, however much or little he accomplishes, his income remains the same? High characters may be moved by devotion to the common welfare under such a system, but does not the average man tend to rest back on his oar, reasoning that it is of no use to make a special effort, since the effort will not increase his income, nor its withholding diminish it?"

"Does it then really seem to you, " answered my companion, "that human nature is insensible to any motives save fear of want and love of luxury, that you should expect security and equality of livelihood to leave them without possible incentives to effort? Your contemporaries did not really think so, though they might fancy they did. When it was a question of the grandest class of efforts, the most absolute self-devotion, they depended on quite other incentives. Not higher wages, but honor and the hope of men's gratitude, patriotism and the inspiration of duty, were the motives which they set before their soldiers when it was a question of dying for the nation, and never was there an age of the world when those motives did not call out what is best and noblest in men. And not only this, but when you come to analyze the love of money which was the general impulse to effort in your day, you find that the dread of want and desire of luxury was but one of several motives which the pursuit of money represented; the others, and with many the more influential, being desire of power, of social position, and reputation for ability and success. So you see that though we have abolished poverty and the fear of it, and inordinate luxury with the hope of it, we have not touched the greater part of the motives which underlay the love of money in former times, or any of those which prompted the supremer sorts of effort. The coarser motives, which no longer move us, have been replaced by higher motives wholly unknown to the mere wage earners of your age. Now that industry, of whatever sort, is no longer self-service, but service of the nation, patriotism, passion for humanity, impel the worker as in your day they did the soldier. The army of industry is an army, not alone by virtue of its perfect organization, but by reason also of the ardor of self-devotion which animates its members.

"But as you used to supplement the motives of patriotism with the love of glory, in order to stimulate the valor of your soldiers, so do we. Based as our industrial system is on the principle of requiring the same unit of effort from every man, that is, the best he can do, you will see that the means by which we spur the workers to do their best must be a very essential part of our scheme. With us, diligence in the national service is the sole and certain way to public repute, social distinction, and official power. The value of a man's services to society fixes his rank in it. Compared with the effort of our social arrangements in impelling men to be zealous in business, we deem the object lessons of biting poverty and wanton luxury on which you depended a device as weak and uncertain as it was barbaric. The lust of honor even in your sordid day notoriously impelled men to more desperate effort than the love of money could."

"I should be extremely interested," I said, "to learn something of what these social arrangements are."

"The scheme in its details," replied the doctor, "is of course very elaborate, for it underlies the entire organization of our industrial army; but a few words will give you a general idea of it."

At this moment our talk was charmingly interrupted by the emergence upon the aerial platform where we sat of Edith Leete. She was dressed for the street, and had come to speak to her father about some commission she was to do for him.

"By the way, Edith," he exclaimed, as she was about to leave us to ourselves, "I wonder if Mr. West would not be interested in visiting the store with you? I have been telling him something about our system of distribution, and perhaps he might like to see it in practical operation.

"My daughter," he added, turning to me, "is an indefatigable shopper, and can tell you more about the stores than I can."

The proposition was naturally very agreeable to me, and Edith being good enough to say that she should be glad to have my company, we left the house together.

"IF I AM GOING TO EXPLAIN OUR WAY OF SHOPPING TO you," said my companion, as we walked along the street, "you must explain your way to me. I have never been able to understand it from all I have read on the subject. For example, when you had such a vast number of shops, each with its different assortment, how could a lady ever settle upon any purchase till she had visited all the shops, for, until she had, she could not know what there was to choose from."

"It was as you suppose. That was the only way she could know," I replied.

"Father calls me an indefatigable shopper, but I should soon be a very fatigued one if I had to do as they did," was Edith's laughing comment.

"The loss of time in going from shop to shop was indeed a waste which the busy bitterly complained of," I said. "But as for the ladies of the idle class, though they complained also, I think the system was really a godsend by furnishing a device to kill time."

"But say there were a thousand shops in a city, hundreds, perhaps, of the same sort, how could even the idlest find time to make their rounds?"

"They really could not visit all, of course," I replied. "Those who did a great deal of buying, learned in time where they might expect to find what they wanted. This class had made a science of the specialties of the shops, and bought at advantage, always getting the most and best for the least money. It required, however, long experience to acquire this knowledge. Those who were too busy, or bought too little to gain it, took their chances and were generally unfortunate, getting the least and worst for the most money. It was the merest chance if persons not experienced in shopping received the value of their money."

"But why did you put up with such a shockingly inconvenient arrangement when you saw its faults so plainly?" Edith asked me.

"It was like all our social arrangements," I replied. "You can see their faults scarcely more plainly than we did, but we saw no remedy for them."

"Here we are at the store of our ward," said Edith, as we turned in at the great portal of one of the magnificent public buildings I had observed in my morning walk. There was nothing in the exterior aspect of the edifice to suggest a store to a representative of the nineteenth century. There was no display of goods in the great windows, or any device to advertise wares, or attract custom. Nor was there any sort of sign or legend on the front of the building to indicate the character of the business carried on there; but instead, above the portal, standing out from the front of the building, a majestic life-size group of statuary, the central figure of which was a female ideal of Plenty, with her cornucopia. Judging from the composition of the throng passing in and out, about the same proportion of the sexes among shoppers obtained as in the nineteenth century. As we entered, Edith said that there was one of these great distributing establishments in each ward of the city, so that no residence was more than five or ten minutes' walk from one of them. It was the first interior of a twentieth-century public building that I had ever beheld, and the spectacle naturally impressed me deeply. I was in a vast hall full of light, received not alone from the windows on all sides, but from the dome, the point of which was a hundred feet above. Beneath it, in the center of the hall, a magnificent fountain played, cooling the atmosphere to a delicious freshness with its spray. The walls and ceiling were frescoed in mellow tints, calculated to soften without absorbing the light which flooded the interior. Around the fountain was a space occupied with chairs and sofas, on which many persons were seated conversing. Legends on the walls all about the hall indicated to what classes of commodities the counters below were devoted. Edith directed her steps toward one of these, where samples of muslin of a bewildering variety were displayed, and proceeded to inspect them.

"Where is the clerk?" I asked, for there was no one behind the counter, and no one seemed coming to attend to the customer.

"I have no need of the clerk yet," said Edith. "I have not made my selection."

"It was the principal business of clerks to help people to make their selections in my day," I replied.

"What! To tell people what they wanted?"

"Yes. And oftener to induce them to buy what they didn't want."

"But did not ladies find that very impertinent?" Edith asked, wonderingly. "What concern could it possibly be to the clerks whether people bought or not?"

"It was their sole concern," I answered. "They were hired for the purpose of getting rid of the goods, and were expected to do their utmost, short of the use of force, to compass that end."

"Ah, yes! How stupid I am to forget!" said Edith. "The storekeeper and his clerks depended for their livelihood on selling the goods in your day. Of course that is all different now. The goods are the nation's. They are here for those who want them, and it is the business of the clerks to wait on people and take their orders; but it is not the interest of the clerk or the nation to dispose of a yard or a pound of anything to anybody who does not want it." She smiled as she added, "How exceedingly odd it must have seemed to have clerks trying to induce one to take what one did not want, or was doubtful about!"

"But even a twentieth-century clerk might make himself useful in giving you information about the goods, though he did not tease you to buy them," I suggested.

"No," said Edith, "that is not the business of the clerk. These printed cards, for which the government authorities are responsible, give us all the information we can possibly need."

I saw then that there was fastened to each sample a card containing in succinct form a complete statement of the make and materials of the goods and all its qualities, as well as price, leaving absolutely no point to hang a question on.

"The clerk has, then, nothing to say about the goods he sells?" I said.

"Nothing at all. It is not necessary that he should know or profess to know anything about them. Courtesy and accuracy in taking orders are all that are required of him."

"What a prodigious amount of lying that simple arrangement saves!" I ejaculated.

"Do you mean that all the clerks misrepresented their goods in your day?" Edith asked.

"God forbid that I should say so!" I replied. "For there were many who did not, and they were entitled to especial credit, for when one's livelihood and that of his wife and babies depended on the amount of goods he could dispose of, the temptation to deceive the customer—or let him deceive himself—was well-nigh overwhelming. But, Miss Leete, I am distracting you from your task with my talk."

"Not at all. I have made my selections." With that she touched a button, and in a moment a clerk appeared. He took down her order on a tablet with a pencil which made two copies, of which he gave one to her, and enclosing the counterpart in a small receptacle, dropped it into a transmitting tube.

"The duplicate of the order," said Edith as she turned away from the counter, after the clerk had punched the value of her purchase out of the credit card she gave him, "is given to the purchaser, so that any mistakes in filling it can be easily traced and rectified."

"You were very quick about your selections," I said. "May I ask how you knew that you might not have found something to suit you better in some of the other stores? But probably you are required to buy in your own district."

"Oh, no," she replied. "We buy where we please, though naturally most often near home. But I should have gained nothing by visiting other stores. The assort-

68

ment in all is exactly the same, representing as it does in each case samples of all the varieties produced or imported by the United States. That is why one can decide quickly, and never need visit two stores."

"And is this merely a sample store? I see no clerks cutting off goods or marking bundles."

"All our stores are sample stores, except as to a few classes of articles. The goods, with these exceptions, are all at the great central warehouse of the city, to which they are shipped directly from the producers. We order from the sample and the printed statement of texture, make, and qualities. The orders are sent to the warehouse, and the goods distributed from there."

"That must be a tremendous saving of handling," I said. "By our system, the manufacturer sold to the wholesaler, the wholesaler to the retailer, and the retailer to the consumer, and the goods had to be handled each time. You avoid one handling of the goods, and eliminate the retailer altogether, with his big profit and the army of clerks it goes to support. Why, Miss Leete, this store is merely the order department of a wholesale house, with no more than a wholesaler's complement of clerks. Under our system of handling the goods, persuading the customer to buy them, cutting them off, and packing them, ten clerks would not do what one does here. The saving must be enormous."

"I suppose so," said Edith, "but of course we have never known any other way. But, Mr. West, you must not fail to ask Father to take you to the central warehouse some day, where they receive the orders from the different sample houses all over the city and parcel out and send the goods to their destinations. He took me there not long ago, and it was a wonderful sight. The system is certainly perfect; for example, over yonder in that sort of cage is the dispatching clerk. The orders, as they are taken by the different departments in the store, are sent by transmitters to him. His assistants sort them and enclose each class in a carrier-box by itself. The dispatching clerk has a dozen pneumatic transmitters before him answering to the general classes of goods, each communicating with the corresponding department at the warehouse. He drops the box of orders into the tube it calls for, and a few moments later it drops on the proper desk in the warehouse, together with all the orders of the same sort from the other sample stores. The orders are read off, recorded, and sent to be filled, like lightning. The filling I thought the most interesting part. Bales of cloth are placed on spindles and turned by machinery, and the cutter, who also has a machine, works right through one bale after another till exhausted, when another man takes his place; and it is the same with those who fill the orders in any other staple. The packages are then delivered by larger tubes to the city districts, and thence distributed to the houses. You may understand how quickly it is all done when I tell you that my order will probably be at home sooner than I could have carried it from here."

"How do you manage in the thinly settled rural districts?" I asked.

"The system is the same," Edith explained, "the village sample shops are connected by transmitters with the central county warehouse, which may be twenty miles away. The transmission is so swift, though, that the time lost on the way is trifling. But, to save expense, in many counties one set of tubes connect several villages with the warehouse, and then there is time lost waiting for one another. Sometimes it is two or three hours before goods ordered are received. It was so where I was staying last summer, and I found it quite inconvenient."*

"There must be many other respects also, no doubt, in which the country stores are inferior to the city stores," I suggested.

"No," Edith answered, "they are otherwise precisely as good. The sample shop of the smallest village, just like this one, gives you your choice of all the varieties

---

* I am informed since the above is in type that this lack of perfection in the distributing service of some of the country districts is to be remedied, and that soon every village will have its own set of tubes.

of goods the nation has, for the county warehouse draws on the same source as the city warehouse."

As we walked home I commented on the great variety in the size and cost of the houses. "How is it," I asked, "that this difference is consistent with the fact that all citizens have the same income?"

"Because," Edith explained, "although the income is the same, personal taste determines how the individual shall spend it. Some like fine houses; others, like myself, prefer pretty clothes; and still others want an elaborate table. The rents which the nation receives for these houses vary, according to size, elegance, and location, so that everybody can find something to suit. The larger houses are usually occupied by large families, in which there are several to contribute to the rent; while small families, like ours, find smaller houses more convenient and economical. It is a matter of taste and convenience wholly. I have read that in old times people often kept up establishments and did other things which they could not afford for ostentation, to make people think them richer than they were. Was it really so, Mr. West?"

"I shall have to admit that it was," I replied.

"Well, you see, it could not be so nowadays; for everybody's income is known, and it is known that what is spent one way must be saved another."

· XI ·

WHEN WE ARRIVED HOME, DOCTOR LEETE HAD NOT YET returned, and Mrs. Leete was not visible. "Are you fond of music, Mr. West?" Edith asked.

I assured her that it was half of life, according to my notion.

"I ought to apologize for inquiring," she said. "It is not a question that we ask one another nowadays; but I have read that in your day, even among the cultured class, there were some who did not care for music."

"You must remember, in excuse," I said, "that we had some rather absurd kinds of music."

"Yes," she said, "I know that. I am afraid I should not have fancied it all myself. Would you like to hear some of ours now, Mr. West?"

"Nothing would delight me so much as to listen to you," I said.

"To me!" she exclaimed, laughing. "Did you think I was going to play or sing to you?"

"I hoped so, certainly," I replied.

Seeing that I was a little abashed, she subdued her merriment and explained. "Of course, we all sing nowadays as a matter of course in the training of the voice, and some learn to play instruments for their private amusement; but the professional music is so much grander and more perfect than any performance of ours, and so easily commanded when we wish to hear it, that we don't think of calling our singing or playing music at all. All the really fine singers and players are in the musical service, and the rest of us hold our peace for the main part. But would you really like to hear some music?"

I assured her once more that I would.

"Come, then, into the music room," she said, and I followed her into an apartment finished, without hangings, in wood, with a floor of polished wood. I was prepared for new devices in musical instruments, but I saw nothing in the room which by any stretch of imagination could be conceived as such. It was evident that my puzzled appearance was affording intense amusement to Edith.

"Please look at today's music," she said, handing me a card, "and tell me what you would prefer. It is now five o'clock, you will remember."

The card bore the date "September 12, 2000," and contained the longest program of music I had ever seen. It was as various as it was long, including a most extraordinary range of vocal and instrumental solos, duets, quartets, and various orchestral combinations. I remained bewildered by the prodigious list until Edith's pink fingertip indicated a particular section of it, where several selections were bracketed, with the words "5 P.M." against them; then I observed that this prodigious program was an all-day one, divided into twenty-four sections answering to the hours. There were but a few pieces of music in the "5 P.M." section, and I indicated an organ piece as my preference.

"I am so glad you like the organ," said she. "I think there is scarcely any music that suits my mood oftener."

She made me sit down comfortably, and, crossing the room, so far as I could see, merely touched one or two screws, and at once the room was filled with the music of a grand organ anthem; filled, not flooded, for, by some means, the volume of melody had been perfectly gradua-ted to the size of the apartment. I listened, scarcely breathing, to the close. Such music, so perfectly ren-dered, I had never expected to hear.

"Grand!" I cried, as the last great wave of sound broke and ebbed away into silence. "Bach must be at the keys of that organ; but where is the organ?"

"Wait a moment, please," said Edith. "I want to have you listen to this waltz before you ask any questions. I think it is perfectly charming." And as she spoke the sound of violins filled the room with the witchery of a summer night. When this had also ceased, she said: "There is nothing in the least mysterious about the music, as you seem to imagine. It is not made by fairies or genii, but by good, honest, and exceedingly clever human hands. We have simply carried the idea of labor-saving by cooperation into our musical service as into everything else. There are a number of music rooms in the city, perfectly adapted acoustically to the different sorts of music. These halls are connected by telephone with all the houses of the city whose people care to pay the small fee, and there are none, you may be sure, who do not. The corps of musicians attached to each hall is so large that, although no individual performer, or group of performers, has more than a brief part, each day's program lasts through the twenty-four hours. There are on that card for today, as you will see if you observe closely, distinct programs of four of these concerts, each of a different order of music from the others, being now simultaneously performed, and any one of the four pieces now going on that you prefer, you can hear by merely pressing the button which will connect your house wire with the hall where it is being rendered. The programs are so coordinated that the pieces at any one time simultaneously proceeding in the different halls usually offer a choice, not only between instrumental and vocal, and between different sorts of instruments, but also between different motives from grave to gay, so that all tastes and moods can be suited."

"It appears to me, Miss Leete," I said, "that if we could have devised an arrangement for providing everybody with music in their homes, perfect in quality, unlimited in quantity, suited to every mood, and beginning and ceasing at will, we should have considered the limit of human felicity already attained, and ceased to strive for further improvements."

"I am sure I never could imagine how those among you who depended at all on music managed to endure the old-fashioned system for providing for it," replied Edith. "Music really worth hearing must have been, I suppose, wholly out of the reach of the masses, and attainable by the most favored only occasionally, at great trouble, prodigious expense, and then for brief periods, arbitrarily fixed by somebody else, and in connection with all sorts of undesirable circumstances. Your concerts, for instance, and operas! How perfectly exasperating it must have been, for the sake of a piece or two of music that suited you, to have to sit for hours listening to what you did not care for! Now, at a dinner one can skip the courses one does not care for. Who would ever dine, however hungry, if required to eat everything brought on the table? And I am sure one's hearing is quite as sensitive as one's taste. I suppose it was these difficulties in the way of commanding really good music which made you endure so much playing and singing in your homes by people who had only the rudiments of the art."

"Yes," I replied, "it was that sort of music or none for most of us."

"Ah, well," Edith sighed, "when one really considers, it is not so strange that people in those days so often did not care for music. I dare say I should have detested it, too."

"Did I understand you rightly," I inquired, "that this musical program covers the entire twenty-four hours? It seems to on this card, certainly; but who is there to listen to music between, say, midnight and morning?"

"Oh, many," Edith replied. "Our people keep all hours; but if the music were provided from midnight to morning for no others, it still would be for the sleepless, the sick, and the dying. All our bedchambers have a telephone attachment at the head of the bed by which any person who may be sleepless can command music at pleasure, of the sort suited to the mood."

"Is there such an arrangement in the room assigned to me?"

"Why, certainly. And how stupid, how very stupid, of me not to think to tell you of that last night! Father will show you about the adjustment before you go to bed tonight, however; and with the receiver at your ear, I am quite sure you will be able to snap your fingers at all sorts of uncanny feelings if they trouble you again."

That evening Doctor Leete asked us about our visit to the store, and in the course of the desultory comparison of the ways of the nineteenth century and the twentieth, which followed, something raised the question of inheritance. "I suppose," I said, "the inheritance of property is not now allowed."

"On the contrary," replied Doctor Leete, "there is no interference with it. In fact, you will find, Mr. West, as you come to know us, that there is far less interference of any sort with personal liberty nowadays than you were accustomed to. We require, indeed, by law that every man shall serve the nation for a fixed period, instead of leaving him his choice, as you did, between working, stealing, or starving. With the exception of this fundamental law, which is, indeed, merely a codification of the law of nature—the edict of Eden—by which it is made equal in its pressure on men, our system depends in no particular upon legislation, but is entirely voluntary, the logical outcome of the operation of human nature under rational conditions. This question of inheritance illustrates just that point. The fact that the nation is the sole capitalist and landowner of course restricts the individual's possessions to his annual credit, and what personal and household belongings he may have procured with it. His credit, like an annuity in your day, ceases on his death, with the allowance of a fixed sum for funeral expenses. His other possessions he leaves as he pleases."

"What is to prevent, in course of time, such accumulations of valuable goods and chattels in the hands of individuals as might seriously interfere with equality in the circumstances of citizens?" I asked.

"That matter arranges itself very simply," was the reply. "Under the present organization of society, accumulations of personal property are merely burdensome the moment they exceed what adds to the real comfort. In your day, if a man had a house crammed full with gold and silver plate, rare china, expensive furniture, and such things, he was considered rich, for these things represented money, and could at any time be turned into it. Nowadays a man whom the legacies of a hundred relatives, simultaneously dying, should place in a similar position, would be considered very unlucky. The articles, not being salable, would be of no value to him except for their actual use or the enjoyment of their beauty. On the other hand, his income remaining the same, he would have to deplete his credit to hire houses to store the goods in, and still further to pay for the service of those who took care of them. You may be very sure that such a man would lose no time in scattering among his friends possessions which only made him the poorer, and that none of those friends would accept more of them than they could easily spare room for and time to attend to. You see, then, that to prohibit the inheritance of personal property with a view to prevent great accumulations would be a superfluous precaution for the nation. The individual citizen can be trusted to see that he is not overburdened. So careful is he in this respect, that the relatives usually waive claim to most of the effects of deceased friends, reserving only particular objects. The nation takes charge of the resigned chattels, and turns such as are of value into the common stock once more."

"You spoke of paying for service to take care of your houses," said I. "That suggests a question I have several times been on the point of asking. How have you disposed of the problem of domestic service? Who are willing to be domestic servants in a community where all are social equals? Our ladies found it hard enough to find such even when there was little pretense of social equality."

"It is precisely because we are all social equals whose equality nothing can compromise, and because service is honorable, in a society whose fundamental principle is that all in turn shall serve the rest, that we could easily provide a corps of domestic servants such as you never dreamed of, if we needed them," replied Doctor Leete. "But we do not need them."

"Who does your housework, then?" I asked.

"There is none to do," said Mrs. Leete, to whom I had addressed this question. "Our washing is all done at public laundries at excessively cheap rates, and our cooking at public kitchens. The making and repairing of all we wear are done outside in public shops. Electricity, of course, takes the place of all fires and lighting. We choose houses no larger than we need, and furnish them so as to involve the minimum of trouble to keep them in order. We have no use for domestic servants."

"The fact," said Doctor Leete, "that you had in the poorer classes a boundless supply of serfs on whom you could impose all sorts of painful and disagreeable tasks, made you indifferent to devices to avoid the necessity for them. But now that we all have to do in turn whatever work is done for society, every individual in the nation has the same interest, and a personal one, in devices for lightening the burden. This fact has given a prodigious impulse to labor-saving inventions in all sorts of industry, of which the combination of the maximum of comfort and minimum of trouble in household arrangements was one of the earliest results.

"In case of special emergencies in the household," pursued Doctor Leete, "such as extensive cleaning or renovation, or sickness in the family, we can always secure assistance from the industrial force."

"But how do you recompense these assistants, since you have no money?"

"We do not pay them, of course, but the nation for them. Their services can be obtained by application at the proper bureau, and their value is pricked off the credit card of the applicant."

"What a paradise for womankind the world must be now!" I exclaimed. "In my day, even wealth and unlimited servants did not enfranchise their possessors from household cares, while the women of the merely well-to-do and poorer classes lived and died martyrs to them."

"Yes," said Mrs. Leete, "I have read something of that; enough to convince me that, badly off as the men, too, were in your day, they were more fortunate than their mothers and wives."

"The broad shoulders of the nation," said Doctor Leete, "bear now like a feather the burden that broke the backs of the women of your day. Their misery came, with all your other miseries, from that incapacity for cooperation which followed from the individualism on which your social system was founded, from your inability to perceive that you could make ten times more profit out of your fellow men by uniting with them than by contending with them. The wonder is, not that you did not live more comfortably, but that you were able to live together at all, who were all confessedly bent on making one another your servants, and securing possession of one another's goods."

"There, there, Father. If you are so vehement, Mr. West will think you are scolding him," laughingly interposed Edith.

"When you want a doctor," I asked, "do you simply

apply to the proper bureau and take any one that may be sent?"

"That rule would not work well in the case of physicians," replied Doctor Leete. "The good a physician can do a patient depends largely on his acquaintance with his constitutional tendencies and condition. The patient must be able, therefore, to call in a particular doctor, and he does so just as patients did in your day. The only difference is that, instead of collecting his fee for himself, the doctor collects it for the nation by pricking off the amount, according to a regular scale for medical attendance, from the patient's credit card."

"I can imagine," I said, "that if the fee is always the same, and a doctor may not turn away patients, as I suppose he may not, the good doctors are called constantly and the poor doctors left in idleness."

"In the first place, if you will overlook the apparent conceit of the remark from a retired physician," replied Doctor Leete, with a smile, "we have no poor doctors. Anybody who pleases to get a little smattering of medical terms is not now at liberty to practice on the bodies of citizens, as in your day. None but students who have passed the severe tests of the schools, and clearly proved their vocation, are permitted to practice. Then, too, you will observe that there is nowadays no attempt of doctors to build up their practice at the expense of other doctors. There would be no motive for that. For the rest, the doctor has to render regular reports of his work to the medical bureau, and if he is not reasonably well employed, work is found for him."

· XII ·

THE QUESTIONS WHICH I NEEDED TO ASK BEFORE I COULD acquire even an outline acquaintance with the institutions of the twentieth century being endless, and Doctor Leete's good-nature appearing equally so, we sat up talking for several hours after the ladies left us. Reminding my host of the point at which our talk had broken off that morning, I expressed my curiosity to learn how the organization of the industrial army was made to afford a sufficient stimulus to diligence in the lack of any anxiety on the worker's part as to his livelihood.

"You must understand in the first place," replied the doctor, "that the supply of incentives to effort is but one of the objects sought in the organization we have adopted for the army. The other, and equally important, is to secure for the file leaders and captains of the force, and the great officers of the nation, men of proved abilities, who are pledged by their own careers to hold their followers up to their highest standard of performance and permit no lagging. With a view to these two ends the industrial army is organized. First comes the unclassified grade of common laborers, men of all work, to which all recruits during their first three years belong. This grade is a sort of school and a very strict one, in which the young men are taught habits of obedience, subordination, and devotion to duty. While the miscellaneous nature of the work done by this force prevents the systematic grading of the workers which is afterward possible, yet individual records are kept, and excellence receives distinction corresponding with the penalties that negligence incurs. It is not, however, policy with us to permit youthful recklessness or indiscretion, when not deeply culpable, to handicap the future careers of young men, and all who have passed through the unclassified grade without serious disgrace have an equal opportunity to choose the life employment they have most liking for. Having selected this, they enter upon it as apprentices. The length of the apprenticeship naturally differs in different occupations. At the end of it the apprentice becomes a full workman, and a member of his trade or guild. Now not only are the individual records of the apprentices for ability and industry strictly kept, and excellence distinguished by suitable distinctions, but upon the average of his record during apprenticeship the standing given the apprentice among the full workmen depends.

"While the internal organizations of different industries, mechanical and agricultural, differ according to their peculiar conditions, they agree in a general division of their workers into first, second, and third grades, according to ability, and these grades are in many cases subdivided into first and second classes. According to his standing as an apprentice, a young man is assigned his place as a first-, second-, or third-grade worker. Of course only young men of unusual ability pass directly from apprenticeship into the first grade of the workers. The most fall into the lower grades, working up as they grow more experienced, at the periodical regradings. These regradings take place in each industry at intervals corresponding with the length of the apprenticeship to that industry, so that merit never need wait long to rise, nor can any rest on past achievements unless they would drop into a lower rank. One of the notable advantages of a high grading is the privilege it gives the worker in electing which of the various branches or processes of his industry he will follow as his specialty. Of course it is not intended that any of these processes shall be disproportionately arduous, but there is often much difference between them, and the privilege of election is accordingly highly prized. So far as possible, indeed, the preferences even of the poorest workmen are considered in assigning them their line of work, because not only their happiness but their usefulness is thus enhanced. While, however, the wish of the lower-grade man is consulted so far as the exigencies of the service permit, he is considered only after the upper-grade men have been provided for, and often he has to put up with second or third choice, or even with an arbitrary assignment when help is needed. This privilege of election attends every regrading, and when a man loses his grade he also risks having to exchange the sort of work he likes for some other less to his taste. The results of each regrading, giving the standing of every man in his industry, are gazetted in the public prints, and those who have won promotion since the last regrading receive the nation's thanks and are publicly invested with the badge of their new rank."

"What may this badge be?" I asked.

"Every industry has its emblematic device," replied Doctor Leete, "and this, in the shape of a metallic badge so small that you might not see it unless you knew where to look, is all the insigns which the men of the army wear, except where public convenience demands a distinctive uniform. This badge is the same in form for all grades of industry, but while the badge of the third grade is iron, that of the second grade is silver, and that of the first is gilt.

"Apart from the grand incentive to endeavor afforded by the fact that the high places in the nation are open only to the highest-class men, and that rank in the army constitutes the only mode of social distinction for the vast majority who are not aspirants in art, literature, and the professions, various incitements of a minor, but perhaps equally effective, sort are provided in the form of special privileges and immunities in the way of discipline, which the superior-class men enjoy. These, while intended to be as little as possible invidious to the less successful, have the effect of keeping constantly before every man's mind the great desirability of attaining the grade next above his own.

"It is obviously important that not only the good but also the indifferent and poor workmen should be able to cherish the ambition of rising. Indeed, the number of the latter being so much greater, it is even more essential that the ranking system should not operate to discourage them than that it should stimulate the others. It is to this end that the grades are divided into classes. The grades as well as the classes being made numerically equal at each regrading, there is not at any time, counting out the officers and the unclassified and apprentice grades, over one-ninth of the industrial army in the lowest class, and most of this number are recent apprentices, all of whom expect to rise. Those who remain during the entire term of service in the lowest class are but a trifling fraction of the industrial army, and likely to be as deficient in sensibility to their position as in ability to better it.

"It is not even necessary that a worker should win promotion to a higher grade to have at least a taste of glory. While promotion requires a general excellence of record as a worker, honorable mention and various sorts of prizes are awarded for excellence less than sufficient for promotion, and also for special feats and single performances in the various industries. There are many minor distinctions of standing, not only within the grades but within the classes, each of which acts as a spur to the efforts of a group. It is intended that no form of merit shall wholly fail of recognition.

"As for actual neglect of work, positively bad work, or other overt remissness on the part of men incapable of generous motives, the discipline of the industrial army is far too strict to allow anything whatever of the sort. A man able to duty, and persistently refusing, is sentenced to solitary imprisonment on bread and water till he consents.

"The lowest grade of the officers of the industrial army, that of assistant foremen, or lieutenants, is appointed out of men who have held their place for two years in the first class of the first grade. Where this leaves too large a range of choice, only the first group of this class are eligible. No one thus comes to the point of commanding men until he is about thirty years old. After a man becomes an officer, his rating of course no longer depends on the efficiency of his own work, but on that of his men. The foremen are appointed from among the assistant foremen, by the same exercise of discretion limited to a small eligible class. In the appointments to the still higher grades another principle is introduced, which it would take too much time to explain now.

"Of course such a system of grading as I have described would have been impracticable applied to the small industrial concerns of your day, in some of which there were hardly enough employees to have left one apiece for the classes. You must remember that, under the national organization of labor, all industries are carried on by great bodies of men, many of your farms or shops being combined as one. It is also owing solely to the vast scale on which industry is organized, with coordinate establishments in every part of the country, that we are able by exchanges and transfers to fit every man so nearly with the sort of work he can do best.

"And now, Mr. West, I will leave it to you, on the bare outline of its features which I have given, if those who need special incentives to do their best are likely to lack them under our system. Does it not seem to you that men who found themselves obliged, whether they wished or not, to work, would under such a system be strongly impelled to do their best?"

I replied that it seemed to me the incentives offered were, if any objection were to be made, too strong; that the pace set for the young men was too hot; and such, indeed, I would add with deference, still remains my opinion, now that by longer residence among you I have become better acquainted with the whole subject.

Doctor Leete, however, desired me to reflect, and I am ready to say that it is perhaps a sufficient reply to my objection, that the worker's livelihood is in no way dependent on his ranking, and anxiety for that never embitters his disappointments; that the working hours are short, the vacations regular, and that all emulation ceases at forty-five, with the attainment of middle life.

"There are two or three other points I ought to refer to," he added, "to prevent your getting mistaken impressions. In the first place, you must understand that this system of preferment given the most efficient workers over the less so, in no way contravenes the fundamental idea of our social system, that all who do their best are equally deserving, whether the best be great or small. I have shown that the system is arranged to encourage the weaker as well as the stronger with the hope of rising, while the fact that the stronger are selected for the leaders is in no way a reflection upon the weaker, but in the interest of the common weal.

"Do not imagine, either, because emulation is given

free play as an incentive under our system, that we deem it a motive likely to appeal to the nobler sort of men, or worthy of them. Such as these find their motives within, not without, and measure their duty by their own endowments, not by those of others. So long as their achievement is proportioned to their powers, they would consider it preposterous to expect praise or blame because it chanced to be great or small. To such natures emulation appears philosophically absurd, and despicable in a moral aspect by its substitution of envy for admiration, and exultation for regret, in one's attitude toward the successes and the failures of others.

"But all men, even in the last year of the twentieth century, are not of this high order, and the incentives to endeavor requisite for those who are not must be of a sort adapted to their inferior natures. For these, then, emulation of the keenest edge is provided as a constant spur. Those who need this motive will feel it. Those who are above its influence do not need it.

"I should not fail to mention," resumed the doctor, "that for those too deficient in mental or bodily strength to be fairly graded with the main body of workers, we have a separate grade, unconnected with the others—a sort of invalid corps, the members of which are provided with a light class of tasks fitted to their strength. All our sick in mind and body, all our deaf and dumb, and lame and blind and crippled, and even our insane, belong to this invalid corps, and bear its insigns. The strongest often do nearly a man's work, the feeblest, of course, nothing; but none who can do anything are willing quite to give up. In their lucid intervals, even our insane are eager to do what they can."

"That is a pretty idea of the invalid corps," I said. "Even a barbarian from the nineteenth century can appreciate that. It is a very graceful way of disguising charity, and must be grateful to the feelings of its recipients."

"Charity!" repeated Doctor Leete. "Did you suppose that we consider the incapable class we are talking of objects of charity?"

"Why, naturally," I said, "inasmuch as they are incapable of self-support."

But here the doctor took me up quickly.

"Who is capable of self-support?" he demanded. "There is no such thing in a civilized society as self-support. In a state of society so barbarous as not even to know family cooperation, each individual may possibly support himself, though even then for a part of his life only; but from the moment that men begin to live together, and constitute even the rudest of society, self-support becomes impossible. As men grow more civilized, and the subdivision of occupations and services is carried out, a complex mutual dependence becomes the universal rule. Every man, however solitary may seem his occupation, is a member of a vast industrial partnership, as large as the nation, as large as humanity. The necessity of mutual dependence should imply the duty and guarantee of mutual support; and that it did not in your day constituted the essential cruelty and unreason of your system."

"That may all be so," I replied, "but it does not touch the case of those who are unable to contribute anything to the product of industry."

"Surely I told you this morning, at least I thought I did," replied Doctor Leete, "that the right of a man to maintenance at the nation's table depends on the fact that he is a man, and not on the amount of health and strength he may have, so long as he does his best."

"You said so," I answered, "but I supposed the rule applied only to the workers of different ability. Does it also hold of those who can do nothing at all?"

"Are they not also men?"

"I am to understand, then, that the lame, the blind, the sick, and the impotent, are as well off as the most efficient, and have the same income?"

"Certainly," was the reply.

"The idea of charity on such a scale," I answered, "would have made our most enthusiastic philanthropists gasp."

"If you had a sick brother at home," replied Doctor

Leete, "unable to work, would you feed him on less dainty food, and lodge and clothe him more poorly, than yourself? More likely far, you would give him the preference; nor would you think of calling it charity. Would not the word, in that connection, fill you with indignation?"

"Of course," I replied, "but the cases are not parallel. There is a sense, no doubt, in which all men are brothers; but this general sort of brotherhood is not to be compared, except for rhetorical purposes, to the brotherhood of blood, either as to its sentiment or its obligations."

"There speaks the nineteenth century!" exclaimed Doctor Leete. "Ah, Mr. West, there is no doubt as to the length of time that you slept. If I were to give you, in one sentence, a key to what may seem the mysteries of our civilization as compared with that of your age, I should say that it is the fact that the solidarity of the race and the brotherhood of man, which to you were but fine phrases, are, to our thinking and feeling, ties as real and as vital as physical fraternity.

"But even setting that consideration aside, I do not see why it so surprises you that those who cannot work are conceded the full right to live on the produce of those who can. Even in your day the duty of military service for the protection of the nation, to which our industrial service corresponds, while obligatory on those able to discharge it, did not operate to deprive of the privileges of citizenship those who were unable. They stayed at home, and were protected by those who fought, and nobody questioned their right to be, or thought less of them. So, now, the requirement of industrial service from those able to render it does not operate to deprive of the privileges of citizenship, which now implies the citizen's maintenance, him who cannot work. The worker is not a citizen because he works, but works because he is a citizen. As you recognize the duty of the strong to fight for the weak, we, now that fighting is gone by, recognize his duty to work for him.

"A solution which leaves an unaccounted-for residuum is no solution at all; and our solution of the problem of human society would have been none at all had it left the lame, the sick, and the blind outside with the beasts, to fare as they might. Better far have left the strong and well unprovided for than these burdened ones, toward whom every heart must yearn, and for whom ease of mind and body should be provided, if for no others. Therefore it is, as I told you this morning, that the title of every man, woman, and child to the means of existence rests on no basis less plain, broad, and simple than the fact that they are fellows of one race—members of one human family. The only coin current is the image of God, and that is good for all we have.

"I think there is no feature of the civilization of your epoch so repugnant to modern ideas as the neglect with which you treated your dependent classes. Even if you had no pity, no feeling of brotherhood, how was it that you did not see that you were robbing the incapable class of their plain right in leaving them unprovided for?"

"I don't quite follow you there," I said. "I admit the claim of this class to our pity, but how could they who produced nothing claim a share of the product as a right?"

"How happened it," was Doctor Leete's reply, "that your workers were able to produce more than so many savages would have done? Was it not wholly on account of the heritage of the past knowledge and achievements of the race, the machinery of society, thousands of years in contriving, found by you ready-made to your hand? How did you come to be possessors of this knowledge and this machinery, which represent nine parts to one contributed by yourself in the value of your product? You inherited it, did you not? And were not these others, these unfortunate and crippled brothers whom you cast out, joint inheritors, coheirs with you? What did you do with their share? Did you not rob them when you put them off with crusts, who were entitled to sit with the

88

heirs, and did you not add insult to robbery when you called the crusts charity?

"Ah, Mr. West," Doctor Leete continued, as I did not respond, "what I do not understand is, setting aside all considerations either of justice or brotherly feeling toward the crippled and defective, how the workers of your day could have had any heart for their work, knowing that their children, or grandchildren, if unfortunate, would be deprived of the comforts and even necessities of life. It is a mystery how men with children could favor a system under which they were rewarded beyond those less endowed with bodily strength or mental power. For, by the same discrimination by which the father profited, the son, for whom he would give his life, being perchance weaker than others, might be reduced to crusts and beggary. How men dared leave children behind them, I have never been able to understand."

NOTE. Although in his talk on the previous evening Doctor Leete had emphasized the pains taken to enable every man to ascertain and follow his natural bent in choosing an occupation, it was not till I learned that the worker's income is the same in all occupations that I realized how absolutely he may be counted on to do so, and thus, by selecting the harness which sets most lightly on himself, find that in which he can pull best. The failure of my age in any systematic or effective way to develop and utilize the natural aptitudes of men for the industries and intellectual avocations was one of the great wastes, as well as one of the most common causes of unhappiness in that time. The vast majority of my contemporaries, though nominally free to do so, never really chose their occupations at all, but were forced by circumstances into work for which they were relatively inefficient, because not naturally fitted for it. The rich, in this respect, had little advantage over the poor. The latter, indeed, being generally deprived of education, had no opportunity even to ascertain the natural aptitudes they might have, and on account of their poverty were unable to develop them by cultivation even when ascertained. The liberal and technical professions, except by favorable accident, were shut to them, to their own great loss and that of the nation. On the other hand, the well-to-do, although they could command education and opportunity, were scarcely less hampered by social prejudice, which forbade them to pursue manual avocations, even when adapted to them, and destined them, whether fit or unfit, to the professions, thus wasting many an excellent handi-

AS EDITH HAD PROMISED HE SHOULD DO, DOCTOR LEETE
accompanied me to my bedroom, to instruct me as to the
adjustment of the musical telephone. He showed how, by
turning a screw, the volume of the music could be made
to fill the room, or die away to an echo so faint and far
that one could scarcely be sure whether he heard or
imagined it. If, of two persons side by side, one desired
to listen to music and the other to sleep, it could be
audible to one and inaudible to another.

"I should strongly advise you to sleep if you can tonight, Mr. West, in preference to listening to the finest
tunes in the world," the doctor said, after explaining
these points. "In the trying experience you are just now
passing through, sleep is a nerve tonic for which there
is no substitute."

Mindful of what had happened to me that very morning, I promised to heed his counsel.

"Very well," he said, "then I will set the telephone at
eight o'clock."

"What do you mean?" I asked.

He explained that, by a clockwork combination, a person could arrange to be awakened at any hour by the
music.

It began to appear, as has since fully proved to be the
case, that I had left my tendency to insomnia behind me
with the other discomforts of existence in the nineteenth
century; for though I took no sleeping draught this time,

craftsman. Mercenary considerations, tempting men to pursue
money-making occupations for which they were unfit, instead of less
remunerative employments for which they were fit, were responsible
for another vast perversion of talent. All these things are now
changed. Equal education and opportunity must needs bring to light
whatever aptitudes a man has, and neither social prejudices nor
mercenary considerations hamper him in the choice of his life work.

yet, as the night before, I had no sooner touched the pillow than I was asleep.

I dreamed that I sat on the throne of the Abencerrages in the banqueting hall of the Alhambra, feasting my lords and generals, who next day were to follow the crescent against the Christian dogs of Spain. The air, cooled by the spray of fountains, was heavy with the scent of flowers. A band of nautch girls, round-limbed and luscious-lipped, danced with voluptuous grace to the music of brazen and stringed instruments. Looking up to the latticed galleries, one caught a gleam now and then from the eye of some beauty of the royal harem, looking down upon the assembled flower of Moorish chivalry. Louder and louder clashed the cymbals, wilder and wilder grew the strain, till the blood of the desert race could no longer resist the martial delirium, and the swart nobles leaped to their feet; a thousand scimitars were bared, and the cry "Allah il Allah!" shook the hall and awoke me, to find it broad daylight, and the room tingling with the electric music of the *Turkish Reveille*.

At the breakfast table, when I told my host of my morning's experience, I learned that it was not a mere chance that the piece of music which awakened me was a reveille. The airs played at one of the halls during the waking hours of the morning were always of an inspiring type.

"By the way," I said, "I have not thought to ask you anything about the state of Europe. Have the societies of the Old World also been remodeled?"

"Yes," replied Doctor Leete, "the great nations of Europe as well as Australia, Mexico, and parts of South America, are now organized industrially like the United States, which was the pioneer of the evolution. The peaceful relations of these nations are assured by a loose form of federal union of worldwide extent. An international council regulates the mutual intercourse and commerce of the members of the union and their joint policy toward the more backward races, which are gradually being educated up to civilized institutions. Complete autonomy within its own limits is enjoyed by every nation."

"How do you carry on commerce without money?" I said. "In trading with other nations, you must use some sort of money, although you dispense with it in the internal affairs of the nation."

"Oh, no. Money is as superfluous in our foreign as in our internal relations. When foreign commerce was conducted by private enterprise, money was necessary to adjust it on account of the multifarious complexity of the transactions; but nowadays it is a function of the nations as units. There are thus only a dozen or so merchants in the world, and their business being supervised by the international council, a simple system of book accounts serves perfectly to regulate their dealings. Customs duties of every sort are of course superfluous. A nation simply does not import what its government does not think requisite for the general interest. Each nation has a bureau of foreign exchange, which manages its trading. For example, the American bureau, estimating such and such quantities of French goods necessary to America for a given year, sends the order to the French bureau, which in turn sends its order to our bureau. The same is done mutually by all the nations."

"But how are the prices of foreign goods settled, since there is no competition?"

"The price at which one nation supplies another with goods," replied Doctor Leete, "must be that at which it supplies its own citizens. So you see there is no danger of misunderstanding. Of course no nation is theoretically bound to supply another with the product of its own labor, but it is for the interest of all to exchange some commodities. If a nation is regularly supplying another with certain goods, notice is required from either side of any important changes in the relation."

"But what if a nation, having a monopoly of some natural product, should refuse to supply it to the others, or to one of them?"

"Such a case has never occurred, and could not without doing the refusing party vastly more harm than the others," replied Doctor Leete. "In the first place, no favoritism could be legally shown. The law requires that each nation shall deal with the others, in all respects, on exactly the same footing. Such a course as you suggest would cut off the nation adopting it from the remainder of the earth for all purposes whatever. The contingency is one that need not give us much anxiety."

"But," said I, "supposing a nation, having a natural monopoly in some product of which it exports more than it consumes, should put the price away up, and thus, without cutting off the supply, make a profit out of its neighbors' necessities? Its own citizens would of course have to pay the higher price on that commodity, but as a body would make more out of foreigners than they would be out of pocket themselves."

"When you come to know how prices of all commodities are determined nowadays, you will perceive how impossible it is that they could be altered, except with reference to the amount or arduousness of the work required respectively to produce them," was Doctor Leete's reply. "This principle is an international as well as a national guarantee; but even without it the sense of community of interest, international as well as national, and the conviction of the folly of selfishness, are too deep nowadays to render possible such a piece of sharp practice as you apprehend. You must understand that we all look forward to an eventual unification of the world as one nation. That, no doubt, will be the ultimate form of society, and will realize certain economic advantages over the present federal system of autonomous nations. Meanwhile, however, the present system works so nearly perfectly that we are quite content to leave to posterity the completion of the scheme. There are, indeed, some who hold that it never will be completed, on the ground that the federal plan is not merely a provisional solution of the problem of human society, but the best ultimate solution."

"How do you manage," I asked, "when the books of any two nations do not balance? Supposing we import more from France than we export to her."

"At the end of each year," replied the doctor, "the books of every nation are examined. If France is found in our debt, probably we are in the debt of some nation which owes France, and so on with all the nations. The balances that remain after the accounts have been cleared by the international council should not be large under our system. Whatever they may be, the council requires them to be settled every few years, and may require their settlement at any time if they are getting too large; for it is not intended that any nation shall run largely in debt to another, lest feelings unfavorable to amity should be engendered. To guard further against this, the international council inspects the commodities interchanged by the nations, to see that they are of perfect quality."

"But what are the balances finally settled with, seeing that you have no money?"

"In national staples—a basis of agreement as to what staples shall be accepted, and in what proportions, for settlement of accounts, being a preliminary to trade relations."

"Emigration is another point I want to ask you about," said I. "With every nation organized as a close industrial partnership, monopolizing all means of production in the country, the emigrant, even if he were permitted to land, would starve. I suppose there is no emigration nowadays."

"On the contrary, there is constant emigration, by which I suppose you mean removal to foreign countries for permanent residence," replied Doctor Leete. "It is arranged on a simple international arrangement of indemnities. For example, if a man at twenty-one emigrates from England to America, England loses all the expense of his maintenance and education, and America gets a worker for nothing. America accordingly makes England an allowance. The same principle, varied to suit the case, applies generally. If the man is near the term of his labor when he emigrates, the country receiving him has the allowance. As to imbecile persons, it is deemed best that each nation should be responsible for its own, and the emigration of such must be under full guarantees of support by his own nation. Subject to these regulations, the right of any man to emigrate at any time is unrestricted."

"But how about mere pleasure trips, tours of observation? How can a stranger travel in a country whose people do not receive money, and are themselves supplied with the means of life on a basis not extended to him? His own credit card cannot, of course, be good in other lands. How does he pay his way?"

"An American credit card," replied Doctor Leete, "is just as good in Europe as American gold used to be, and on precisely the same condition, namely, that it be exchanged into the currency of the country you are traveling in. An American in Berlin takes his credit card to the local office of the international council, and receives in exchange for the whole or part of it a German credit card, the amount being charged against the United States in favor of Germany on the international account."

"Perhaps Mr. West would like to dine at the Elephant today," said Edith, as we left the table.

"That is the name we give to the general dining house of our ward," explained her father. "Not only is our cooking done at the public kitchens, as I told you last night, but the service and quality of the meals are much more satisfactory if taken at the dining house. The two minor meals of the day are usually taken at home, as not worth the trouble of going out, but it is general to go out to dine. We have not done so since you have been with us, from a notion that it would be better to wait till you had become a little more familiar with our ways. What do you think? Shall we take dinner at the dining house today?"

I said that I should be very much pleased to do so.

Not long after, Edith came to me, smiling, and said:

"Last night, as I was thinking what I could do to make you feel at home until you came to be a little more used to us and our ways, an idea occurred to me. What would you say if I were to introduce you to some very nice people of your own times, whom I am sure you used to be well acquainted with?''

I replied, rather vaguely, that it would certainly be very agreeable, but I did not see how she was going to manage it.

"Come with me," was her smiling reply, "and see if I am not as good as my word."

My susceptibility to surprise had been pretty well exhausted by the numerous shocks it had received, but it was with some wonderment that I followed her into a room which I had not before entered. It was a small, cosy apartment, walled with cases filled with books.

"Here are your friends," said Edith, indicating one of the cases, and as my eye glanced over the names on the backs of the volumes, Shakespeare, Milton, Wordsworth, Shelley, Tennyson, Defoe, Dickens, Thackeray, Hugo, Hawthorne, Irving, and a score of other great writers of my time and all time, I understood her meaning. She had indeed made good her promise in a sense compared with which its literal fulfillment would have been a disappointment. She had introduced me to a circle of friends whom the century that had elapsed since last I communed with them had aged as little as it had myself. Their spirit was as high, their wit as keen, their laughter and their tears as contagious, as when their speech had whiled away the hours of a former century. Lonely I was not and could not be more, with this goodly companionship, however wide the gulf of years that gaped between me and my old life.

"You are glad I brought you here," exclaimed Edith, radiant, as she read in my face the success of her experiment. "It was a good idea, was it not, Mr. West? How stupid of me not to think of it before! I will leave you now with your old friends, for I know there will be no company for you like them just now; but remember you must not let old friends make you quite forget new ones!" And with that smiling caution she left me.

Attracted by the most familiar of the names before me, I laid my hand on a volume of Dickens, and sat down to read. He had been my prime favorite among the book writers of the century—I mean the nineteenth century—and a week had rarely passed in my old life during which I had not taken up some volume of his works to while away an idle hour. Any volume with which I had been familiar would have produced an extraordinary impression, read under my present circumstances, but my exceptional familiarity with Dickens, and his consequent power to call up the associations of my former life, gave to his writings an effect no others could have had, to intensify, by force of contrast, my appreciation of the strangeness of my present environment. However new and astonishing one's surroundings, the tendency is to become a part of them so soon that almost from the first the power to see them objectively and fully measure their strangeness is lost. That power, already dulled in my case, the pages of Dickens restored by carrying me back through their associations to the standpoint of my former life. With a clearness which I had not been able before to attain, I saw now the past and present, like contrasting pictures, side by side.

The genius of the great novelist of the nineteenth century, like that of Homer, might indeed defy time; but the setting of his pathetic tales, the misery of the poor, the wrongs of power, the pitiless cruelty of the system of society, had passed away as utterly as Circe and the sirens, Charybdis and Cyclops.

During the hour or two that I sat there with Dickens open before me, I did not actually read more than a couple of pages. Every paragraph, every phrase, brought up some new aspect of the world-transformation which had taken place, and led my thoughts on long and widely ramifying excursions. As meditating thus in Doctor Leete's library I gradually attained a more clear and coherent idea of the prodigious spectacle which I had been so strangely enabled to view, I was filled with a deepening wonder at the seeming capriciousness of the fate that had given to one who so little deserved it, or seemed in any way set apart for it, the power alone among his contemporaries to stand upon the earth in this latter day. I had neither foreseen the new world nor toiled for it, as many about me had done regardless of the scorn of fools or the misconstruction of the good. Surely it would have been more in accordance with the fitness of things had one of those prophetic and strenuous souls been enabled to see the travail of his soul and be satisfied; he, for example, a thousand times rather than I, who, having beheld in a vision the world I looked on, sang of it in words that again and again, during these last wondrous days, had rung in my mind:

For I dipped into the future, far as human eye could see,
Saw the vision of the world, and all the wonder that
    would be; . . .

Till the war-drum throbbed no longer, and the battle-
    flags were furled.
In the Parliament of man, the Federation of the world.

Then the common sense of most shall hold a fretful
    realm in awe,
And the kindly earth shall slumber, lapped in univer-
    sal law. . . .

Yet I doubt not through the ages one increasing pur-
    pose runs,
And the thoughts of men are widened with the process
    of the suns.*

What though, in his old age, he momentarily lost faith in his own prediction, as prophets in their hours of depression and doubt generally do; the words had remained eternal testimony to the seership of a poet's heart, the insight that is given to faith.

I was still in the library when some hours later Doctor Leete sought me there. "Edith told me of her idea," he said, "and I thought it an excellent one. I had a little curiosity what writer you would first turn to. Ah, Dickens! You admired him, then! That is where we moderns

*Tennyson, "Locksley Hall."

agree with you. Judged by our standards, he overtops all the writers of his age, not because his literary genius was highest, but because his great heart beat for the poor, because he made the cause of the victims of society his own, and devoted his pen to exposing its cruelties and shams. No man of his time did so much as he to turn men's minds to the wrong and wretchedness of the old order of things, and open their eyes to the necessity of the great change that was coming, although he himself did not clearly foresee it."

· XIV ·

A HEAVY RAINSTORM CAME UP DURING THE DAY, AND I had concluded that the condition of the streets would be such that my hosts would have to give up the idea of going out to dinner, although the dining hall I had understood to be quite near. I was much surprised when at the dinner hour the ladies appeared prepared to go out, but without either rubbers or umbrellas.

The mystery was explained when we found ourselves on the street, for a continuous waterproof covering had been let down so as to enclose the sidewalk and turn it into a well-lighted and perfectly dry corridor, which was filled with a stream of ladies and gentlemen dressed for dinner. At the corners the entire open space was similarly roofed in. Edith Leete, with whom I walked, seemed much interested in learning what appeared to be entirely new to her, that in the stormy weather the streets of the Boston of my day had been impassable, except to persons protected by umbrellas, boots, and heavy clothing. "Were sidewalk coverings not used at all?" she asked. They were used, I explained, but in a scattered and utterly unsystematic way, being private enterprises. She said to me that at the present time all the streets were provided against inclement weather in the manner I saw, the apparatus being rolled out of the way when it was unnecessary. She intimated that it would be considered an extraordinary imbecility to permit the weather to have any effect on the social movements of the people.

Doctor Leete, who was walking ahead, overhearing something of our talk, turned to say that the difference between the age of individualism and that of concert was well characterized by the fact that, in the nineteenth century, when it rained, the people of Boston put up three hundred thousand umbrellas over as many heads, and in the twentieth century they put up one umbrella over all the heads.

As we walked on, Edith said, "The private umbrella is Father's favorite figure to illustrate the old way when everybody lived for himself and his family. There is a nineteenth-century painting at the art gallery representing a crowd of people in the rain, each one holding his umbrella over himself and his wife, and giving his neighbors the drippings, which he claims must have been meant by the artist as a satire on his times."

We now entered a large building into which a stream of people was pouring. I could not see the front, owing to the awning, but, if in correspondence with the interior, which was even finer than the store I visited the day before, it would have been magnificent. My companion said that the sculptured group over the entrance was especially admired. Going up a grand staircase, we walked some distance along a broad corridor with many doors opening upon it. At one of these, which bore my host's name, we turned in, and I found myself in an elegant dining room containing a table for four. Windows opened on a courtyard where a fountain played to a great height and music made the air electric.

"You seem at home here," I said, as we seated ourselves at table, and Doctor Leete touched an annunciator.

"This is, in fact, a part of our house, slightly detached from the rest," he replied. "Every family in the ward has a room set apart in this great building for its permanent and exclusive use for a small annual rental. For transient guests and individuals there is accommodation on another floor. If we expect to dine here, we put in our orders the night before, selecting anything in market, according to the daily reports in the papers. The meal is as expensive or as simple as we please, though of course everything is vastly cheaper as well as better than it would be if prepared at home. There is actually nothing which our people take more interest in than the perfection of the catering and cooking done for them, and I admit that we are a little vain of the success that has been attained by this branch of the service. Ah, my dear Mr. West, though other aspects of your civilization were more tragical, I can imagine that none could have been more depressing than the poor dinners you had to eat, that is, all of you who had not great wealth."

"You would have found none of us disposed to disagree with you on that point," I said.

The waiter, a fine-looking young fellow, wearing a slightly distinctive uniform, now made his appearance. I observed him closely, as it was the first time I had been able to study particularly the bearing of one of the enlisted members of the industrial army. This young man, I knew from what I had been told, must be highly educated, and the equal, socially and in all respects, of those he served. But it was perfectly evident that to neither side was the stipulation in the slightest degree embarrassing. Doctor Leete addressed the young man in a tone devoid, of course, as any gentleman's would be, of superciliousness, but at the same time not in any way deprecatory, while the manner of the young man was simply that of a person intent on discharging correctly the task he was engaged in, equally without familiarity or obsequiousness. It was, in fact, the manner of a soldier on duty, but without the military stiffness. As the youth left the room, I said, "I cannot get over my wonder at seeing a young man like that serving so contentedly in a menial position."

"What is that word 'menial'? I never heard of it," said Edith.

"It is obsolete now," remarked her father. "If I understand it rightly, it applied to persons who performed particularly disagreeable and unpleasant tasks for others, and carried with it an implication of contempt. Was it not so, Mr. West?"

"That is about it," I said. "Personal service, such as waiting on tables, was considered menial, and held in such contempt, in my day, that persons of culture and refinement would suffer hardship before condescending to it."

"What a strangely artificial idea," exclaimed Mrs. Leete, wonderingly.

"And yet these services had to be rendered," said Edith.

"Of course," I replied. "But we imposed them on the poor, and those who had no alternative but starvation."

"And increased the burden you imposed on them by adding your contempt," remarked Doctor Leete.

"I don't think I clearly understand," said Edith. "Do you mean that you permitted people to do things for you which you despised them for doing, or that you accepted services from them which you would have been unwilling to render them? You can't surely mean that, Mr. West?"

I was obliged to tell her that the fact was just as she had stated. Doctor Leete, however, came to my relief.

"To understand why Edith is surprised," he said, "you must know that nowadays it is an axiom of ethics that to accept a service from another which we would be unwilling to return in kind, if need were, is like borrowing with the intention of not repaying, while to enforce such a service by taking advantage of the poverty or necessity of a person would be an outrage like forcible robbery. It is the worst thing about any system which divides men, or allows them to be divided, into classes and castes, that it weakens the sense of a common humanity. Unequal distribution of wealth, and, still more effectually, unequal opportunities of education and culture, divided society in your day into classes which in many respects regarded each other as distinct races. There is not, after all, such a difference as might appear between our ways of looking at this question of service. Ladies and gentlemen of the cultured class in your day would no more have permitted persons of their own class to render them services they would scorn to return than we would permit anybody to do so. The poor and the uncultured, however, they looked upon as of another kind from themselves. The equal wealth and equal opportunities of culture which all persons now enjoy have simply made us all members of one class, which corresponds to the most fortunate class with you. Until this equality of condition had come to pass, the idea of the solidarity of humanity, the brotherhood of all men, could never have become the real conviction and practical principle of action it is nowadays. In your day the same phrases were indeed used, but they were phrases merely."

"Do the waiters, also, volunteer?"

"No," replied Doctor Leete. "The waiters are young men in the unclassified grade of the industrial army who are assignable to all sorts of miscellaneous occupations not requiring special skill. Waiting on table is one of these, and every young recruit is given a taste of it. I myself served as a waiter for several months in this very dining house some forty years ago. Once more you must remember that there is recognized no sort of difference between the dignity of the different sorts of work required by the nation. The individual is never regarded, nor regards himself, as the servant of those he serves, nor is he in any way dependent upon them. It is always the nation which he is serving. No difference is recognized between a waiter's functions and those of any other worker. The fact that his is a personal service is indifferent from our point of view. So is a doctor's. I should as soon expect our waiter today to look down on me because I served him as a doctor, as think of looking down on him because he serves me as a waiter."

After dinner my entertainers conducted me about the building, of which the extent, the magnificent architecture and richness of embellishment, astonished me. It seemed that it was not merely a dining hall, but likewise a great pleasure house and social rendezvous of the quarter, and no appliance of entertainment or recreation seemed lacking.

"You find illustrated here," said Doctor Leete, when I had expressed my admiration, "what I said to you in our first conversation, when you were looking out over the city, as to the splendor of our public and common life as compared with the simplicity of our private and home life, and the contrast which, in this respect, the twentieth bears to the nineteenth century. To save ourselves useless burdens, we have as little gear about us at home as is consistent with comfort, but the social side of our life is ornate and luxurious beyond anything the world ever knew before. All the industrial and professional guilds have clubhouses as extensive as this, as well as country, mountain, and seaside houses for sport and rest in vacations."

NOTE. In the latter part of the nineteenth century it became a practice of needy young men at some of the colleges of the country to earn a little money for their term bills by serving as waiters on tables at hotels during the summer vacation. It was claimed, in reply to critics who expressed the prejudices of the time in asserting that persons voluntarily following such an occupation could not be gentlemen, that they were entitled to praise for vindicating, by their example, the dignity of all honest and necessary labor. The use of this argument illustrates a common confusion in thought on the part of my former contemporaries. The business of waiting on tables was in no more need of defense than most of the other ways of getting a living in that day, but to talk of dignity attaching to labor of any sort under the system then prevailing was absurd. There is no way in which selling labor for the highest price it will fetch is more dignified than selling goods for what can be got. Both were commercial transactions to be judged by the commercial standard. By setting a price in money on his service, the worker accepted the money measure for it, and renounced all clear claim to be judged by any other. The sordid taint which this necessity imparted to the noblest and the highest sorts of service was bitterly resented by generous souls, but there was no evading it. There was no exemption, however transcendent the quality of one's service, from the necessity of haggling for its price in the marketplace. The physician must sell his healing and the apostle his preaching like the rest. The prophet, who had guessed the meaning of God, must dicker for the price of his revelation, and the poet hawk his visions in printers' row. If I

XV

WHEN, IN THE COURSE OF OUR TOUR OF INSPECTION, WE came to the library, we succumbed to the temptation of the luxurious leather chairs with which it was furnished, and sat down in one of the book-lined alcoves to rest and chat awhile.*

"Edith tells me that you have been in the library all the morning," said Mrs. Leete. "Do you know, it seems to me, Mr. West, that you are the most enviable of mortals."

"I should like to know just why," I replied.

"Because the books of the last hundred years will be new to you," she answered. "You will have so much of the most absorbing literature to read as to leave you scarcely time for meals these five years to come. Ah, what would I give if I had not already read Berrian's novels."

"Or Nesmyth's, Mamma," added Edith.

"Yes, or Oates' poems, or *Past and Present,* or *In the Beginning,* or—oh, I could name a dozen books, each worth a year of one's life," declared Mrs. Leete, enthusiastically.

were asked to name the most distinguishing felicity of this age, as compared to that in which I first saw the light, I should say that to me it seems to consist in the dignity you have given to labor by refusing to set a price upon it and abolishing the marketplace forever. By requiring of every man his best you have made God his task master, and by making honor the sole reward of achievement you have imparted to all service the distinction peculiar in my day to the soldier's.

*I cannot sufficiently celebrate the glorious liberty that reigns in the public libraries of the twentieth century as compared with the intolerable management of those of the nineteenth century, in which the books were jealously railed away from the people, and obtainable only at an expenditure of time and red tape calculated to discourage any ordinary taste for literature.

"I judge, then, that there has been some notable liter ature produced in this century."

"Yes," said Doctor Leete. "It has been an era of un-exampled intellectual splendor. Probably humanity never before passed through a moral and material evolution, at once so vast in its scope and brief in its time of accomplishment, as that from the old order to the new in the early part of this century. When men came to realize the greatness of the felicity which had befallen them, and that the change through which they had passed was not merely an improvement in details of their condition, but the rise of the race to a new plane of existence with an illimitable vista of progress, their minds were affected in all their faculties with a stimulus, of which the outburst of the medieval Renaissance offers a suggestion but faint indeed. There ensued an era of mechanical invention, scientific discovery, art, musical and literary productiveness to which no previous age of the world offers anything comparable."

"By the way," said I, "talking of literature, how are books published now? Is that also done by the nation?"

"Certainly."

"But how do you manage it? Does the government publish everything that is brought it as a matter of course, at the public expense, or does it exercise a censorship and print only what it approves?"

"Neither way. The printing department has no censorial powers. It is bound to print all that is offered it, but prints it only on condition that the author defray the first cost out of his credit. He must pay for the privilege of the public ear, and if he has any message worth hearing we consider that he will be glad to do it. Of course, if incomes were unequal, as in the old times, this rule would enable only the rich to be authors, but the resources of citizens being equal, it merely measures the strength of the author's motive. The cost of an edition of an average book can be saved out of a year's credit by the practice of economy and some sacrifices. The book, on being published, is placed on sale by the nation."

"The author receiving a royalty on the sales as with us, I suppose," I suggested.

"Not as with you, certainly," replied Doctor Leete, "but nevertheless in one way. The price of every book is made up of the cost of its publication with a royalty for the author. The author fixes this royalty at any figure he pleases. Of course if he puts it unreasonably high it is his own loss, for the book will not sell. The amount of this royalty is set to his credit and he is discharged from other service to the nation for so long a period as this credit at the rate of allowance for the support of citizens shall suffice to support him. If his book be moderately successful, he has thus a furlough for several months, a year, two or three years, and if he in the meantime produces other successful work, the remission of service is extended so far as the sale of that may justify. An author of much acceptance succeeds in supporting himself by his pen during the entire period of service, and the degree of any writer's literary ability, as determined by the popular voice, is thus the measure of the opportunity given him to devote his time to literature. In this respect the outcome of our system is not very dissimilar to that of yours, but there are two notable differences. In the first place, the universally high level of education nowadays gives the popular verdict a conclusiveness on the real merit of literary work which in your day it was as far as possible from having. In the second place, there is no such thing now as favoritism of any sort to interfere with the recognition of true merit. Every author has precisely the same facilities for bringing his work before the popular tribunal. To judge from the complaints of the writers of your day, this absolute equality of opportunity would have been greatly prized."

"In the recognition of merit in other fields of original genius, such as music, art, invention, design," I said, "I suppose you follow a similar principle."

"Yes," he replied, "although the details differ. In art, for example, as in literature, the people are the sole judges. They vote upon the acceptance of statues and paintings for the public buildings, and their favorable verdict carries with it the artist's remission from other tasks to devote himself to his vocation. On copies of his work disposed of, he also derives the same advantage as the author on sales of his books. In all these lines of original genius the plan pursued is the same—to offer a free field to aspirants, and as soon as exceptional talent is recognized, to release it from all trammels and let it have free course. The remission of other service in these cases is not intended as a gift or reward, but as the means of obtaining more and higher service. Of course there are various literary, art, and scientific institutes to which membership comes to the famous and is greatly prized. The highest of all honors in the nation, higher than the presidency, which calls merely for good sense and devotion to duty, is the red ribbon awarded by the vote of the people to the great authors, artists, engineers, physicians, and inventors of the generation. Not over a certain number wear it at any one time, though every bright young fellow in the country loses innumerable nights' sleep dreaming of it. I even did myself."

"Just as if Mamma and I would have thought any more of you with it," exclaimed Edith, "not that it isn't, of course, a very fine thing to have."

"You have no choice, my dear, but to take your father as you found him and make the best of him," Doctor Leete replied. "But as for your mother, there, she would never have had me if I had not assured her that I was bound to get the red ribbon or at least the blue."

On this extravagance Mrs. Leete's only comment was a smile.

"How about periodicals and newspapers?" I said. "I won't deny that your book-publishing system is a considerable improvement on ours, both as to its tendency to encourage a real literary vocation, and, quite as important, to discourage mere scribblers; but I don't see how it can be made to apply to magazines and newspapers. It is very well to make a man pay for publishing a book, because the expense will be only occasional; but no man could afford the expense of publishing a newspaper every day in the year. It took the deep pockets of our private capitalists to do that, and often exhausted even them before the returns came in. If you have newspapers at all, they must, I fancy, be published by the government at the public expense, with government editors, reflecting government opinions. Now, if your system is so perfect that there is never anything to criticize in the conduct of affairs, this arrangement may answer. Otherwise I should think the lack of an independent unofficial medium for the expression of public opinion would have most unfortunate results. Confess, Doctor Leete, that a free newspaper press, with all that it implies, was a redeeming incident of the old system when capital was in private hands, and that you have to set off the loss of that against your gains in other respects."

"I am afraid I can't give you even that consolation," replied Doctor Leete, laughing. "In the first place, Mr. West, the newspaper press is by no means the only or, as we look at it, the best vehicle for serious criticism of public affairs. To us, the judgments of your newspapers on such themes seem generally to have been crude and flippant, as well as deeply tinctured with prejudice and bitterness. Insofar as they may be taken as expressing public opinion, they give an unfavorable impression of the popular intelligence, while so far as they may have formed public opinion, the nation was not to be felicitated. Nowadays, when a citizen desires to make a serious impression upon the public mind as to any aspect of public affairs, he comes out with a book or pamphlet, published as other books are. But this is not because we lack newspapers and magazines, or that they lack the most absolute freedom. The newspaper press is organized so as to be a more perfect expression of public opinion than it possibly could be in your day, when private capital controlled and managed it primarily as a money-making business, and secondarily only as a mouthpiece for the people."

"But," said I, "if the government prints the papers at the public expense, how can it fail to control their policy? Who appoints the editors, if not the government?"

"The government does not pay the expense of the papers, nor appoint their editors, nor in any way exert the slightest influence on their policy," replied Doctor Leete. "The people who take the paper pay the expense of its publication, choose its editor, and remove him when unsatisfactory. You will scarcely say, I think, that such a newspaper press is not a free organ of popular opinion."

"Decidedly I shall not," I replied, "but how is it practicable?"

"Nothing could be simpler. Supposing some of my neighbors or myself think we ought to have a newspaper reflecting our opinions, and devoted especially to our locality, trade, or profession. We go about among the people till we get the names of such a number that their annual subscriptions will meet the cost of the paper, which is little or big according to the largeness of its constituency. The amount of the subscriptions marked off the credits of the citizens guarantees the nation against loss in publishing the paper, its business, you understand, being that of a publisher purely, with no option to refuse the duty required. The subscribers to the paper now elect somebody as editor, who, if he accepts the office, is discharged from other service during his incumbency. Instead of paying a salary to him, as in your day, the subscribers pay the nation an indemnity equal to the cost of his support for taking him away from the general service. He manages the paper just as one of your editors did, except that he has no counting room to obey, or interests of private capital as against the public good to defend. At the end of the first year, the subscribers for the next either re-elect the former editor or choose anyone else to his place. An able editor, of course, keeps his place indefinitely. As the subscription list enlarges, the funds of the paper increase, and it is improved by the securing of more and better contributors, just as your papers were."

"How is the staff of contributors recompensed, since they cannot be paid in money?"

"The editor settles with them the price of their wares.

The amount is transferred to their individual credit from the guarantee credit of the paper, and a remission of service is granted the contributor for a length of time corresponding to the amount credited him, just as to other authors. As to magazines, the system is the same. Those interested in the prospectus of a new periodical pledge enough subscriptions to run it for a year; select their editor, who recompenses his contributors just as in the other case, the printing bureau furnishing the necessary force and material for publication, as a matter of course. When an editor's services are no longer desired, if he cannot earn the right to his time by other literary work, he simply resumes his place in the industrial army. I should add that, though ordinarily the editor is elected only at the end of the year, and as a rule is continued in office for a term of years, in case of any sudden change he should give to the tone of the paper, provision is made for taking the sense of the subscribers as to his removal at any time."

"However earnestly a man may long for leisure for purposes of study or meditation," I remarked, "he cannot get out of the harness, if I understand you rightly, except in these two ways you have mentioned. He must either by literary, artistic, or inventive productiveness indemnify the nation for the loss of his services, or must get a sufficient number of other people to contribute to such an indemnity."

"It is most certain," replied Doctor Leete, "that no able-bodied man nowadays can evade his share of work and live on the toil of others, whether he calls himself by the fine name of student or confesses to being simply lazy. At the same time our system is elastic enough to give free play to every instinct of human nature which does not aim at dominating others or living on the fruit of others' labor. There is not only the remission by indemnification but the remission by abnegation. Any man in his thirty-third year, his term of service being then half done, can obtain an honorable discharge from the army, provided he accepts for the rest of his life one-half the rate of maintenance other citizens receive. It is quite possible to live on this amount, though one must forego the luxuries and elegancies of life, with some, perhaps, of its comforts."

When the ladies retired that evening, Edith brought me a book and said:

"If you should be wakeful tonight, Mr. West, you might be interested in looking over this story by Berrian. It is considered his masterpiece, and will at least give you an idea what the stories nowadays are like."

I sat up in my room that night reading *Penthesilia* till it grew gray in the east, and did not lay it down till I had finished it. And yet let no admirer of the great romancer of the twentieth century resent my saying that at the first reading what most impressed me was not so much what was in the book as what was left out of it. The story writers of my day would have deemed the making of bricks without straw a light task compared with the construction of a romance from which should be excluded all effects drawn from the contrasts of wealth and poverty, education and ignorance, coarseness and refinement, high and low, all motives drawn from social pride and ambition, the desire of being richer or the fear of being poorer, together with sordid anxieties of any sort for one's self or others; a romance in which there should, indeed, be love galore, but love unfretted by artificial barriers created by differences of station or possessions, owning no other law but that of the heart. The reading of *Penthesilia* was of more value than almost any amount of explanation would have been in giving me something like a general impression of the social aspect of the twentieth century. The information Doctor Leete had imparted was indeed extensive as to facts, but they had affected my mind as so many separate impressions, which I had as yet succeeded but imperfectly in making cohere. Berrian put them together for me in a picture.

XVI

NEXT MORNING I ROSE SOMEWHAT BEFORE THE BREAKFAST hour. As I descended the stairs, Edith stepped into the hall from the room which had been the scene of the morning interview between us described some chapters back.

"Ah!" she exclaimed, with a charmingly arch expression, "you thought to slip out unbeknown for another of those solitary morning rambles which have such nice effects on you. But you see I am up too early for you this time. You are fairly caught."

"You discredit the efficacy of your own cure," I said, "by supposing that such a ramble would now be attended with bad consequences."

"I am very glad to hear that," she said. "I was in here arranging some flowers for the breakfast table when I heard you come down, and fancied I detected something surreptitious in your step on the stairs."

"You did me injustice," I replied. "I had no idea of going out at all."

Despite her effort to convey an impression that my interception was purely accidental, I had at the time a dim suspicion of what I afterward learned to be the fact, namely, that this sweet creature, in pursuance of her self-assumed guardianship over me, had risen for the last two or three mornings at an unheard-of hour, to insure against the possibility of my wandering off alone in case I should be affected as on the former occasion. Receiving permission to assist her in making up the breakfast bouquet, I followed her into the room from which she had emerged.

"Are you sure," she asked, "that you are quite done with those terrible sensations you had that morning?"

"I can't say that I do not have times of feeling decidedly queer," I replied, "moments when my personal identity seems an open question. It would be too much to expect after my experience that I should not have such sensations occasionally, but as for being carried entirely off my feet, as I was on the point of being that morning, I think the danger is past."

"I shall never forget how you looked that morning," she said.

"If you had merely saved my life," I continued, "I might, perhaps, find words to express my gratitude, but it was my reason you saved, and there are no words that would not belittle my debt to you." I spoke with emotion, and her eyes grew suddenly moist.

"It is too much to believe all this," she said, "but it is very delightful to hear you say it. What I did was very little. I was very much distressed for you, I know. Father never thinks anything ought to astonish us when it can be explained scientifically, as I suppose this long sleep of yours can be, but even to fancy myself in your place makes my head swim. I know that I could not have borne it at all."

"That would depend," I replied, "on whether an angel came to support you with her sympathy in the crisis of your condition, as one came to me." If my face at all expressed the feelings I had a right to have toward this sweet and lovely young girl, who had played so angelic a role toward me, its expression must have been very worshipful just then. The expression or the words, or both together, caused her now to drop her eyes with a charming blush.

"For the matter of that," I said, "if your experience has not been as startling as mine, it must have been rather overwhelming to see a man belonging to a strange century, and apparently a hundred years dead, raised to life."

"It seemed indeed strange beyond any describing at first," she said, "but when we began to put ourselves in your place, and realize how much stranger it must seem to you, I fancy we forgot our own feelings a good deal, at least I know I did. It seemed then not so much astounding as interesting and touching beyond anything ever heard of before."

"But does it not come over you as astounding to sit at table with me, seeing who I am?"

"You must remember that you do not seem so strange to us as we must to you," she answered. "We belong to a future of which you could not form an idea, a generation of which you knew nothing until an you saw us. But you belong to a generation of which our forefathers were a part. We know all about it; the names of many of its members are household words with us. We have made a study of your ways of living and thinking; which does not seem strange to you. So you see, Mr. West, that if you feel that you can, in time, get accustomed to us, you must not be surprised that from the first we have scarcely found you strange at all."

"I had not thought of it in that way," I replied. "There is indeed much in what you say. One can look back a thousand years easier than forward fifty. A century is not so very long a retrospect. I might have known your great-grandparents. Possibly I did. Did they live in Boston?"

"I believe so."

"You are not sure, then?"

"Yes," she replied. "Now I think, they did."

"I had a very large circle of acquaintances in the city," I said. "It is not unlikely that I knew or knew of some of them. Perhaps I may have known them well. Wouldn't it be interesting if I should chance to be able to tell you all about your great-grandfather, for instance?"

"Very interesting."

"Do you know your genealogy well enough to tell me who your forebears were in the Boston of my day?"

"Oh, yes."

"Perhaps, then, you will some time tell me what some of their names were."

She was engrossed in arranging a troublesome spray of green, and did not reply at once. Steps upon the stairway indicated that the other members of the family were descending.

"Perhaps, some time," she said.

After breakfast, Doctor Leete suggested taking me to

inspect the central warehouse and observe actually in operation the machinery of distribution, which Edith had described to me. As we walked away from the house I said, "It is now several days that I have been living in your household on a most extraordinary foot, or rather on none at all. I have not spoken of this aspect of my position before because there were so many other aspects yet more extraordinary. But now that I am beginning a little to feel my feet under me, and to realize that, however I came here, I am here, and must make the best of it, I must speak to you on this point."

"As for your being a guest in my house," replied Doctor Leete, "I pray you not to begin to be uneasy on that point, for I mean to keep you a long time yet. With all your modesty, you can but realize that such a guest as yourself is an acquisition not willingly to be parted with."

"Thanks, Doctor," I said. "It would be absurd, certainly, for me to affect any oversensitiveness about accepting the temporary hospitality of one to whom I owe it that I am not still awaiting the end of the world in a living tomb. But if I am to be a permanent citizen of this century I must have some standing in it. Now, in my time a person more or less entering the world, however he got in, would not be noticed in the unorganized throng of men, and might make a place for himself anywhere he chose if he were strong enough. But nowadays everybody is a part of a system with a distinct place and function. I am outside the system, and don't see how I can get in; there seems no way to get in, except to be born in or to come in as an emigrant from some other system."

Doctor Leete laughed heartily.

"I admit," he said, "that our system is defective in lacking provision for cases like yours, but you see nobody anticipated additions to the world except by the usual process. You need, however, have no fear that we shall be unable to provide both a place and occupation for you in due time. You have as yet been brought in contact only with the members of my family, but you must not suppose that I have kept your secret. On the contrary, your case, even before your resuscitation, and vastly more since, has excited the profoundest interest in the nation. In view of your precarious nervous condition, it was thought best that I should take exclusive charge of you at first, and that you should, through me and my family, receive some general idea of the sort of world you had come back to before you began to make the acquaintance generally of its inhabitants. As to finding a function for you in society, there was no hesitation as to what that would be. Few of us have it in our power to confer so great a service on the nation as you will be able to when you leave my roof, which, however, you must not think of doing for a good time yet."

"What can I possibly do?" I asked. "Perhaps you imagine I have some trade, or art, or special skill. I assure you I have none whatever. I never earned a dollar in my life, or did an hour's work. I am strong, and might be a common laborer, but nothing more."

"If that were the most efficient service you were able to render the nation, you would find that avocation considered quite as respectable as any other," replied Doctor Leete, "but you can do something else better. You are easily the master of all our historians on questions relating to the social condition of the latter part of the nineteenth century, to us one of the most absorbingly interesting periods of history; and whenever in due time you have sufficiently familiarized yourself with our institutions, and are willing to teach us something concerning those of your day, you will find an historical lectureship in one of our colleges awaiting you."

"Very good! Very good indeed," I said, much relieved by so practical a suggestion on a point which had begun to trouble me. "If your people are really so much interested in the nineteenth century, there will indeed be an occupation ready-made for me. I don't think there is anything else that I could possibly earn my salt at, but I certainly may claim without conceit to have some special qualifications for such a post as you describe."

XVII

I FOUND THE PROCESSES AT THE WAREHOUSE QUITE AS interesting as Edith had described them, and became even enthusiastic over the truly remarkable illustration which is seen there of the prodigiously multiplied efficiency which perfect organization can give to labor. It is like a gigantic mill, into the hopper of which goods are being constantly poured by the trainload and shipload, to issue at the other end in packages of pounds and ounces, yards and inches, pints and gallons, corresponding to the infinitely complex personal needs of half a million people. Doctor Leete, with the assistance of data furnished by me as to the way goods were sold in my day, figured out some astounding results in the way of the economies effected by the modern system.

As we set out homeward, I said: "After what I have seen today, together with what you have told me, and what I learned under Miss Leete's tutelage at the sample store, I have a tolerably clear idea of your system of distribution, and how it enables you to dispense with a circulating medium. But I should like very much to know something more about your system of production. You have told me in general how your industrial army is levied and organized, but who directs its efforts? What supreme authority determines what shall be done in every department, so that enough of everything is produced and yet no labor wasted? It seems to me that this must be a wonderfully complex and difficult function, requiring very unusual endowments."

"Does it indeed seem so to you?" responded Doctor Leete. "I assure you that it is nothing of the kind, but on the other hand so simple, and depending on principles so obvious and easily applied, that the functionaries at Washington to whom it is trusted require to be nothing more than men of fair abilities to discharge it to the entire satisfaction of the nation. The machine which they direct is indeed a vast one, but so logical in its principles and direct and simple in its workings, that it all but runs itself; and nobody but a fool could derange it, as I think you will agree after a few words of explanation. Since you already have a pretty good idea of the working of the distributive system, let us begin at the end. Even in your day statisticians were able to tell you the number of yards of cotton, velvet, woolen, the number of barrels of flour, potatoes, butter, number of pairs of shoes, hats, and umbrellas annually consumed by the nation. Owing to the fact that production was in private hands, and that there was no way of getting statistics of actual distribution, these figures were not exact, but they were nearly so. Now that every pin which is given out from a national warehouse is recorded, of course the figures of consumption for any week, month, or year, in the possession of the department of distribution at the end of that period, are precise. On these figures, allowing for tendencies to increase or decrease and for any causes likely to affect demand, the estimates, say, for a year ahead, are based. These estimates, with a proper margin for security, having been accepted by the general administration, the responsibility of the distributive department ceases until the goods are delivered to it. I speak of the estimates being furnished for an entire year ahead, but in reality they cover that much time only in case of the great staples for which the demand can be calculated on as steady. In the great majority of smaller industries for the product of which popular taste fluctuates, and novelty is frequently required, production is kept barely ahead of consumption, the distributive department furnishing frequent estimates based on the weekly state of demand.

"Now the entire field of productive and constructive industry is divided into ten great departments, each representing a group of allied industries, each particular industry being in turn represented by a subordinate bureau, which has a complete record of the plant and force under its control, of the present product, and means of increasing it. The estimates of the distributive department, after adoption by the administration, are sent as mandates to the ten great departments, which allot them to the subordinate bureaus representing the particular industries, and these set the men at work. Each bureau is responsible for the task given it, and this responsibility is enforced by departmental oversight and that of the administration; nor does the distributive department accept the product without its own inspection; while even if in the hands of the consumer an article turns out unfit, the system enables the fault to be traced back to the original workman. The production of the commodities for actual public consumption does not, of course, require by any means all the national force of workers. After the necessary contingents have been detailed for the various industries, the amount of labor left for other employment is expended in creating fixed capital, such as buildings, machinery, engineering works, and so forth."

"One point occurs to me," I said, "on which I should think there might be dissatisfaction. Where there is no opportunity for private enterprise, how is there any assurance that the claims of small minorities of the people to have articles produced, for which there is no wide demand, will be respected? An official decree at any moment may deprive them of the means of gratifying some special taste, merely because the majority does not share it."

"That would be tyranny indeed," replied Doctor Leete, "and you may be very sure that it does not happen with us, to whom liberty is as dear as equality or fraternity. As you come to know our system better, you will see that our officials are in fact, and not merely in name, the agents and servants of the people. The administration has no power to stop the production of any commodity for which there continues to be a demand. Suppose the demand for any article declines to such a point that its production becomes very costly. The price has to be raised in proportion, of course, but as long as the consumer cares to pay it, the production goes on. Again, suppose an article not before produced is demanded. If the administration doubts the reality of the demand, a popular petition guaranteeing a certain basis of consumption compels it to produce the desired article. A government, or a majority, which should undertake to tell the people, or a minority, what they were to eat, drink, or wear, as I believe governments in America did in your day, would be regarded as a curious anachronism indeed. Possibly you had reasons for tolerating these infringements of personal independence, but we should not think them endurable. I am glad you raised this point, for it has given me a chance to show you how much more direct and efficient is the control over production exercised by the individual citizen now than it was in your day, when what you called private initiative prevailed, though it should have been called capitalist initiative, for the average private citizen had little enough share in it."

"You speak of raising the price of costly articles," I said. "How can prices be regulated in a country where there is no competition between buyers or sellers?"

"Just as they were with you," replied Doctor Leete. "You think that needs explaining," he added, as I looked incredulous, "but the explanation need not be long; the cost of the labor which produced it was recognized as the legitimate basis of the price of an article in your day, and so it is in ours. In your day, it was the difference in wages that made the difference in the cost of labor; now it is the relative number of hours constituting a day's work in different trades, the maintenance of the worker being equal in all cases. The cost of a man's work in a trade so difficult that in order to attract volunteers the hours have to be fixed at four a day is twice as great as that in a trade where the men work eight hours. The result as to the cost of labor, you see, is just the same as if the man working four hours were paid, under your system, twice the wages the other gets. This calculation applied to the labor employed in the various processes of a manufactured article gives its price relatively to other articles. Besides the cost of production and transportation, the factor of scarcity affects the prices of some commodities. As regards the great staples of life, of which an abundance can always be secured, scarcity is eliminated as a factor. There is always a large surplus kept on hand from which any fluctuations of demand or supply can be corrected, even in most cases of bad crops. The prices of the staples grow less year by year, but rarely, if ever, rise. There are, however, certain classes of articles permanently, and others temporarily, unequal to the demand, as, for example, fresh fish or dairy products in the latter category, and the products of high skill and rare materials in the other. All that can be done here is to equalize the inconvenience of the scarcity. This is done by temporarily raising the price if the scarcity be temporary, or fixing it high if it be permanent. High prices in your day meant restriction of the articles affected to the rich, but nowadays, when the means of all are the same, the effect is only that those to whom the articles seem most desirable are the ones who purchase them. Of course the nation, as any other caterer for the public needs must be, is frequently left with small lots of goods on its hands by changes in taste, unseasonable weather, and various other causes. These it has to dispose of at a sacrifice just as merchants often did in your day, charging up the loss to the expenses of the business. Owing, however, to the vast body of consumers to which such lots can be simultaneously offered, there is rarely any difficulty in getting rid of them at trifling loss. I have given you now some general notion of our system of production, as well as distribution. Do you find it as complex as you expected?"

I admitted that nothing could be much simpler.

"I am sure," said Doctor Leete, "that it is within the truth to say that the head of one of the myriad private businesses of your day, who had to maintain sleepless vigilance against the fluctuations of the market, the machinations of his rivals, and the failure of his debtors, had a far more trying task than the group of men at Washington who nowadays direct the industries of the entire nation. All this merely shows, my dear fellow, how much easier it is to do things the right way than the wrong. It is easier for a general up in a balloon, with perfect survey of the field, to maneuver a million men to victory than for a sergeant to manage a platoon in a thicket."

"The general of this army, including the flower of the manhood of the nation, must be the foremost man in the country, really greater even than the President of the United Stares," I said.

"He is the President of the United States," replied Doctor Leete, "or rather the most important function of the presidency is the headship of the industrial army."

"How is he chosen?" I asked.

"I explained to you before," replied Doctor Leete, "when I was describing the force of the motive of emulation among all grades of the industrial army, that the line of promotion for the meritorious lies through three grades to the officer's grade, and thence up through the lieutenancies to the captaincy, or foremanship, and superintendency, or colonel's rank. Next, with an intervening grade in some of the larger trades, comes the general of the guild, under whose immediate control all the operations of the trade are conducted. This officer is at the head of the national bureau representing his trade, and is responsible for its work to the administration. The general of his guild holds a splendid position, and one which amply satisfies the ambition of most men, but above his rank, which may be compared—to follow the military analogies familiar to you—to that of a general of division, or major-general, is that of the chiefs of the ten great departments, or groups of allied trades. The chiefs of these ten grand divisions of the industrial army may be compared to your commanders of army corps, or lieutenant generals, each having from a dozen to a score of generals of separate guilds reporting to him. Above these ten great officers, who form his council, is the general-in-chief, who is the President of the United States.

"The general-in-chief of the industrial army must have passed through all the grades below him, from the common laborers up. Let us see how he rises. As I have told you, it is simply by the excellence of his record as a worker that one rises through the grades of the privates and becomes a candidate for a lieutenancy. Through the lieutenancies he rises to the colonelcy, or superintendent's position, by appointment from above, strictly limited to the candidates of the best records. The general of the guild appoints to the ranks under him, but he himself is not appointed, but chosen by suffrage."

"By suffrage!" I exclaimed. "Is not that ruinous to the discipline of the guild, by tempting the candidates to intrigue for the support of the workers under them?"

"So it would be, no doubt," replied Doctor Leete, "if the workers had any suffrage to exercise, or anything to say about the choice. But they have nothing. Just here comes in a peculiarity of our system. The general of the guild is chosen from among the superintendents by vote of the honorary members of the guild, that is, of those who have served their time in the guild and received their discharge. As you know, at the age of forty-five we are mustered out of the army of industry, and have the residue of life for the pursuit of our own improvement or recreation. Of course, however, the associations of our active lifetime retain a powerful hold on us. The companionships we formed then remain our companionships till the end of life. We always continue honorary members of our former guilds, and retain the keenest and most jealous interest in their welfare and repute in the hands of the following generation. In the clubs maintained by the honorary members of the several guilds, in which we meet socially, there are no topics of conversation so common as those which relate to these matters, and the young aspirants for guild leadership who can pass the criticism of us old fellows are likely to be pretty well equipped. Recognizing this fact, the nation entrusts to the honorary members of each guild the election of its general, and I venture to claim that no previous form of society could have developed a body of electors so ideally adapted to their office, as regards absolute impartiality, knowledge of the special qualifications and record of candidates, solicitude for the best result, and complete absence of self-interest.

"Each of the ten lieutenant generals, or heads of departments, is himself elected from among the generals of the guilds grouped as a department, by vote of the honorary members of the guilds thus grouped. Of course there is a tendency on the part of each guild to vote for its own general, but no guild of any group has nearly enough votes to elect a man not supported by most of the others. I assure you that these elections are exceedingly lively."

"The President, I suppose, is selected from among the ten heads of the great departments," I suggested.

"Precisely, but the heads of departments are not eligible to the presidency till they have been a certain number of years out of office. It is rarely that a man passes through all the grades to the headship of a department much before he is forty, and at the end of a five years' term he is usually forty-five. If more, he still serves through his term, and if less, he is nevertheless discharged from the industrial army at its termination. It would not do for him to return to the ranks. The interval before he is a candidate for the presidency is intended to give time for him to recognize fully that he has returned into the general mass of the nation, and is identified with it rather than with the industrial army. Moreover, it is expected that he will employ this period in studying the general condition of the army, instead of that of the special group of guilds of which he was the head. From among the former heads of departments who may be eligible at the time, the President is elected by vote of all the men of the nation who are connected with the industrial army."

"The army is not allowed to vote for the President?"

"Certainly not. That would be perilous to its discipline, which it is the business of the President to maintain as the representative of the nation at large. His right hand for this purpose is the inspectorate, a highly important department of our system; to the inspectorate come all complaints or information as to defects in goods, insolence or inefficiency of officials, or dereliction of any sort in the public service. The inspectorate, however, does not wait for complaints. Not only is it on the alert to catch and sift every rumor of a fault in the service, but it is its business, by systematic and constant oversight and inspection of every branch of the army, to find out what is going wrong before anybody else does. The President is usually not far from fifty when elected, and serves five years, forming an honorable exception to the rule of retirement at forty-five. At the end of his term of office, a national Congress is called to receive his report and approve or condemn it. If it is approved, Congress usually elects him to represent the nation for five years more in the international council. Congress, I should also say, passes on the reports of the outgoing heads of departments, and a disapproval renders any one of them ineligible for President. But it is rare, indeed, that the nation has occasion for other sentiments than those of gratitude toward its high officers. As to their ability, to have risen from the ranks, by tests so various and severe, to their positions, is proof in itself of extraordinary qualities, while as to faithfulness, our social system leaves them absolutely without any other motive than that of winning the esteem of their fellow citizens. Corruption is impossible in a society where there is neither poverty to be bribed nor wealth to bribe, while as to demagoguery or intrigue for office, the conditions of promotion render them out of the question."

"One point I do not quite understand," I said. "Are the members of the liberal professions eligible to the presidency? And if so, how are they ranked with those who pursue the industries proper?"

"They have no ranking with them," replied Doctor Leete. "The members of the technical professions, such as engineers and architects, have a ranking with the constructive guilds; but the members of the liberal professions, the doctors and teachers, as well as the artists and men of letters who obtain remissions of industrial service, do not belong to the industrial army. On this ground they vote for the President, but are not eligible to his office. One of its main duties being the control and discipline of the industrial army, it is essential that the President should have passed through all its grades to understand his business."

"That is reasonable," I said, "but if the doctors and teachers do not know enough of industry to be President, neither, I should think, can the President know enough of medicine and education to control those departments."

"No more does he," was the reply. "Except in the general way that he is responsible for the enforcement of the laws as to all classes, the President has nothing to do with the faculties of medicine and education, which are controlled by boards of regents of their own, in which the President is ex-officio chairman, and has the casting vote. These regents, who, of course, are responsible to Congress, are chosen by the honorary members of the guilds of education and medicine, the retired teachers and doctors of the country."

"Do you know," I said, "the method of electing officials by votes of the retired members of the guilds is nothing more than the application on a national scale of the plan of government by alumni, which we used to a slight extent occasionally in the management of our higher educational institutions."

"Did you, indeed?" exclaimed Doctor Leete, with animation. "That is quite new to me, and I fancy will be to most of us, and of much interest as well. There has been great discussion as to the germ of the idea, and we fancied that there was for once something new under the sun. Well! Well! In your higher educational institutions! That is interesting indeed. You must tell me more of that."

"Truly, there is very little more to tell than I have told already," I replied. "If we had the germ of your idea, it was but as a germ."

XVIII

THAT EVENING I SAT UP FOR SOME TIME AFTER THE LADIES had retired, talking with Doctor Leete about the effect of the plan of exempting men from further service to the nation after the age of forty-five, a point brought up by his account of the part taken by the retired citizens in the government.

"At forty-five," said I, "a man still has ten years of good manual labor in him, and twice ten years of good intellectual service. To be superannuated at that age and laid on the shelf must be regarded rather as a hardship than a favor by men of energetic dispositions."

"My dear Mr. West," exclaimed Doctor Leete, beaming upon me, "you cannot have any idea of the piquancy your nineteenth-century ideas have for us of this day, the rare quaintness of their effect. Know; O child of another race and yet the same, that the labor we have to render as our part in securing for the nation the means of a comfortable physical existence is by no means regarded as the most important, the most interesting, or the most dignified employment of our powers. We look upon it as a necessary duty to be discharged before we can fully devote ourselves to the higher exercise of our faculties, the intellectual and spiritual enjoyments and pursuits which alone mean life. Everything possible is indeed done by the distribution of burdens, and by all manner of special attractions and incentives to relieve our labor of irksomeness, and, except in a comparative sense, is not usually irksome, and is often inspiring. But it is not our labor, but the higher and larger activities which the performance of our task will leave us free to enter upon, that are considered the main business of existence.

"Of course not all, nor the majority, have those scientific, artistic, literary, or scholarly interests which make leisure the one thing valuable to their possessors. Many look upon the last half of life chiefly as a period for enjoyment of other sorts; for travel, for social relaxation in the company of their lifetime friends; a time for the cultivation of all manner of personal idiosyncrasies and special tastes, and the pursuit of every imaginable form of recreation; in a word, a time for the leisurely and unperturbed appreciation of the good things of the world which they have helped to create. But whatever the differences between our individual tastes as to the use we shall put our leisure to, we all agree in looking forward to the date of our discharge as the time we shall first enter upon the full enjoyment of our birthright, the period when we shall first really attain our majority and become enfranchised from discipline and control, with the fee of our lives vested in ourselves. As eager boys in your day anticipated twenty-one, so men nowadays look forward to forty-five. At twenty-one we become men, but at forty-five we renew youth. Middle age and what you would have called old age are considered, rather than youth, the enviable time of life. Thanks to the better conditions of existence nowadays, and above all the freedom of everyone from care, old age approaches many years later and has an aspect far more benign than in past times. Persons of average constitution usually live to eighty-five or ninety, and at forty-five we are physically and mentally younger, I fancy, than you were at thirty-five. It is a strange reflection that at forty-five, when we are just entering upon the most enjoyable period of life, you already began to think of growing old and to look backward. With you it was the forenoon, with us it is the afternoon, which is the brighter half of life."

After this I remember that our talk branched into the subject of popular sports and recreations at the present time as compared with those of the nineteenth century.

"In one respect," said Doctor Leete, "there is a marked difference. The professional sportsmen, which were such a curious feature of your day, we have nothing answering to, nor are the prizes for which our athletes contend money prizes, as with you. Our contests are always for glory only. The generous rivalry existing between the various guilds, and the loyalty of each worker to his own, afford a constant stimulation to all sorts of games and matches by sea and land, in which the young men take scarcely more interest than the honorary guildsmen who have served their time. The guild yacht races off Marblehead take place next week, and you will be able to judge for yourself of the popular enthusiasm which such events nowadays call out as compared with your day. The demand for *panem et circenses* preferred by the Roman populace is recognized nowadays as a wholly reasonable one. If bread is the first necessity of life, recreation is a close second, and the nation caters for both. Americans of the nineteenth century were as unfortunate in lacking an adequate provision for the one sort of need as for the other. Even if the people of that period had enjoyed larger leisure, they would, I fancy, have often been at a loss how to pass it agreeably. We are never in that predicament."

· XIX ·

IN THE COURSE OF AN EARLY MORNING CONSTITUTIONAL I visited Charleston. Among the changes, too numerous to attempt to indicate, which mark the lapse of a century in that quarter, I particularly noted the total disappearance of the old state prison.

"That went before my day, but I remember hearing about it," said Doctor Leete, when I alluded to the fact at the breakfast table. "We have no jails nowadays. All cases of atavism are treated in the hospitals."

"Of atavism!" I exclaimed, staring.

"Why, yes," replied Doctor Leete. "The idea of dealing punitively with those unfortunates was given up at least fifty years ago, and I think more."

"I don't quite understand you," I said. "Atavism in

my day was a word applied to the cases of persons in whom some trait of a remote ancestor recurred in a noticeable manner. Am I to understand that crime is nowadays looked upon as the recurrence of an ancestral trait?"

"I beg your pardon," said Doctor Leete with a smile half-humorous, half-deprecating, "but since you have so explicitly asked the question, I am forced to say that the fact is precisely that."

After what I had already learned of the moral contrasts between the nineteenth and the twentieth centuries, it was doubtless absurd in me to begin to develop sensitiveness on the subject, and probably if Doctor Leete had not spoken with that apologetic air and Mrs. Leete and Edith shown a corresponding embarrassment, I should not have flushed, as I was conscious I did.

"I was not in much danger of being vain of my generation before," I said, "but, really—"

"This is your generation, Mr. West," interposed Edith. "It is the one in which you are living, you know, and it is only because we are alive now that we call it ours."

"Thank you. I will try to think of it so," I said, and as my eyes met hers their expression quite cured my senseless sensitiveness. "After all," I said, with a laugh, "I was brought up a Calvinist, and ought not to be startled to hear crime spoken of as an ancestral trait."

"In point of fact," said Doctor Leete, "our use of the word is no reflection at all on your generation, if, begging Edith's pardon, we may call it yours, so far as seeming to imply that we think ourselves, apart from our circumstances, better than you were. In your day, fully nineteen-twentieths of the crime, using the word broadly to include all sorts of misdemeanors, resulted from the inequality in the possessions of individuals. Want tempted the poor; lust of greater gains, or the desire to preserve former gains, tempted the well-to-do. Directly or indirectly, the desire for money, which then meant every good thing, was the motive of all this crime, the taproot of a vast poison growth, which the machinery of law, courts and police could barely prevent from choking your civilization outright. When we made the nation the sole trustee of the wealth of the people, and guaranteed to all abundant maintenance, on the one hand abolishing want, and on the other checking the accumulation of riches, we cut this root, and the poison tree that overshadowed your society withered, like Jonah's gourd, in a day. As for the comparatively small class of violent crimes against persons, unconnected with any idea of gain, they were almost wholly confined, even in your day, to the ignorant and bestial; and in these days, when education and good manners are not the monopoly of a few, but universal, such atrocities are scarcely ever heard of. You now see why the word 'atavism' is used for crime. It is because nearly all forms of crime known to you are motiveless now, and when they appear can only be explained as the outcropping of ancestral traits. You used to call persons who stole, evidently without any rational motive, kleptomaniacs, and when the case was clear, deemed it absurd to punish them as thieves. Your attitude toward the genuine kleptomaniac is precisely ours toward the victim of atavism, an attitude of compassion and firm but gentle restraint."

"Your courts must have an easy time of it," I observed. "With no private property to speak of, no disputes between citizens over business relations, no real estate to divide or debts to collect, there must be absolutely no civil business at all for them; and with no offenses against property, and mighty few of any sort to provide criminal cases, I should think you might almost do without judges and lawyers altogether."

"We do without the lawyers, certainly," was Doctor Leete's reply. "It would not seem reasonable to us, in a case where the only interest of the nation is to find out the truth, that persons should take part in the proceedings who had an acknowledged motive to color it."

"But who defends the accused?"

"If he is a criminal he needs no defense, for he pleads guilty in most instances," replied Doctor Leete. "The plea of the accused is not a mere formality with us, as with you. It is usually the end of the case."

"You don't mean that the man who pleads not guilty is thereupon discharged?"

"No, I do not mean that. He is not accused on light grounds, and if he denies his guilt, must still be tried. But trials are few, for in most cases the guilty man pleads guilty. When he makes a false plea and is clearly proved guilty, his penalty is doubled. Falsehood, is, however, so despised among us that few offenders would lie to save themselves."

"That is the most astounding thing you have yet told me," I exclaimed. "If lying has gone out of fashion, this is indeed the 'new heavens and the new earth wherein dwelleth righteousness,' which the prophet foretold."

"Such is, in fact, the belief of some persons nowadays," was the doctor's answer. "They hold that we have entered upon the millennium, and the theory from their point of view does not lack plausibility. But as to your astonishment at finding that the world has outgrown lying, there is really no ground for it. Falsehood, even in your day, was not common between gentlemen and ladies, social equals. The lie of fear was the refuge of cowardice, and the lie of fraud the device of the cheat. The inequalities of men and the lust of acquisition offered a constant premium on lying at that time. Yet even then, the man who neither feared another nor desired to defraud him scorned falsehood. Because we are now all social equals, and no man either has anything to fear from another or can gain anything by deceiving him, the contempt of falsehood is so universal that it is rarely, as I told you, that even a criminal in other respects will be found willing to lie. When, however, a plea of not guilty is returned, the judge appoints two colleagues to state the opposite sides of the case. How far these men are from being like your hired advocates and prosecutors, determined to acquit or convict, may appear from the fact that unless both agree that the verdict found is just, the case is tried over, while anything like bias in the tone of either of the judges stating the case would be a shocking scandal."

"Do I understand," I said, "that it is a judge who hears it?"

"Certainly. The judges take turns in serving on the bench and at the bar, and are expected to maintain the judicial temper equally whether in stating or deciding a case. The system is indeed in effect that of trial by three judges occupying different points of view as to the case. When they agree upon a verdict, we believe it to be as near to absolute truth as men well can come."

"You have given up the jury system, then?"

"It was well enough as a corrective in the days of hired advocates, and a bench sometimes venal, and often with a tenure that made it dependent, but is needless now. No conceivable motive but justice could actuate our judges."

"How are these magistrates selected?"

"They are an honorable exception to the rule which discharges all men from service at the age of forty-five. The President of the nation appoints the necessary judges year by year from the class reaching that age. The number appointed is, of course, exceedingly few, and the honor so high that it is held an offset to the additional term of service which follows, and though a judge's appointment may be declined, it rarely is. The term is five years, without eligibility to reappoint. The members of the Supreme Court, which is the guardian of the constitution, are selected from among the lower judges, whose terms expire that year, and who select, as their last official act, the one of their colleagues left on the bench whom they deem fittest to fill it."

"There being no legal profession to serve as a school for judges," I said, "they must, of course, come directly from the law school to the bench."

"We have no such thing as law schools," replied the doctor, smiling. "The law as a special science is obsolete. It was a system of casuistry which the elaborate artificiality of the old order of society absolutely required to interpret it, but only a few of the plainest and simplest legal maxims have any application to the existing state of the world. Everything touching the relations of men to one another is now simpler, beyond any comparison, than in your day. We should have no sort of use for the hair-splitting experts who presided and argued in your courts. You must not imagine, however, that we have any disrespect for those ancient worthies because we have no use for them. On the contrary, we entertain an unfeigned respect, amounting almost to awe, for the men who alone understood and were able to expound the interminable complexity of the rights of property, and the relations of commercial and personal dependence involved in your system. What, indeed, could possibly give a more powerful impression of the intricacy and artificiality of that system than the fact that it was necessary to set apart from other pursuits the cream of the intellect of every generation, in order to provide a body of pundits able to make it even vaguely intelligible to those whose fates it determined. The treatises of your great lawyers, the works of Blackstone and Chitty, of Story and Parsons, stand in our museums, side by side with the tomes of Duns Scotus and his fellow scholastics, as curious monuments of intellectual subtlety devoted to subjects equally remote from the interests of modern men. Our judges are simply widely informed, judicious, and discreet men of ripe years.

"I should not fail to speak of one important function of the minor judges," added Doctor Leete. "This is to adjudicate all cases where a private of the industrial army makes a complaint of unfairness against an officer. All such questions are heard and settled without appeal by a single judge, three judges being required only in graver cases. The efficiency of industry requires the strictest discipline in the army of labor, but the claim of the workman to just and considerate treatment is backed by the whole power of the nation. The officer commands and the private obeys, but no officer is so high that he would dare display an overbearing manner toward a workman of the lowest class. As for churlishness or rudeness by an official of any sort, in his relations to the public, not one among minor offenses is more sure of a prompt penalty than this. Not only justice but civility is enforced by our judges in all sorts of intercourse. No value of service is accepted as a set-off to boorish or offensive manners."

It occurred to me, as Doctor Leete was speaking, that in all his talk I had heard much of the nation and nothing of the state governments. Had the organization of the nation as an industrial unit done away with the states? I asked.

"Necessarily," he replied. "The state governments would have interfered with the control and discipline of the industrial army, which, of course, required to be central and uniform. Even if the state governments had not become inconvenient for other reasons, they were rendered superfluous by the prodigious simplification in the task of government since your day. Almost the sole function of the administration now is that of directing the industries of the country. Most of the purposes for which governments formerly existed no longer remain to be subserved. We have no army or navy, and no military organization. We have no departments of state or treasury, no excise or revenue services, no taxes or tax collectors. The only function proper of government, as known to you, which still remains, is the judiciary and police system. I have already explained to you how simple is our judicial system as compared with your huge and complex machine. Of course the same absence of crime and temptation to it, which makes the duties of judges so light, reduces the number and duties of the police to a minimum."

"But with no state legislatures, and Congress meeting only once in five years, how do you get your legislation done?"

"We have no legislation," replied Doctor Leete, "that is, next to none. It is rarely that Congress, even when it meets, considers any new laws of consequence, and then it only has power to commend them to the following Congress, lest anything be done hastily. If you will consider a moment, Mr. West, you will see that we have nothing to make laws about. The fundamental principles on which our society is founded settle for all time the strifes and misunderstandings which in your day called for legislation.

"Fully ninety-nine hundredths of the laws of that time concerned the definition and protection of private property and the relations of buyers and sellers. There is neither private property, beyond personal belongings, now, nor buying and selling, and therefore the occasion of nearly all the legislation formerly necessary has passed away. Formerly, society was a pyramid posed on its apex. All the gravitations of human nature were constantly tending to topple it over, it could be maintained upright, or rather upwrong (if you will pardon the feeble witticism), by an elaborate system of constantly renewed props and buttresses and guy-ropes in the form of laws. A central Congress and forty state legislatures, turning out some twenty thousand laws a year, could not make new props fast enough to take the place of those which were constantly breaking down or becoming ineffectual through some shifting of the strain. Now society rests on its base, and is in as little need of artificial supports as the everlasting hills."

"But you have at least municipal governments besides the one central authority?"

"Certainly, and they have important and extensive functions in looking out for the public comfort and recreation, and the improvement and embellishment of the villages and cities."

"But having no control over the labor of their people, or means of hiring it, how can they do anything?"

"Every town or city is conceded the right to retain, for its own public works, a certain proportion of the quota of labor its citizens contribute to the nation. This proportion, being assigned it as so much credit, can be applied in any way desired."

· XX ·

THAT AFTERNOON EDITH CASUALLY INQUIRED IF I HAD YET revisited the underground chamber in the garden in which I had been found.

"Not yet," I replied. "To be frank, I have shrunk thus far from doing so, lest the visit might revive old associations rather too strongly for my mental equilibrium."

"Ah, yes!" she said. "I can imagine that you have done well to stay away. I ought to have thought of that."

"No," I said, "I am glad you spoke of it. The danger, if there was any, existed only during the first day or two. Thanks to you, chiefly and always, I feel my footing now so firm in this new world, that if you will go with me to keep the ghosts off, I should really like to visit the place this afternoon."

Edith demurred at first, but, finding that I was in earnest, consented to accompany me. The rampart of earth thrown up from the excavation was visible among the trees from the house, and a few steps brought us to the spot. All remained as it was at the point when work was interrupted by the discovery of the tenant of the chamber, save that the door had been opened and the slab from the roof replaced. Descending the sloping sides of the excavation, we went in at the door and stood within the dimly-lighted room.

Everything was just as I had beheld it last on that evening one hundred and thirteen years previous, just before closing my eyes for that long sleep. I stood for some time silently looking about me. I saw that my companion was furtively regarding me with an expression of awed and sympathetic curiosity. I put out my hand to her and she placed hers in it, the soft fingers responding with a reassuring pressure to my clasp. Finally she whispered, "Had we better go out now? You must not try yourself too far. Oh, how strange it must be to you!"

"On the contrary," I replied, "it does not seem strange; that is the strangest part of it."

"Not strange?" she echoed.

"Even so," I replied. "The emotions with which you evidently credit me, and which I anticipated would attend this visit, I simply do not feel. I realize all that these surroundings suggest, but without the agitation I expected. You can't be nearly as much surprised at this as I am myself. Ever since that terrible morning when you came to my help, I have tried to avoid thinking of my former life, just as I have avoided coming here, for fear of the agitating effects. I am for all the world like a man who has permitted an injured limb to lie motionless under the impression that it is exquisitely sensitive, and on trying to move it finds that it is paralyzed."

"Do you mean your memory is gone?"

"Not at all. I remember everything connected with my former life, but with a total lack of keen sensation. I remember it for clearness as if it had been but a day since then, but my feelings about what I remember are as faint as if to my consciousness, as well as in fact, a hundred years had intervened. Perhaps it is possible to explain this, too. The effect of change in surroundings is like that of lapse of time in making the past seem remote. When I first woke from that trance, my former life appeared as yesterday, but now, since I have learned to know my new surroundings, and I realize the prodigious changes that have transformed the world, I no longer find it hard, but very easy, to realize that I have slept a century. Can you conceive of such a thing as living a hundred years in four days? It really seems to me that I have done just that, and that it is this experience which has given so remote and unreal an appearance to my former life. Can you see how such a thing might be?"

"I can conceive it," replied Edith, meditatively, "and I think we ought to be thankful it is so, for it will save you much suffering, I am sure."

"Imagine," I said, in an effort to explain, as much to myself as to her, the strangeness of my mental condition, "that a man first heard of a bereavement many, many years, half a lifetime perhaps, after the event occurred. I fancy his feeling would be perhaps something as mine is. When I think of my friends in the world of that former day, and the sorrow they must have felt for me, it is with a pensive pity, rather than keen anguish, as of a sorrow long, long ago ended."

"You have told us nothing yet of your friends," said Edith. "Had you many to mourn you?"

"Thank God, I had very few relatives, none nearer than cousins," I replied. "But there was one, not a relative, but dearer to me than any kind of blood. She had your name. She was to have been my wife soon. Ah me!"

"Ah me!" sighed the Edith by my side. "Think of the heartache she must have had."

Something in the deep feeling of this gentle girl touched a chord in my benumbed heart. My eyes, before so dry, were flooded with the tears that had till now refused to come. When I had regained my composure, I saw that she too had been weeping freely.

"God bless your tender heart," I said. "Would you like to see her picture?"

A small locket with Edith Bartlett's picture, secured about my neck with a gold chain, had lain upon my breast all through that long sleep, and removing this I opened and gave it to my companion. She took it with eagerness, and after poring long over the sweet face, touched the picture with her lips.

"I know that she was good and lovely enough to well deserve your tears," she said, "but remember her heartache was over long ago, and she has been in heaven for nearly a century."

It was indeed so. Whatever her sorrow had once been, for nearly a century she had ceased to weep, and, my sudden passion spent, my own tears dried away. I had loved her very dearly in my other life, but it was a hundred years ago! I do not know but some may find in this confession evidence of lack of feeling, but I think, perhaps, that none can have had an experience sufficiently like mine to enable them to judge me. As we were about to leave the chamber, my eye rested upon the great iron safe which stood in one corner. Calling my companion's attention to it, I said:

"This was my strong room as well as my sleeping room. In the safe yonder are several thousand dollars in gold, and any amount of securities. If I had known when I went to sleep that night just how long my nap would be, I should still have thought that the gold was a safe provision for my needs in any country or any century, however distant. That a time would ever come when it would lose its purchasing power, I should have considered the wildest of fancies. Nevertheless, here I wake up to find myself among a people of whom a cartload of gold will not procure a loaf of bread."

As might be expected, I did not succeed in impressing Edith that there was anything remarkable in this fact. "Why in the world should it?" she merely asked.

· XXI ·

IT HAD BEEN SUGGESTED BY DOCTOR LEETE THAT WE should devote the next morning to an inspection of the schools and colleges of the city, with some attempt on his own part at an explanation of the educational system of the twentieth century.

"You will see," said he, as we set out after breakfast, "many very important differences between our methods of education and yours, but the main difference is that nowadays all persons equally have those opportunities of higher education which in your day only an infinitesimal portion of the population enjoyed. We should think we had gained nothing worth speaking of, in equalizing the physical comfort of men, without this educational equality."

"The cost must be very great," I said.

"If it took half the revenue of the nation, nobody would grudge it," replied Doctor Leete, "nor even if it took it all save a bare pittance. But in truth the expense of educating ten thousand youths is not ten nor five times that of educating one thousand. The principle which makes all operations on a large scale proportionally cheaper than on a small scale holds as to education also."

"College education was terribly expensive in my day," said I.

"If I have not been misinformed by our historians," Doctor Leete answered, "it was not college education but college dissipation and extravagance which cost so highly. The actual expense of your colleges appears to have been very low, and would have been far lower if their patronage had been greater. The higher education nowadays is as cheap as the lower, as all grades of teachers, like all other workers, receive the same support. We have simply added to the common school system of compulsory education, in vogue in Massachusetts a hundred years ago, a half-dozen higher grades, carrying the youth to the age of twenty-one and giving him what you used to call the education of a gentleman, instead of turning him loose at fourteen or fifteen with no mental equipment beyond reading, writing, and the multiplication table."

"Setting aside the actual cost of these additional years of education," I replied, "we should not have thought we could afford the loss of time from industrial pursuits. Boys of the poorer classes usually went to work at sixteen or younger, and knew their trade at twenty."

"We should not concede you any gain even in material product by that plan," Doctor Leete replied. "The greater efficiency which education gives to all sorts of labor, except the rudest, makes up a short period for the time lost in acquiring it."

"We should also have been afraid," said I, "that a high education, while it adapted men to the professions, would set them against manual labor of all sorts."

"That was the effect of high education in your day, I have read," replied the doctor, "and it was no wonder, for manual labor meant association with a rude, coarse, and ignorant class of people. There is no such class now. It was inevitable that such a feeling should exist then, for the further reason that all men receiving a high education were understood to be destined for the professions or for wealthy leisure, and such an education in one neither rich nor professional was a proof of disappointed aspirations, an evidence of failure, a badge of inferiority rather than superiority. Nowadays, of course, when the highest education is deemed necessary to fit a man merely to live, without any reference to the sort of work he may do, its possession conveys no such implication."

"After all," I remarked, "no amount of education can cure natural dullness or make up for original mental deficiencies. Unless the average natural mental capacity of men is much above its level in my day, a high education must be pretty nearly thrown away on a large element of the population. We used to hold that a certain amount of susceptibility to educational influences is required to make a mind worth cultivating, just as a certain natural fertility in soil is required if it is to repay tilling."

"Ah," said Doctor Leete, "I am glad you used that illustration, for it is just the one I would have chosen to set forth the modern view of education. You say that land so poor that the product will not repay the labor of tilling is not cultivated. Nevertheless, much land that does not begin to repay tilling by its product was cultivated in your day and is in ours. I refer to gardens, parks, lawns, and, in general, to pieces of land so situated that, were they left to grow up to weeds and briers, they would be eyesores and inconveniences to all about. They are therefore tilled, and though their product is little, there is yet no land that, in a wider sense, better repays cultivation. So it is with the men and women with whom we mingle in the relations of society, whose voices are always in our ears, whose behavior in innumerable ways affects our enjoyment—who are, in fact, as much conditions of our lives as the air we breathe, or any of the physical elements on which we depend. If, indeed, we could not afford to educate everybody, we should choose the coarsest and dullest by nature, rather than the brightest, to receive what education we could give. The naturally refined and intellectual can better dispense with aids to culture than those less fortunate in natural endowments.

"To borrow a phrase which was often used in your day, we should not consider life worth living if we had to be surrounded by a population of ignorant, boorish, coarse, wholly uncultivated men and women, as was the plight of the few educated in your day. Is a man satisfied, merely because he is perfumed himself, to mingle with a malodorous crowd? Could he take more than a very limited satisfaction, even in a palatial apartment, if the windows on all four sides opened into stableyards? And yet just that was the situation of those considered most fortunate as to culture and refinement in your day. I know that the poor and ignorant envied the rich and cultured then; but to us the latter, living as they did, surrounded by squalor and brutishness, seem little better off than the former. The cultured man in your age was like one up to the neck in a nauseous bog solacing himself with a smelling bottle. You see, perhaps, now, how we look at this question of universal high education. No single thing is so important to every man as to have for neighbors intelligent, companionable persons. There is nothing, therefore, which the nation can do for him that will enhance so much his own happiness as to educate his neighbors. When it fails to do so, the value of his own education to him is reduced by half, and many of the tastes he has cultivated are made positive sources of pain.

"To educate some to the highest degree, and leave the mass wholly uncultivated, as you did, made the gap between them almost like that between different natural species, which have no means of communication. What could be more inhuman than this consequence of a partial enjoyment of education! Its universal and equal enjoyment leaves, indeed, the differences between men as to natural endowments as marked as in a state of nature, but the level of the lowest is vastly raised. Brutishness is eliminated. All have some inkling of the humanities, some appreciation of the things of the mind, and an admiration for the still higher culture they have fallen short of. They have become capable of receiving and imparting, in various degrees, but all in some measure, the pleasures and inspirations of a refined social life. The cultured society of the nineteenth century—what did it consist of but here and there a few microscopic oases in a vast, unbroken wilderness? The proportion of individuals capable of intellectual sympathies or refined intercourse, to the mass of their contemporaries, used to be so infinitesimal as to be in any broad view of humanity scarcely worth mentioning. One generation of the world today represents a greater volume of intellectual life than any five centuries ever did before.

"There is still another point I should mention in stating the grounds on which nothing less than the universality of the best education could now be tolerated," continued Doctor Leete, "and that is, the interest of the coming generation in having educated parents. To put the matter in a nutshell, there are three main grounds on which our educational system rests: first, the right of every man to the completest education the nation can give him on his own account, as necessary to his enjoyment of himself; second, the right of his fellow citizens to have him educated, as necessary to their enjoyment of his society; third, the right of the unborn to be guaranteed an intelligent and refined parentage."

I shall not describe in detail what I saw in the schools that day. Having taken but slight interest in educational matters in my former life, I could offer few comparisons of interest. Next to the fact of the universality of the higher as well as the lower education, I was most struck with the prominence given to physical culture, and the fact that proficiency in athletic feats and games as well as in scholarship had a place in the rating of the youth.

"The faculty of education," Doctor Leete explained, "is held to the same responsibility for the bodies as for the minds of its charges. The highest possible physical, as well as mental, development of everyone is the double object of a curriculum which lasts from the age of six to that of twenty-one."

The magnificent health of the young people in the schools impressed me strongly. My previous observations, not only of the notable personal endowments of the family of my host, but of the people I had seen in my walks abroad, had already suggested the idea that there must have been something like a general improvement in the physical standard of the race since my day, and now, as I compared these stalwart young men and fresh, vigorous maidens with the young people I had seen in the schools of the nineteenth century, I was moved to impart my thoughts to Doctor Leete. He listened with great interest to what I said.

"Your testimony on this point," he declared, "is invaluable. We believe that there has been such an improvement as you speak of, but of course it could only be a matter of theory with us. It is an incident of your unique position that you alone in the world of today can speak with authority on this point. Your opinion, when you state it publicly, will, I assure you, make a profound sensation. For the rest it would be strange, certainly, if the race did not show an improvement. In your day, riches debauched one class with idleness of mind and body, while poverty sapped the vitality of the masses by overwork, bad food, and pestilent homes. The labor required of children, and the burdens laid on women, enfeebled the very springs of life. Instead of these maleficent circumstances, all now enjoy the most favorable conditions of physical life; the young are carefully nurtured and studiously cared for; the labor which is required of all is limited to the period of greatest bodily vigor, and is never excessive; care for one's self and one's family, anxiety as to livelihood, the strain of a ceaseless battle for life—all these influences, which once did so much to wreck the minds and bodies of men and women, are known no more. Certainly, an improvement of the species ought to follow such a change. In certain specific respects we know, indeed, that the improvement has taken place. Insanity, for instance, which in the nineteenth century was so terribly common a product of your insane mode of life, has almost disappeared, with its alternative, suicide."

· XXII ·

WE HAD MADE AN APPOINTMENT TO MEET THE LADIES AT the dining hall for dinner, after which, having some engagement, they left us sitting at table there, discussing our wine and cigars with a multitude of other matters.

"Doctor," said I, in the course of our talk, "morally speaking, your social system is one which I should be insensate not to admire in comparison with any previously in vogue in the world, and especially with that of my own most unhappy century. If I were to fall into a mesmeric sleep tonight as lasting as that other, and meanwhile the course of time were to take a turn backward instead of forward, and I were to wake up again in the nineteenth century, when I had told my friends what I had seen, they would every one admit that your world was a paradise of order, equity, and felicity. But they were a very practical people, my contemporaries, and after expressing their admiration for the moral beauty and material splendor of the system, they would presently begin to cipher and ask how you got the money to make everybody so happy; for certainly, to support the whole nation at a rate of comfort, and even luxury, such as I see around me, must involve vastly greater wealth than the nation produced in my day. Now, while I could explain to them pretty nearly everything else of the main features of your system, I should quite fail to answer this question, and failing there, they would tell me, for they were very close ciphers, that I had been dreaming; nor would they ever believe anything else. In my day, I know that the total annual product of the nation, although it might have been divided with absolute equality, would not have come to more than three or four hundred dollars per head, not very much more than enough to supply the necessities of life with few or any of its comforts. How is it that you have so much more?"

"That is a very pertinent question, Mr. West," replied Doctor Leete, "and I should not blame your friends, in the case you supposed, if they declared your story all moonshine, failing a satisfactory reply to it. It is a question which I cannot answer exhaustively at any one sitting, and as for the exact statistics to bear out my general statements, I shall have to refer you for them to books in my library, but it would certainly be a pity to leave you to be put to confusion by your old acquaintances, in case of the contingency you speak of, for lack of a few suggestions.

"Let us begin with a number of small items wherein we economize wealth as compared with you. We have no national, state, county, or municipal debts, or payments on their account. We have no sort of military or naval expenditures for men or materials, no army, navy, or militia. We have no revenue service, no swarm of tax assessors and collectors. As regards our judiciary, police, sheriffs, and jailers, the force which Massachusetts alone kept on foot in your day far more than suffices for the nation now. We have no criminal class preying upon the wealth of society as you had. The number of persons, more or less absolutely lost to the working force through physical disability, or the lame, sick, and debilitated, which constituted such a burden on the able-bodied in your day, now that all live under conditions of health and comfort, has shrunk to scarcely perceptible proportions, and with every generation is becoming more completely eliminated.

"Another item wherein we save is the disuse of money and the thousand occupations connected with financial operations of all sorts, whereby an army of men was formerly taken away from useful employments. Also consider that the waste of the very rich in your day on inordinate personal luxury has ceased, though, indeed, this item might easily be overestimated. Again, consider that there are no idlers now, rich or poor—no drones.

"A very important cause of former poverty was the vast waste of labor and materials which resulted from domestic washing and cooking, and the performing separately of innumerable other tasks to which we apply the cooperative plan.

"A larger economy than any of these—yes, of all together—is effected by the organization of our distributing system, by which the work done once by the merchants, traders, storekeepers, with their various grades of jobbers, wholesalers, retailers, agents, commercial travelers, and middlemen of all sorts, with an excessive waste of energy in needless tranportation and interminable handlings, is performed by one-tenth the number of hands and an unnecessary turn of not one wheel. Something of what our distributing system is like you know. Our statisticians calculate that one-eightieth part of our workers suffices for all the processes of distribution which in your day required one-eighth of the population, so much being withdrawn from the force engaged in productive labor."

"I begin to see," I said, "where you get your greater wealth."

"I beg your pardon," replied Doctor Leete, "but you scarcely do as yet. The economies I have mentioned thus far, in the aggregate, considering the labor they would save directly and indirectly through saving of material, might possibly be equivalent to the addition to your annual production of wealth of one-half its former total. These items are, however, scarcely worth mentioning in comparison with other prodigious wastes, now saved, which resulted inevitably from leaving the industries of the nation to private enterprise. However great the economies your contemporaries might have devised in the consumption of products, and however marvelous the progress of mechanical invention, they could never have raised themselves out of the slough of poverty so long as they held to that system.

"No mode more wasteful for utilizing human energy could be devised, and for the credit of the human intellect it should be remembered that the system never was devised, but was merely a survival from the rude ages when the lack of social organization made any sort of cooperation impossible."

"I will readily admit," I said, "that our industrial system was ethically very bad, but as a mere wealth-making machine, apart from moral aspects, it seemed to us admirable."

"As I said," responded the doctor, "the subject is too large to discuss at length now, but if you are really interested to know the main criticisms which we moderns make on your industrial system as compared with our own, I can touch briefly on some of them.

"The wastes which resulted from leaving the conduct of industry to irresponsible individuals, wholly without mutual understanding or concert, were mainly four: first, the waste by mistaken undertakings; second, the waste from the competition and mutual hostility of those engaged in industry; third, the waste by periodical gluts and crises, with the consequent interruptions of industry; fourth, the waste from idle capital and labor, at all times. Any one of these four great leaks, were all the others stopped, would suffice to make the difference between wealth and poverty on the part of a nation.

"Take the waste by mistaken undertakings, to begin with. In your day the production and distribution of commodities being without concert or organization, there was no means of knowing just what demand there was for any class of products, or what was the rate of supply. Therefore, any enterprise by a private capitalist was always a doubtful experiment. The projector having no general view of the field of industry and consumption, such as our government has, could never be sure either what the people wanted, or what arrangements other capitalists were making to supply them. In view of this, we are not surprised to learn that the chances were considered several to one in favor of the failure of any given business enterprise, and that it was common for persons who at last succeeded in making a hit to have failed repeatedly. If a shoemaker, for every pair of shoes he succeeded in completing, spoiled the leather of four or five pair, besides losing the time spent on them, he would stand about the same chance of getting rich as your contemporaries did with their system of private enterprise, and its average of four or five failures to one success.

"The next of the great wastes was that from competition. The field of industry was a battlefield as wide as the world, in which the workers wasted, in assailing one another, energies which, if expended in concerted effort, as today, would have enriched all. As for mercy or quarter in this warfare, there was absolutely no suggestion of it. To deliberately enter a field of business and destroy the enterprises of those who had occupied it previously, in order to plant one's own enterprise on their ruins, was an achievement which never failed to command popular admiration. Nor is there any stretch of fancy in comparing this sort of struggle with actual warfare, so far as concerns the mental agony and physical suffering which attended the struggle, and the misery which overwhelmed the defeated and those dependent on them. Now nothing about your age is, at first sight, more astounding to a man of modern times than the fact that men engaged in the same industry, instead of fraternizing as comrades and colaborers to a common end, should have regarded each other as rivals and enemies to be throttled and overthrown. This certainly seems like sheer madness, a scene from bedlam. But more closely regarded, it is seen to be no such thing. Your contemporaries, with their mutual throat-cutting, knew very well what they were at. The producers of the nineteenth century were not, like ours, working together for the maintenance of the community, but each solely for his own maintenance at the expense of the community. If, in working to this end, he at the same time increased the aggregate wealth, that was merely incidental. It was just as feasible and as common to increase one's private hoard by practices injurious to the general welfare. One's worst enemies were necessarily those of his own trade, for, under your plan of making private profit the motive of production, a scarcity of the article he produced was what each particular producer desired. It was for his interest that no more of it should be produced than he himself could produce. To secure this consummation as far as circumstances permitted, by killing off and discouraging those engaged in his line of industry, was his constant effort. When he had killed off all he could, his policy was to combine with those he could not kill, and convert their mutual warfare into a warfare upon the public at large by cornering the market, as I believe you used to call it, and putting up prices to the highest point people would stand before going without the goods. The daydream of the nineteenth-century producer was to gain absolute control of the supply of some necessity of life, so that he might keep the public at the verge of starvation, and always command famine prices for what he supplied. This, Mr. West, is what was called in the nineteenth century a system of production. I will leave it to you if it does not seem, in some of its aspects, a great deal more like a system for preventing production. Some time when we have plenty of leisure I am going to ask you to sit down with me and try to make me comprehend, as I never yet could, though I have studied the matter a great deal, how such shrewd fellows as your contemporaries appear to have been in many respects ever came to entrust the business of providing for the community to a class whose interest it was to starve it. I assure you that the wonder with us is, not that the world did not get rich under such a system, but that it did not perish outright from want. This wonder increases as we go on to consider some of the other prodigious wastes that characterized it.

"Apart from the waste of labor and capital by misdirected industry, and that from the constant bloodletting of your industrial warfare, your system was liable to periodical convulsions, overwhelming alike the wise and unwise, the successful cutthroat as well as his victim. I refer to the business crises at intervals of five to ten years, which wrecked the industries of the nation, prostrating all weak enterprises and crippling the strongest, and were followed by long periods, often of many years, of so-called dull times, during which the capitalists slowly regathered their dissipated strength while the laboring classes starved and rioted. Then would ensue another brief season of prosperity, followed in turn by another crisis and the ensuing years of exhaustion. As commerce developed, making the nations mutually dependent, these crises became worldwide, while the obstinacy of the ensuing state of collapse increased with the area affected by the convulsions, and the consequent lack of rallying centers. In proportion as the industries of the world multiplied and became complex, and the volume of capital involved was increased, these business cataclysms became more frequent, till, in the latter part of the nineteenth century, there were two years of bad times to one of good, and the system of industry, never before so extended or so imposing, seemed in danger of collapsing by its own weight. After endless discussions, your economists appear by that time to have settled down to the despairing conclusion that there was no more possibility of preventing or controlling these crises than if they had been droughts or hurricanes. It only remained to endure them as necessary evils, and when they had passed over to build up again the shattered structure of industry, as dwellers in an earthquake country keep on rebuilding their cities on the same site.

"So far as considering the causes of the trouble inherent in their industrial system, your contemporaries were certainly correct. They were in its very basis, and must needs become more and more maleficent as the business fabric grew in size and complexity. One of these causes was the lack of any common control of the different industries, and the consequent impossibility of their orderly and coordinate development. It inevitably resulted from this lack that they were continually getting out of step with one another and out of relation with the demand.

"Of the latter there was no criterion such as organized distribution gives us, and the first notice that it had been exceeded in any group of industries was a crash of prices, bankruptcy of producers, stoppage of production, reduction of wages, or discharge of workmen. This process was constantly going on in many industries, even in what were called good times, but a crisis took place only when the industries affected were extensive. The markets then were glutted with goods, of which nobody wanted beyond a sufficiency at any price. The wages and profits of those making the glutted classes of goods being reduced or wholly stopped, their purchasing power as consumers of other classes of goods, of which there was no natural glut, was taken away, and, as a consequence, goods of which there was no natural glut became artificially glutted, till their prices also were broken down, and their makers thrown out of work and deprived of income. The crisis was by this time fairly under way, and nothing could check it till a nation's ransom had been wasted.

"A cause, also inherent in your system, which often produced and always terribly aggravated crises, was the machinery of money and credit. Money was essential when production was in many private hands, and buying and selling were necessary to secure what one wanted. It was, however, open to the obvious objection of substituting for food, clothing, and other things a merely conventional representative of them. The confusion of mind which this favored, between goods and their representative, led the way to the credit system and its prodigious illusions. Already accustomed to accept money for commodities, the people next accepted promises for money, and ceased to look at all behind the representative for the thing represented. Money was a sign of real commodities, but credit was but the sign of a sign. There was a natural limit to gold and silver, that is, money proper, but none to credit, and the result was that the volume of credit, that is, the promises of money, ceased to bear any ascertainable proportion to the money, still less to the commodities, actually in existence. Under such a system, frequent and periodical crises were necessitated by a law as absolute as that which brings to the ground a structure overhanging its center of gravity. It was one of your fictions that the government and the banks authorized by it alone issued money; but everybody who gave a dollar's credit issued money to that extent, which was as good as any to swell the circulation till the next crisis. The great extension of the credit system was a characteristic of the latter part of the nineteenth century, and accounts largely for the almost incessant business crises which marked that period. Perilous as credit was, you could not dispense with its use, for, lacking any national or other public organization of the capital of the country, it was the only means you had for concentrating and directing it upon industrial enterprises. It was in this way a most potent means for exaggerating the chief peril of the private-enterprise system of industry by enabling particular industries to absorb disproportionate amounts of the disposable capital of the country, and thus prepare disaster. Business enterprises were always vastly in debt for advances of credit, both to one another and to the banks and capitalists, and the prompt withdrawal of this credit at the first sign of a crisis was generally the precipitating cause of it.

"It was the misfortune of your contemporaries that they had to cement their business fabric with a material which an accident might at any moment turn into an explosive. They were in the plight of a man building a house with dynamite for mortar, for credit can be compared with nothing else.

"If you would see how needless were these convulsions of business which I have been speaking of, and how entirely they resulted from leaving industry to private and unorganized management, just consider the working of our system. Overproduction in special lines, which was the great hobgoblin of your day, is impossible now, for by the connection between distribution and production supply is geared to demand like an engine to the governor which regulates its speed. Even suppose by an error of judgment an excessive production of some commodity. The consequent slackening or cessation of production in that line throws nobody out of employment. The suspended workers are at once found occupation in some other department of the vast workshop and lose only the time spent in changing, while, as for the glut, the business of the nation is large enough to carry any amount of product manufactured in excess of demand till the latter overtakes it. In such a case of overproduction, as I have supposed, there is not with us, as with you, any complex machinery to get out of order and magnify a thousand times the original mistake. Of course, having not even money, we still less have credit. All estimates deal directly with the real things, the flour, iron, wood, wool, and labor, of which money and credit were for you the very misleading representatives. In our calculations of cost there can be no mistakes. Out of the annual product the amount necessary for the support of the people is taken, and the requisite labor to produce the next year's consumption provided for. The residue of the material and labor represents what can be safely expended in improvements. If the crops are bad, the surplus for that year is less than usual, that is all. Except for slight occasional effects of such natural causes, there are no fluctuations of business, the material prosperity of the nation flows on uninterruptedly from generation to generation, like an ever broadening and deepening river.

"Your business crises, Mr. West," continued the doctor, "like either of the great wastes I mentioned before, were enough, alone, to have kept your noses to the grindstone forever; but I have still to speak of one other great cause of your poverty, and that was the idleness of a great part of your capital and labor. With us it is the business of the administration to keep in constant employment every ounce of available capital and labor in the country. In your day there was no general control of either capital or labor, and a large part of both failed to find employment. 'Capital,' you used to say, 'is naturally timid,' and it would certainly have been reckless if it had not been timid in an epoch when there was a large preponderance of probability that any particular business venture would end in failure. There was no time when, if security could have been guaranteed it, the amount of capital devoted to productive industry could not have been greatly increased. The proportion of it so employed underwent constant extraordinary fluctuations, according to the greater or less feeling of uncertainty as to the stability of the industrial situation, so that the output of the national industries greatly varied in different years. But for the same reason that the amount of capital employed at times of special insecurity was far less than at times of somewhat greater security, a very large proportion was never employed at all, because the hazard of business was always very great in the best of times.

"It should be also noted that the great amount of capital always seeking employment where tolerable safety could be insured terribly embittered the competition between capitalists when a promising opening presented itself. The idleness of capital, the result of its timidity, of course meant the idleness of labor in corresponding degree. Moreover, every change in the adjustments of business, every slightest alteration in the condition of commerce or manufactures, not to speak of the innumerable business failures that took place yearly, even in the best of times, were constantly throwing a multitude of men out of employment for periods of weeks or months, or even years. A great number of these seekers after employment were constantly traversing the country, becoming in time professional vagabonds, then criminals. 'Give us work!' was the cry of an army of the unemployed at nearly all seasons, and in seasons of dullness in business this army swelled to a host so vast and desperate as to threaten the stability of the government. Could there conceivably be a more conclusive demonstration of the imbecility of the system of private enterprise as a method for enriching a nation than the fact that, in an age of such general poverty and want of everything, capitalists had to throttle one another to find a safe chance to invest their capital and workmen rioted and burned because they could find no work to do?

"Now, Mr. West," continued Doctor Leete, "I want you to bear in mind that these points of which I have been speaking indicate only negatively the advantages of the national organization of industry by showing certain fatal defects and prodigious imbecilities of the systems of private enterprise which are not found in it. These alone, you must admit, would pretty well explain why the nation is so much richer than in your day. But the larger half of our advantage over you, the positive side of it, I have yet barely spoken of. Supposing the system of private enterprise in industry were without any of the great leaks I have mentioned; that there were no waste on account of misdirected effort growing out of mistakes as to the demand, and inability to command a general view of the industrial field. Suppose, also, there were no neutralizing and duplicating of effort from competition. Suppose, also, there were no waste from business panics and crises through bankruptcy and long interruptions of industry, and also none from the idleness of capital and labor. Supposing these evils, which are essential to the conduct of industry by capital in private hands, could all be miraculously prevented, and the system yet retained; even then the superiority of the results attained by the modern industrial system of national control would remain overwhelming.

"You used to have some pretty large textile manufacturing establishments, even in your day, although not comparable with ours. No doubt you have visited these great mills in your time, covering acres of ground, employing thousands of hands, and combining under one roof, under one control, the hundred distinct processes between, say, the cotton bale and the bale of glossy calicoes. You have admired the vast economy of labor as of mechanical force resulting from the perfect interworking with the rest of every wheel and every hand. No doubt you have reflected how much less the same force of workers employed in that factory would accomplish if they were scattered, each man working independently. Would you think it an exaggeration to say that the utmost product of those workers, working thus apart, however amicable their relations might be, was increased not merely by a percentage, but many fold, when their efforts were organized under one control? Well now, Mr.

West, the organization of the industry of the nation under a single control, so that all its processes interlock, has multiplied the total product over the utmost that could be done under the former system, even leaving out of account the four great wastes mentioned, in the same proportion that the product of those mill workers was increased by cooperation. The effectiveness of the working force of a nation, under the myriad-headed leadership of private capital, even if the leaders were not mutual enemies, as compared with that which it attains under a single head, may be likened to the military efficiency of a mob, or a horde of barbarians with a thousand petty chiefs, as compared with that of a disciplined army under one general—such a fighting machine, for example, as the German army in the time of Von Moltke."

"After what you have told me," I said, "I do not so much wonder that the nation is richer now than then, but that you are not all Crœsuses."

"Well," replied Doctor Leete, "we are pretty well off. The rate at which we live is as luxurious as we could wish. The rivalry of ostentation, which in your day led to extravagance in no way conducive to comfort, finds no place, of course, in a society of people absolutely equal in resources, and our ambition stops at the surroundings which minister to the enjoyment of life. We might, indeed, have much larger incomes, individually, if we chose so to use the surplus of our product, but we prefer to expend it upon public works and pleasures in which all share, upon public halls and buildings, art galleries, bridges, statuary, means of transit, and the conveniences of our cities, great musical and theatrical exhibitions, and in providing on a vast scale for the recreations of the people. You have not begun to see how we live yet, Mr. West. At home we have comfort, but the splendor of our life is, on its social side, that which we share with our fellows. When you know more of it you will see where the money goes, as you used to say, and I think you will agree that we do well so to extend it."

"I suppose," observed Doctor Leete, as we strolled homeward from the dining hall, "that no reflection would have cut the men of your wealth-worshiping century more keenly than the suggestion that they did not know how to make money. Nevertheless, that is just the verdict history has passed on them. Their system of unorganized and antagonistic industries was as absurd economically as it was morally abominable. Selfishness was their only science, and in industrial production selfishness is suicide. Competition, which is the instinct of selfishness, is another word for dissipation of energy, while combination is the secret of efficient production; and not till the idea of increasing the common stock can industrial combination be realized, and the acquisition of wealth really begin. Even if the principle of share-and-share-alike for all men were not the only humane and rational basis for a society, we should still enforce it as economically expedient, seeing that until the disintegrating influence of self-seeking is suppressed no true concert of industry is possible."

· XXIII ·

THAT EVENING, AS I SAT WITH EDITH IN THE MUSIC ROOM, listening to some pieces in the program of that day which had attracted my notice, I took advantage of an interval in the music to say, "I have a question to ask you which I fear is rather indiscreet."

"I am quite sure it is not that," she replied, encouragingly.

"I am in the position of an eavesdropper," I continued, "who, having overheard a little of a matter not intended for him, though seeming to concern him, has the impudence to come to the speaker for the rest."

"An eavesdropper!" she repeated, looking puzzled.

"Yes," I said, "but an excusable one, as I think you will admit."

"This is very mysterious," she replied.

"Yes," said I, "so mysterious that often I have doubted whether I really overheard at all what I am going to ask you about, or only dreamed it. I want you to tell me. The matter is this: When I was coming out of that sleep of a century, the first impression of which I was conscious was of voices talking around me, voices that afterward I recognized as your father's, your mother's, and your own. First, I remember your father's voice saying, 'He is going to open his eyes. He had better see but one person at first.' Then you said, if I did not dream it all, 'Promise me, then, that you will not tell him.' Your father seemed to hesitate about promising, but you insisted, and your mother interposing, he finally promised, and when I opened my eyes I saw only him."

I had been quite serious when I said that I was not sure that I had not dreamed the conversation I fancied I had overheard, so incomprehensible was it that these people should know anything of me, a contemporary of their great-grandparents, which I did not know myself. But when I saw the effect of my words upon Edith, I knew, I knew that it was no dream, but another mystery, and a more puzzling one than any I had before encountered. For from the moment that the drift of my question became apparent, she showed indications of the most acute embarrassment. Her eyes, always so frank and direct in expression, had dropped in a panic before mine, while her face crimsoned from neck to forehead.

"Pardon me," I said, as soon as I had recovered from bewilderment at the extraordinary effect of my words. "It seems, then, that I was not dreaming. There is some secret, something about me, which you are withholding from me. Really, doesn't it seem a little hard that a person in my position should not be given all the information possible concerning himself?"

"It does not concern you—that is, not directly. It is not about you—exactly," she replied, scarcely audibly.

"But it concerns me in some way," I persisted. "It must be something that would interest me."

"I don't know even that," she replied, venturing a momentary glance at my face, furiously blushing, and yet with a quaint smile flickering about her lips which betrayed a certain perception of humor in the situation despite its embarrassment—"I am not sure that it would even interest you."

"Your father would have told me," I insisted, with an accent of reproach. "It was you who forbade him. He thought I ought to know."

She did not reply. She was so entirely charming in her confusion that I was now prompted, as much by the desire to prolong the situation as by my original curiosity, to importune her further.

"Am I never to know? Will you never tell me?" I said.

"It depends," she answered, after a long pause.

"On what?" I persisted.

"Ah, you ask too much," she replied. Then, raising to mine a face which inscrutable eyes, flushed cheeks, and smiling lips combined to render perfectly bewitching, she added, "What should you think if I said that it depended on—yourself?"

"On myself?" I echoed. "How can that possibly be?"

"Mr. West, we are losing some charming music," was her only reply to this, and turning to the telephone, at a touch of her finger she set the air to swaying to the rhythm of an adagio. After that she took good care that the music should leave no opportunity for conversation. She kept her face averted from me, and pretended to be absorbed in the airs, but that it was a mere pretense the crimson tide standing at flood in her cheeks sufficiently betrayed.

When at length she suggested that I might have heard all I cared to, for that time, and we rose to leave the room, she came straight up to me and said, without raising her eyes, "Mr. West, you say I have been good to you. I have not been particularly so, but if you think I have, I want you to promise me that you will not try again to make me tell you this thing you have asked tonight, and that you will not try to find it out from anyone else—my father or mother, for instance."

To such an appeal there was but one reply possible. "Forgive me for distressing you. Of course I will promise," I said. "I would never have asked you if I had fancied it could distress you. But do you blame me for being curious?"

"I do not blame you at all."

"And some time," I added, "if I do not tease you, you may tell me of your own accord. May I not hope so?"

"Perhaps," she murmured.

"Only perhaps?"

Looking up, she read my face with a quick, deep glance. "Yes," she said, "I think I may tell you—some time." And so our conversation ended, for she gave me no chance to say anything more.

That night I don't think even Doctor Pillsbury could have put me to sleep, till toward morning at least. Mysteries had been my accustomed food for days now, but none had before confronted me at once so mysterious and so fascinating as this, the solution of which Edith Leete had forbidden me even to seek. It was a double mystery. How, in the first place, was it conceivable that she should know any secret about me, a stranger from a strange age? In the second place, even if she should know such a secret, how account for the agitating effect which the knowledge of it seemed to have upon her? There are puzzles so difficult that one cannot even get so far as a conjecture as to the solution, and this seemed one of them. I am usually of too practical a turn to waste time on such conundrums; but the difficulty of a riddle embodied in a beautiful young girl does not detract from its fascination. In general, no doubt, maidens' blushes may be safely assumed to tell the same tale to young men in all ages and races, but to give that interpretation to Edith's crimson cheeks would, considering my position and the length of time I had known her, and still more the fact that this mystery dated from before I had known her at all, be a piece of utter fatuity. And yet she was an angel, and I should not have been a young man if reason and common sense had been able quite to banish a roseate tinge from my dreams that night.

IN THE MORNING I WENT DOWNSTAIRS EARLY IN THE HOPE of seeing Edith alone. In this, however, I was disappointed. Not finding her in the house, I sought her in the garden, but she was not there. In the course of my wanderings I visited the underground chamber, and sat down there to rest. Upon the reading table in the chamber several periodicals and newspapers lay, and thinking that Doctor Leete might be interested in glancing over a Boston daily of 1887, I brought one of the papers with me into the house when I came.

At breakfast I met Edith. She blushed as she greeted me, but was perfectly self-possessed. As we sat at table, Doctor Leete amused himself with looking over the paper I had brought in. There was in it, as in all the newspapers of that date, a great deal about the labor troubles, strikes, lockouts, boycotts, the programs of labor parties, and the wild threats of the anarchists.

"By the way," said I, as the doctor read aloud to us some of these items, "what part did the followers of the red flag take in the establishment of the new order of things? They were making considerable noise the last thing that I knew."

"They had nothing to do with it except to hinder it, of course," replied Doctor Leete. "They did that very effectually while they lasted, for their talk so disgusted people as to deprive the best-considered projects for social reform of a hearing. The subsidizing of those fellows was one of the shrewdest moves of the opponents of reform."

"Subsidizing them!" I exclaimed in astonishment.

"Certainly," replied Doctor Leete. "No historical authority nowadays doubts that they were paid by the great monopolies to wave the red flag and talk about burning, sacking, and blowing people up, in order, by alarming the timid, to head off any real reforms. What astonishes me most is that you should have fallen into the trap so unsuspectingly."

"What are your grounds for believing that the red-flag party was subsidized?" I inquired.

"Why, simply because they must have seen that their course made a thousand enemies of their professed cause to one friend. Not to suppose that they were hired for the work is to credit them with an inconceivable folly.* In the United States, of all countries, no party could intelligently expect to carry its point without first winning over to its ideas a majority of the nation, as the national party eventually did."

"The national party!" I exclaimed. "That must have arisen after my day. I suppose it was one of the labor parties."

"Oh no!" replied the doctor. "The labor parties, as such, never could have accomplished anything on a large or permanent scale. For purposes of national scope, their basis as merely class organizations was too narrow. It was not till a rearrangement of the industrial and social system on a higher ethical basis, and for the more efficient production of wealth, was recognized as the interest, not of one class, but equally of all classes, of rich and poor, cultured and ignorant, old and young, weak and strong, men and women, that there was any prospect that it would be achieved. Then the national party arose to carry it out by political methods. It probably took that name because its aim was to nationalize the functions of production and distribution. Indeed, it could not well have had any other name, for its purpose was to realize the idea of the nation with a grandeur and completeness never before conceived, not as an association of men for certain merely political functions affecting their happiness only remotely and superficially, but as a family, a vital union, a common life, a mighty heaven-touching

*I fully admit the difficulty of accounting for the course of the anarchists on any other theory than that they were subsidized by the capitalists, but, at the same time, there is no doubt that the theory is wholly erroneous. It certainly was not held at the time by anyone, though it may seem so obvious in the retrospect.

tree whose leaves are its people, fed from its veins, and feeding it in turn. The most patriotic of all possible parties, it sought to justify patriotism and raise it from an instinct to a rational devotion, by making the native land truly a father-land, a father who kept the people alive and was not merely an idol for which they were expected to die."

· XXV ·

THE PERSONALITY OF EDITH LEETE HAD NATURALLY IMpressed me strongly ever since I had come, in so strange a manner, to be an inmate of her father's house, and it was to be expected that after what had happened the night previous, I should be more than ever preoccupied with thoughts of her. From the first I had been struck with the air of serene frankness and ingenuous directness, more like that of a noble and innocent boy than any girl I had ever known, which characterized her. I was curious to know how far this charming quality might be peculiar to herself, and how far possibly a result of alterations in the social position of women which might have taken place since my time. Finding an opportunity that day, when alone with Doctor Leete, I turned the conversation in that direction.

"I suppose," I said, "that women nowadays, having been relieved of the burden of house work, have no employment but the cultivation of their charms and graces."

"So far as we men are concerned," replied Doctor Leete, "we should consider that they amply paid their way, to use one of your forms of expression, if they confined themselves to that occupation, but you may be very sure that they have quite too much spirit to consent to be mere beneficiaries of society, even as a return for ornamenting it. They did, indeed, welcome their riddance from housework, because that was not only exceptionally wearing in itself, but also wasteful, in the extreme, of energy, as compared with the cooperative plan; but they accepted relief from that sort of work only that they might contribute in other and more effectual, as well as more agreeable, ways to the common weal. Our women, as well as our men, are members of the industrial army, and leave it only when maternal duties claim them. The result is that most women, at one time or another of their lives, serve industrially some five or ten or fifteen years, while those who have no children fill out the full term."

"A woman does not, then, necessarily leave the industrial service on marriage?" I queried.

"No more than a man," replied the doctor. "Why on earth should she? Married women have no housekeeping responsibilities now, you know, and a husband is not a baby that he should be cared for."

"It was thought one of the most grievous features of our civilization that we required so much toil from women," I said, "but it seems to me you get more out of them than we did."

Doctor Leete laughed. "Indeed we do, just as we do out of our men. Yet the women of this age are very happy, and those of the nineteenth century, unless contemporary references greatly mislead us, were very miserable. The reason that women nowadays are so much more efficient colaborers with the men, and at the same time are so happy, is that, in regard to their work as well as men's, we follow the principle of providing every one the kind of occupation he or she is best adapted to. Women being inferior in strength to men, and further disqualified industrially in special ways, the kinds of occupation reserved for them, and the conditions under which they pursue them, have reference to these facts. The heavier sorts of work are everywhere reserved for men, the lighter occupations for women. Under no circumstances is a woman permitted to follow any employment not perfectly adapted, both as to kind and degree of labor, to her sex. Moreover, the hours of women's work are considerably shorter than those of men, more frequent vacations are granted, and the most careful provision is made for rest when needed. The men of this day so well appreciate that they owe to the beauty and grace of women the chief zest of their lives and their main incentive to effort, that they permit them to work at all only because it is fully understood that a certain regular requirement of labor, of a sort adapted to their powers, is well for body and mind, during the period of maximum physical vigor. We believe that the magnificent health which distinguishes our women from those of your day, who seem to have been so generally sickly, is owing largely to the fact that all alike are furnished with healthful and inspiriting occupation."

"I understood you," I said, "that the women workers belong to the army of industry, but how can they be under the same system of ranking and discipline with the men, when the conditions of their labor are so different?"

"They are under an entirely different discipline," replied Doctor Leete, "and constitute rather an allied force than an integral part of the army of the men. They have a woman general-in-chief and are under exclusively feminine regime. This general, as also the higher officers, is chosen by the body of women who have passed the time of service, in correspondence with the manner in which the chiefs of the masculine army and the President of the nation are elected. The general of the women's army sits in the cabinet of the President and has a veto on measures respecting women's work, pending appeals to Congress. I should have said, in speaking of the judiciary, that we have women on the bench, appointed by the general of the women, as well as men. Causes in which both parties are women are determined by women judges, and where a man and a woman are parties to a case, a judge of either sex must consent to the verdict."

"Womanhood seems to be organized as a sort of *imperium in imperio* in your system," I said.

"To some extent," Doctor Leete replied, "but the inner *imperium* is one from which you will admit there is not likely to be much danger to the nation. The lack of some such recognition of the distinct individuality of the sexes was one of the innumerable defects of your society. The passional attraction between men and women has too often prevented a perception of the profound differences which make the members of each sex in many things strange to the other, and capable of sympathy only with their own. It is in giving full play to the differences of sex rather than in seeking to obliterate them, as was apparently the effort of some reformers in your day, that the enjoyment of each by itself and the piquancy which each has for the other, are alike enhanced. In your day there was no career for women except in an unnatural rivalry with men. We have given them a world of their own, with its emulations, ambitions, and careers, and I assure you they are very happy in it. It seems to us that women were more than any other class the victims of your civilization. There is something which, even at this distance of time, penetrates one with pathos in the spectacle of their ennuied, underdeveloped lives, stunted at marriage, their narrow horizon, bounded so often, physically, by the four walls of home, and morally by a petty circle of personal interests. I speak now, not of the poorer classes, who were generally worked to death, but also of the well-to-do and rich. From the great sorrows, as well as the petty frets of life, they had no refuge in the breezy outdoor world of human affairs, nor any interests save those of the family. Such an existence would have softened men's brains or driven them mad. All that is changed today. No woman is heard nowadays wishing she were a man, nor parents desiring boy rather than girl children. Our girls are as full of ambition for their careers as our boys. Marriage, when it comes, does not mean incarceration for them, nor does it separate them in any way from the larger interests of society, the bustling life of the world. Only when maternity fills a woman's mind with new interests does she withdraw from the world for a time. Afterward, and at any time, she may return to her place among her comrades, nor need she ever lose touch with them. Women are a very happy race nowadays, as compared with what they ever were before in the world's history, and their power of giving happiness to men has been of course increased in proportion."

"I should imagine it possible," I said, "that the interest which girls take in their careers as members of the industrial army and candidates for its distinctions might have an effect to deter them from marriage."

Doctor Leete smiled. "Have no anxiety on that score, Mr. West," he replied. "The Creator took very good care that whatever other modifications the dispositions of men and women might with time take on, their attraction for each other should remain constant. The mere fact that in an age like yours, when the struggle for existence must have left people little time for other thoughts, and the future was so uncertain that to assume parental responsibilities must have often seemed like a criminal risk, there was even then marrying and giving in marriage, should be conclusive on this point. As for love nowadays, one of our authors says that the vacuum left in the minds of men and women by the absence of care for one's livelihood has been entirely taken up by the tender passion. That, however, I beg you to believe, is something of an exaggeration. For the rest, so far is marriage from being an interference with a woman's career, that the higher positions in the feminine army of industry are entrusted only to women who have been both wives and mothers, as they alone fully represent their sex."

"Are credit cards issued to the women just as to the men?"

"Certainly."

"The credits of the women, I suppose, are for smaller sums, owing to the frequent suspension of their labor on account of family responsibilities."

"Smaller!" exclaimed Doctor Leete. "Oh, no! The maintenance of all our people is the same. There are no exceptions to that rule, but if any difference were made on account of the interruptions you speak of, it would be by making the woman's credit larger, not smaller. Can you think of any service constituting a stronger claim on the nation's gratitude than bearing and nursing the nation's children? According to our view, none deserve so well of the world as good parents. There is no task so unselfish, so necessarily without return, though the heart is well rewarded, as the nurture of the children who are to make the world for one another when we are gone."

"It would seem to follow, from what you have said, that wives are in no way dependent on their husbands for maintenance."

"Of course they are not," replied Doctor Leete, "nor children on their parents either, that is, for means of support, though of course they are for the offices of affection. The child's labor, when he grows up, will go to increase the common stock, not his parents', who will be dead, and therefore he is properly nurtured out of the common stock. The account of every person, man, woman, and child, you must understand, is always with the nation directly, and never through any intermediary, except, of course, that parents, to a certain extent, act for children as their guardians. You see that it is by virtue of the relation of individuals to the nation, of their membership in it, that they are entitled to support; and this title is no way connected with or affected by their relations to other individuals who are fellow members of the nation with them. That any person should be dependent for the means of support upon another would be shocking to the moral sense as well as indefensible on any rational social theory. What would become of personal liberty and dignity under such an arrangement? I am aware that you called yourselves free in the nineteenth century. The meaning of the word could not then, however, have been at all what it is at present, or you certainly would not have applied it to a society of which nearly every member was in a position of galling personal dependence upon others as to the very means of life, the poor upon rich, or employed upon employer, women upon men, children upon parents. Instead of distributing the product of the nation directly to its members, which would seem the most natural and obvious method, it would actually appear that you had given your minds to devising a plan of hand-to-hand distribution, involving the maximum of personal humiliation to all classes of recipients.

"As regards the dependence of women upon men for support, which then was usual, of course natural attraction in case of marriages of love may often have made it endurable, though for spirited women I should fancy it must always have remained humiliating. What, then, must it have been in the innumerable cases where women, with or without the form of marriage, had to sell themselves to men to get their living? Even your contemporaries, callous as they were to most of the revolting aspects of their society, seem to have had an idea that this was not quite as it should be; but, it was still only for pity's sake that they deplored the lot of the women. It did not occur to them that it was robbery as well as cruelty when men seized for themselves the whole product of the world and left women to beg and wheedle for their share. Why—But bless me, Mr. West, I am really running on at a remarkable rate, just as if the robbery, the sorrow, and the shame which those poor women endured were not over a century since, or as if you were responsible for what you no doubt deplored as much as I do."

"I must bear my share of responsibility for the world as it then was," I replied. "All I can say in extenuation is that until the nation was ripe for the present system of organized production and distribution, no radical improvement in the position of woman was possible. The root of her disability, as you say, was her personal dependence upon man for her livelihood, and I can imagine no other mode of social organization than that you have adopted, which would have set woman free of man at the same time that it set men free of one another. I suppose, by the way, that so entire a change in the position of women cannot have taken place without affecting in marked ways the social relations of the sexes. That will be a very interesting study for me."

"The change you will observe," said Doctor Leete, "will chiefly be, I think, the entire frankness and unconstraint which now characterize those relations, as compared with the artificiality which seems to have marked them in your time. The sexes now meet with the ease of perfect equals, suitors to each other for nothing but love. In your time the fact that women were dependent for support on men made the woman in reality the one chiefly benefited by marriage. This fact, so far as we can judge from contemporary records, appears to have been coarsely enough recognized among the lower classes, while among the more polished it was glossed over by a system of elaborate conventionalities which aimed to carry the precisely opposite meaning, namely, that the man was the party chiefly benefited. To keep up this convention it was essential that he should always seem the suitor. Nothing was therefore considered more shocking to the proprieties than that a woman should betray a fondness for a man before he had indicated a desire to marry her. Why, we actually have in our libraries books, by authors of your day, written for no other purpose than to discuss the question whether, under any conceivable circumstances, a woman might, without discredit to her sex, reveal an unsolicited love. All this seems exquisitely absurd to us, and yet we know that, given your circumstances, the problem might have a serious side. When for a woman to proffer her love to a man was in effect to invite him to assume the burden of her support, it is easy to see that pride and delicacy might well have checked the promptings of the heart. When you go out into our society, Mr. West, you must be prepared to be often cross-questioned on this point by our young people, who are naturally much interested in this aspect of old-fashioned manners."*

"And so the girls of the twentieth century tell their love."

"If they choose," replied Doctor Leete. "There is no

*I may say that Doctor Leete's warning has been fully justified by my experience. The amount and intensity of amusement which the young people of this day, and the young women especially, are able to extract from what they are pleased to call the oddities of courtship in the nineteenth century, appear unlimited.

more pretense of a concealment of feeling on their part than on the part of their lovers. Coquetry would be as much despised in a girl as in a man. Affected coldness, which in your day rarely deceived a lover, would deceive him wholly now, for no one thinks of practicing it."

"One result which must follow from the independence of women I can see for myself," I said. "There can be no marriages now except those of inclination."

"That is a matter of course," replied Doctor Leete.

"Think of a world in which there are nothing but matches of pure love! Ah me, Doctor Leete, how far you are from being able to understand what an astonishing phenomenon such a world seems to a man of the nineteenth century!"

"I can, however, to some extent, imagine it," replied the doctor. "But the fact you celebrate, that there are nothing but love matches, means even more, perhaps, than you probably at first realize. It means that for the first time in human history the principle of sexual selection, with its tendency to preserve and transmit the better types of the race, and let the inferior types drop out, has unhindered operation. The necessities of poverty, the need of having a home, no longer tempt women to accept as the fathers of their children men whom they neither can love nor respect. Wealth and rank no longer divert attention from personal qualities. Gold no longer 'gilds the straitened forehead of the fool.' The gifts of person, mind, and disposition—beauty, wit, eloquence, kindness, generosity, geniality, courage—are sure of transmission to posterity. Every generation is sifted through a little finer mesh than the last. The attributes that human nature admires are preserved, those that repel it are left behind. There are, of course, a great many women who with love must mingle admiration, and seek to wed greatly, but these not the less obey the same law, for to wed greatly now is not to marry men of fortune or title, but those who have risen above their fellows by the solidity or brilliance of their services to humanity. These form nowadays the only aristocracy with which alliance is distinction.

"You were speaking, a day or two ago, of the physical superiority of our people to your contemporaries. Perhaps more important than any of the causes I mentioned then as tending to race purification has been the effect of untrammeled sexual selection upon the quality of two or three successive generations. I believe that when you make a fuller study of our people you will find in them not only a physical, but a mental and moral improvement. It would be strange if it were not so, for not only is one of the great laws of nature now freely working out the salvation of the race, but a profound moral sentiment has come to its support. Individualism, which in your day was the animating idea of society, not only was fatal to any vital sentiment of brotherhood and common interest among living men, but equally to any realization of the responsibility of the living for the generation to follow. Today this sense of responsibility, practically unrecognized in all previous ages, has become one of the great ethical ideas of the race, reinforcing, with an intense conviction of duty, the natural impulse to seek in marriage the best and noblest of the other sex. The result is, that not all the encouragements and incentives of every sort which we have provided to develop industry, talent, genius, excellence of whatever kind, are comparable in their effect on our young men with the fact that our women sit aloft as judges of the race and reserve themselves to reward the winners. Of all the whips, and spurs, and baits, and prizes, there is none like the thought of the radiant faces which the laggards will find averted.

"Celibates nowadays are almost invariably men who have failed to acquit themselves creditably in the work of life. The woman must be a courageous one, with a very evil sort of courage, too, whom pity for one of these unfortunates should lead to defy the opinion of her generation—for otherwise she is free—so far as to accept him for a husband. I should add that, more exacting and difficult to resist than any other element in that opinion, she would find the sentiment of her own sex. Our women have risen to the full height of their responsibility as the wardens of the world to come, to whose keeping the keys of the future are confided. Their feeling of duty in this respect amounts to a sense of religious consecration. It is a cult in which they educate their daughters from childhood."

After going to my room that night, I sat up late to read a romance of Berrian, handed me by Doctor Leete, the plot of which turned on a situation suggested by his last words, concerning the modern view of parental responsibility. A similar situation would almost certainly have been treated by a nineteenth-century romancist so as to excite the morbid sympathy of the reader with the sentimental selfishness of the lovers, and his resentment toward the unwritten law which they outraged. I need not describe—for who has not read *Ruth Elton*?—how different is the course which Berrian takes, and with what tremendous effect he enforces the principle which he states: "Over the unborn our power is that of God, and our responsibility like His toward us. As we acquit ourselves toward them, so let Him deal with us."

· XXVI ·

I THINK IF A PERSON WERE EVER EXCUSABLE FOR LOSING track of the days of the week, the circumstances excused me. Indeed, if I had been told that the method of reckoning time had been wholly changed and the days were now counted in lots of five, ten, or fifteen instead of seven, I should have been in no way surprised after what I had already heard and seen of the twentieth century. The first time that any inquiry as to the days of the week occurred to me was the morning following the conversation related in the last chapter. At the breakfast table Doctor Leete asked me if I would care to hear a sermon.

"Is it Sunday, then?" I exclaimed.

"Yes," he replied. "It was on Friday, you see, when we made the lucky discovery of the buried chamber to which we owe your society this morning. It was on Saturday morning, soon after midnight, that you first awoke, and Sunday afternoon when you awoke the second time with faculties fully regained."

"So you still have Sundays and sermons," I said. "We had prophets who foretold that long before this time the world would have dispensed with both. I am very curious to know how the ecclesiastical systems fit in with the rest of your social arrangements. I suppose you have a sort of national church with official clergymen."

Doctor Leete laughed, and Mrs. Leete and Edith seemed greatly amused.

"Why, Mr. West," Edith said, "what odd people you must think us. You were quite done with national religious establishments in the nineteenth century, and did you fancy we had gone back to them?"

"But how can voluntary churches and an unofficial clerical profession be reconciled with national ownership of all buildings, and the industrial service required of all men?" I answered.

"The religious practices of the people have naturally changed considerably in a century," replied Doctor Leete, "but supposing them to have remained unchanged, our social system would accommodate them perfectly. The nation supplies any person or number of persons with buildings on guarantee of the rent, and they remain tenants while they pay it. As for the clergymen, if a number of persons wish the services of an individual for any particular end of their own, apart from the general service of the nation, they can always secure it, with that individual's own consent, of course, just as we secure the service of our editors, by contributing from their credit cards an indemnity to the nation for the loss of his services in general industry. This indemnity paid the nation for the individual answers to the salary in your day paid to the individual himself; and the various applications of this principle leave private initiative full play in all details to which national control is not applicable. Now, as to hearing a sermon today, if you wish to do so, you can either go to church to hear it or stay at home."

"How am I to hear it if I stay at home?"

"Simply by accompanying us to the music room at the proper hour and selecting an easy chair. There are some who still prefer to hear sermons in church, but most of our preaching, like our musical performances, is not in public, but delivered in acoustically prepared chambers, connected by wire with subscribers' houses. If you prefer to go to a church I shall be glad to accompany you, but I really don't believe you are likely to hear anywhere a better discourse than you will at home. I see by the paper that Mr. Barton is to preach this morning, and he preaches only by telephone, and to audiences often reaching 150,000."

"The novelty of the experience of hearing a sermon under such circumstances would incline me to be one of Mr. Barton's hearers, if for no other reason," I said.

An hour or two later, as I sat reading in the library, Edith came for me, and I followed her to the music room, where Doctor and Mrs. Leete were waiting. We had not more than seated ourselves comfortably when the tinkle of a bell was heard, and a few moments after the voice of a man, at the pitch of ordinary conversation, addressed us, with an effect of proceeding from an invisible person in the room. This was what the voice said:

MR. BARTON'S SERMON

"We have had among us, during the past week, a critic from the nineteenth century, a living representative of the epoch of our great-grandparents. It would be strange if a fact so extraordinary had not somewhat strongly affected our imaginations. Perhaps most of us have been stimulated to some effort to realize the society of a century ago, and figure to ourselves what it must have been like to live then. In inviting you now to consider certain reflections upon this subject which have occurred to me, I presume that I shall rather follow than divert the course of your own thoughts."

Edith whispered something to her father at this point, to which he nodded assent and turned to me.

"Mr. West," he said, "Edith suggests that you may find it slightly embarrassing to listen to a discourse on the lines Mr. Barton is laying down, and if so, you need not be cheated out of a sermon. She will connect us with Mr. Sweetser's speaking room if you say so, and I can still promise you a very good discourse."

"No, no," I said. "Believe me, I would much rather hear what Mr. Barton has to say."

"As you please," replied my host.

When her father spoke to me Edith had touched a screw, and the voice of Mr. Barton had ceased abruptly. Now at another touch the room was once more filled with the earnest, sympathetic tones which had already impressed me most favorably.

"I venture to assume that one effect has been common with us as a result of this effort at retrospection, and that it has been to leave us more than ever amazed at the stupendous change which one brief century has made in the material and moral conditions of humanity.

"Still, as regards the contrast between the poverty of the nation and the world in the nineteenth century and their wealth now, it is not greater, possibly, than had been before seen in human history, perhaps not greater, for example, than that between the poverty of this country during the earliest colonial period of the seventeenth century and the relatively great wealth it had attained at the close of the nineteenth, of between the England of William the Conqueror and that of Victoria. Although the aggregate riches of a nation did not then, as now, afford any accurate criterion of the masses of its people, yet instances like these afford partial parallels for the merely material side of the contrast between the nineteenth and the twentieth centuries. It is when we contemplate the moral aspect of that contrast that we find ourselves in the presence of a phenomenon for which history offers no precedent, however far back we may cast our eye. One might almost be excused who should exclaim, 'Here, surely, is something like a miracle!' Nevertheless, when we give over idle wonder, and begin to examine the seeming prodigy critically, we find it no prodigy at all, much less a miracle. It is not necessary to suppose a moral new birth of humanity, or a wholesale destruction of the wicked and survival of the good, to account for the fact before us. It finds its simple and obvious explanation in the reaction of a changed environment upon human nature. It means merely that a form of society which was founded on the pseudo-self-interest of selfishness, and appealed solely to the antisocial and brutal side of human nature, has been replaced by institutions based on the true self-interest of a rational unselfishness, and appealing to the social and generous instincts of men.

"My friends, if you would see men again the beasts of prey they seemed in the nineteenth century, all you have to do is to restore the old social and industrial system, which taught them to view their natural prey in their fellow men, and find their gain in the loss of others. No doubt it seems to you that no necessity, however dire, would have tempted you to subsist on what superior skill or strength enabled you to wrest from others equally needy. But suppose it were not merely your own life that you were responsible for. I know well that there must have been many a man among our ancestors who, if it had been merely a question of his own life, would sooner have given it up than nourished it by bread snatched from others. But this he was not permitted to do. He had dear lives dependent on him. Men loved women in those days, as now. God knows how they dared be fathers, but they had babies as sweet, no doubt, to them as ours to us, whom they must feed, clothe, educate. The gentlest creatures are fierce when they have young to provide for, and in that wolfish society the struggle for bread borrowed a peculiar desperation from the tenderest sentiments. For the sake of those dependent on him, a man might not choose, but must plunge into the foul fight—cheat, overreach, supplant, defraud, buy below worth and sell above, break down the business by which his neighbor fed his young ones, tempt men to buy what they ought not and to sell what they should not, grind his laborers, sweat his debtors, cozen his creditors. Though a man sought it carefully with tears, it was hard to find a way in which he could earn a living and provide for his family except from his mouth. Even the ministers of religion were not exempt from this cruel necessity. While they warned their flocks against the love of money, regard for their families compelled them to keep an outlook for the pecuniary prizes of their calling. Poor fellows, theirs was indeed a trying business, preaching to men a generosity and unselfishness which they and everybody knew would, in the existing state of the world, reduce to poverty those who should practice them, laying down laws of conduct which the law of self-preservation compelled men to break. Looking on the inhuman spectacle of society, these worthy men bitterly bemoaned the depravity of human nature; as if angelic nature would not have been debauched in such a devil's school! Ah, my friends, believe me, it is not now in this happy age that humanity is proving the divinity within it. It was rather in those evil days when not even the fight for life with one another, the struggle for mere existence, in which mercy was folly, could wholly banish generosity and kindness from the earth.

"It is not hard to understand the desperation with which men and women, who under other conditions would have been full of gentleness and ruth, fought and tore each other in the scramble for gold, when we realize what it meant to miss it, what poverty was in that day. For the body it was hunger and thirst, torment by heat and frost, in sickness neglect, in health unremitting toil; for the moral nature it meant oppression, contempt, and the patient endurance of indignity, brutish associations from infancy, the loss of all the innocence of childhood, the grace of womanhood, the dignity of manhood; for the mind it meant the death of ignorance, the torpor of all those faculties which distinguish us from brutes, the reduction of life to a round of bodily functions.

"Ah, my friends, if such a fate as this were offered you and your children as the only alternative of success in the accumulation of wealth, how long do you fancy would you be in a sinking to the moral level of your ancestors?

"Some two or three centuries ago an act of barbarity was committed in India, which, though the number of lives destroyed was but a few score, was attended by such peculiar horrors that its memory is likely to be perpetual. A number of English prisoners were shut up in a room containing not enough air to supply one-tenth their number. The unfortunates were gallant men, devoted comrades in service, but, as the agonies of suffocation began to take hold on them, they forgot all else, and became involved in a hideous struggle, each one for himself, and against all others, to force a way to one of the small apertures of the prison at which alone it was possible to get a breath of air. It was a struggle in which men became beasts, and the recital of its horrors by the few survivors so shocked our forefathers that for a century later we find it a stock reference in their literature as a typical illustration of the extreme possibilities of human misery, as shocking in its moral as its physical aspect. They could scarcely have anticipated that to us the Black Hole of Calcutta, with its press of maddened men tearing and trampling one another in the struggle to win a place at the breathing holes, would seem a striking type of the society of their age. It lacked something of being a complete type, however, for in the Calcutta Black Hole there were no tender women, no little children and old men and women, no cripples. They were at least all men, strong to bear, who suffered.

"When we reflect that the ancient order of which I have been speaking was prevalent up to the end of the nineteenth century, while to us the new order which succeeded it already seems antique, even our parents having known no other, we cannot fail to be astounded at the suddenness with which a transition so profound beyond all previous experience of the race must have been effected. Some observation of the state of men's minds during the last quarter of the nineteenth century will, however, in great measure, dissipate this astonishment. Though general intelligence in the modern sense could not be said to exist in any community at that time, yet, as compared with previous generations, the one then on the stage was intelligent. The inevitable consequence of even this comparative degree of intelligence had been a perception of the evils of society, such as had never before been general. It is quite true that these evils had been even worse, much worse, in previous ages. It was the increased intelligence of the masses which made the difference, as the dawn reveals the squalor of surroundings which in the darkness may have seemed tolerable. The keynote of the literature of the period was one of compassion for the poor and unfortunate, and indignant outcry against the failure of the social machinery to ameliorate the miseries of men. It is plain from these outbursts that the moral hideousness of the spectacle about them was, at least by flashes, fully realized by the best of the men of that time, and that the lives of some of the more sensitive and generous-hearted of them were rendered well-nigh unendurable by the intensity of their sympathies.

"Although the idea of the vital unity of the family of mankind, the reality of human brotherhood, was very far from being apprehended by them as the moral axiom it seems to us, yet it is a mistake to suppose that there was no feeling at all corresponding to it. I could read you passages of great beauty from some of their writers which show that the conception was clearly attained by a few, and no doubt vaguely by many more. Moreover, it must not be forgotten that the nineteenth century was in name Christian, and the fact that the entire commercial and industrial frame of society was the embodiment of the anti-Christian spirit must have had some weight, though I admit it was strangely little, with the nominal followers of Jesus Christ.

"When we inquire why it did not have more, why, in general, long after a vast majority of men had agreed as to the crying abuses of the existing social arrangement, they still tolerated it or contented themselves with talking of petty reforms in it, we come upon an extraordinary fact. It was the sincere belief of even the best of men at that epoch that the only stable elements in human nature, on which a social system could be safely founded, were its worst propensities. They had been taught and believed that greed and self-seeking were all that held mankind together, and that all human associations would fall to pieces if anything were done to blunt the edge of these motives or curb their operation. In a word, they believed—even those who longed to believe otherwise—the exact reverse of what seems to us self-evident; they believed, that is, that the antisocial qualities of men, and not their social qualities, were what furnished the cohesive force of society. It seemed reasonable to them that men lived together solely for the purpose of overreaching and oppressing one another, and of being overreached and oppressed, and that while a society that gave full scope to these propensities could stand, there would be little chance for one based on the idea of cooperation for the benefit of all. It seems absurd to expect any one to believe that convictions like these were ever seriously entertained by men; but that they were not only entertained by our great-grandfathers, but were responsible for the long delay in doing away with the ancient order, after a conviction of its intolerable abuses had become general, is as well established as any fact in history can be. Just here you will find the explanation of the profound pessimism of the literature of the last quarter of the nineteenth century, the note of melancholy in its poetry, and the cynicism of its humor.

"Feeling that the condition of the race was unendurable, they had no clear hope of anything better. They believed that the evolution of humanity had resulted in leading it into a *cul de sac,* and that there was no way of getting forward. The frame of men's minds at this time is strikingly illustrated by treaties which have come down to us, and may even now be consulted in our libraries by the curious, in which laborious arguments are pursued to prove that despite the evil plight of men, life was still, by some slight preponderance of considerations, probably better worth living than leaving. Despising themselves, they despised their Creator. There was a general decay of religious belief. Pale and watery gleams, from skies thickly veiled by doubt and dread, alone lighted up the chaos of earth. That men should doubt Him whose breath is in their nostrils, or dread the hands that molded them, seems to us indeed a pitiable insanity; but we must remember that children who are brave by day have sometimes foolish fears at night. The dawn has come since then. It is very easy to believe in the fatherhood of God in the twentieth century.

"Briefly, as must needs be a discourse of this character, I have adverted to some of the causes which had prepared men's minds for the change from the old to the new order, as well as some causes of the conservatism of despair which for a while held it back after the time was ripe. To wonder at the rapidity with which the change was completed after its possibility was first entertained is to forget the intoxicating effect of hope upon minds long accustomed to despair. The sunburst, after so long and dark a night, must needs have had a dazzling effect. From the moment men allowed themselves to believe that humanity after all had not been meant for a dwarf, that its squat stature was not the measure of its possible growth, but that it stood upon the verge of an avatar of limitless development, the reaction must needs have been overwhelming. It is evident that nothing was able to stand against the enthusiasm which the new faith inspired.

"Here, at last, men must have felt, was a cause compared with which the grandest of historic causes had been trivial. It was doubtless because it could have commanded millions of martyrs, that none were needed. The change of a dynasty in a petty kingdom of the old world often cost more lives than did the revolution which set the feet of the human race at last in the right way.

"Doubtless it ill beseems one to whom the boon of life in our resplendent age has been vouchsafed to wish his destiny other, and yet I have often thought that I would fain exchange my share in this serene and golden day for a place in that stormy epoch of transition, when heroes burst the barred gate of the future and revealed to the kindling gaze of a hopeless race, in place of the blank wall that had closed its path, a vista of progress whose end, for very excess of light, still dazzles us. Ah, my friends! who will say that to have lived then, when the weakest influence was a lever to whose touch the centuries trembled, was not worth a share even in this era of fruition?

"You know the story of that last, greatest, and most bloodless of revolutions. In the time of one generation men laid aside the social traditions and practices of barbarians, and assumed a social order worthy of rational and human beings. Ceasing to be predatory in their habits, they became coworkers, and found in fraternity, at once, the science of wealth and happiness. 'What shall I eat and drink, and wherewithal shall I be clothed?' stated as a problem beginning and ending in self, had been an anxious and an endless one. But when once it was conceived, not from the individual, but the fraternal standpoint, 'What shall we eat and drink, and wherewithal shall we be clothed?'—its difficulties vanished.

"Poverty with servitude had been the result, for the mass of humanity, of attempting to solve the problem of maintenance from the individual standpoint, but no sooner had the nation become the sole capitalist and employer than not alone did plenty replace poverty, but the last vestige of the serfdom of man to man disappeared from earth. Human slavery, so often vainly scotched, at last was killed. The means of subsistence no longer doled out by men to women, by employer to employed, by rich to poor, was distributed from a common stock as among children at the father's table. It was impossible for a man any longer to use his fellow men as tools for his own profit. His esteem was the only sort of gain he could thenceforth make out of him. There was no more either arrogance or servility in the relations of human beings to one another. For the first time since the Creation every man stood up straight before God. The fear of want and the lust of gain became extinct motives when abundance was assured to all and immoderate possessions made impossible of attainment. There were no more beggars nor almoners. Equity left charity without an occupation. The ten commandments became well-nigh obsolete in a world where there was no temptation to theft, no occasion to lie either for fear or favor, no room for envy where all were equal, and little provocation to violence where men were disarmed of power to injure one another. Humanity's ancient dream of liberty, equality, fraternity, mocked by so many ages, at last was realized.

"As in the old society the generous, the just, the tender-hearted had been placed at a disadvantage by the possession of those qualities, so in the new society the cold-hearted, the greedy, and self-seeking found themselves out of joint with the world. Now that the conditions of life for the first time ceased to operate as a forcing process to develop the brutal qualities of human nature, and the premium which had heretofore encouraged selfishness was not only removed, but placed upon unselfishness, it was for the first time possible to see what unperverted human nature really was like. The depraved tendencies, which had previously overgrown and obscured the better to so large an extent, now withered like cellar fungi in the open air, and the nobler qualities showed a sudden luxuriance which turned cynics into panegyrists and for the first time in human history tempted mankind to fall in love with itself. Soon was fully revealed, what the divines and philosophers of the old world never would have believed, that human nature in its essential qualities is good, not bad, that men by their natural intention and structure are generous, not selfish, pitiful, not cruel, sympathetic, not arrogant, godlike in aspirations, instinct with divinest impulses of tenderness and self-sacrifice, images of God indeed, not the travesties upon Him they had seemed. The constant pressure, through numberless generations, of conditions of life which might have perverted angels, had not been able to essentially alter the natural nobility of the stock, and these conditions once removed, like a bent tree, it had sprung back to its normal uprightness.

"To put the whole matter in the nutshell of a parable, let me compare humanity in the olden time to a rosebush planted in a swamp, watered with black bog water, breathing miasmatic fogs by day, and chilled with poison dews at night. Innumerable generations of gardeners had done their best to make it bloom, but beyond an occasional half-opened bud with a worm at the heart, their efforts had been unsuccessful. Many, indeed, claimed that the bush was no rosebush at all, but a noxious shrub, fit only to be uprooted and burned. The gardeners, for the most part, however, held that the bush belonged to the rose family, but had some ineradicable taint about it, which prevented the buds from coming out, and accounted for its generally sickly condition. There were a few, indeed, who maintained that the stock was good enough, that the trouble was in the bog, and that under more favorable conditions the plant might be expected to do better. But these persons were not regular gardeners, and being condemned by the latter as mere theorists and daydreamers, were, for the most part, so regarded by the people. Moreover, urged some eminent moral philosophers, even conceding for the sake of the argument that the bush might possibly do better elsewhere, it was a more valuable discipline for the buds to try to bloom in a bog than it would be under more favorable conditions. The buds that succeeded in opening might indeed be very rare, and the flowers pale and scentless, but they represented far more moral effort than if they had bloomed spontaneously in a garden.

"The regular gardeners and the moral philosophers had their way. The bush remained rooted in the bog, and the old course of treatment went on. Continually new varieties of forcing mixtures were applied to the roots, and more recipes than could be numbered, each declared by its advocates the best and only suitable preparation, were used to kill the vermin and remove the mildew. This went on a very long time. Occasionally someone claimed to observe a slight improvement in the appearance of the bush, but there were quite as many who declared that it did not look so well as it used to. On the whole there could not be said to be any marked change. Finally, during a period of general despondency as to the prospects of the bush where it was, the idea of transplanting it was again mooted, and this time found favor. 'Let us try it,' was the general voice. 'Perhaps it may thrive better elsewhere, and here it is certainly doubtful if it be worth cultivating longer.' So it came about that the rosebush of humanity was transplanted, and set in sweet, warm, dry earth, where the sun bathed it, the stars wooed it, and the south wind caressed it. Then it appeared that it was indeed a rosebush. The vermin and the mildew disappeared, and the bush was covered with most beautiful red roses, whose fragrance filled the world.

"It is a pledge of the destiny appointed for us that the Creator has set in our hearts an infinite standard of achievement, judged by which our past attainments seem always insignificant, and the goal never nearer. Had our forefathers conceived a state of society in which men should live together like brethren dwelling in unity, without strife or envying, violence or overreaching, and where, at the price of a degree of labor not greater than health demands, in their chosen occupations, they should be wholly freed from care for the morrow and left with no more concern for their livelihood than trees which are watered by unfailing streams—had they conceived such a condition, I say, it would have seemed to them nothing less than paradise. They would have confounded it with their idea of heaven, nor dreamed that there could possibly lie further beyond anything to be desired or striven for.

"But how is it with us who stand on this height which they gazed up to? Already we have well-nigh forgotten, except when it is especially called to our minds by some occasion like the present, that it was not always with men as it is now. It is a strain on our imaginations to conceive the social arrangements of our immediate ancestors. We find them grotesque. The solution of the problem of physical maintenance so as to banish care and crime, so far from seeming to us an ultimate attainment, appears but as a preliminary to anything like real human progress. We have but relieved ourselves of an impertinent and needless harassment which hindered our ancestors from undertaking the real ends of existence. We are merely stripped for the race; no more. We are like a child which has just learned to stand upright and walk. It is a great event, from the child's point of view, when he first walks. Perhaps he fancies that there can be little beyond that achievement, but a year later he has forgotten that he could not always walk. His horizon did but widen when he rose, and enlarge as he moved. A great event indeed, in one sense, was his first step, but only as a beginning, not as the end. His true career was but then first entered on. The enfranchisement of humanity in the last century, from mental and physical absorption in working and scheming for the mere bodily necessities, may be regarded as a species of second birth of the race, without which its first birth to an existence that was but a burden would forever have remained unjustified, but whereby it is now abundantly vindicated. Since then, humanity has entered on a new phase of spiritual development, an evolution of higher faculties, the very existence of which in human nature our ancestors scarcely suspected. In place of the dreary hopelessness of the nineteenth century, its profound pessimism as to the future of humanity, the animating idea of the present age is an enthusiastic conception of the opportunities of our earthly existence, and the unbounded possibilities of human nature. The betterment of mankind from generation to generation, physically, mentally, morally, is recognized as the one great object supremely worthy of effort and of sacrifice. We believe the race for the first time to have entered on the realization of God's ideal of it, and each generation must now be a step upward.

"Do you ask what we look for when unnumbered generations shall have passed away? I answer, the way stretches far before us, but the end is lost in light. For twofold is the return of man to God 'who is our home,' the return of the individual by the way of death, and the return of the race by the fulfilment of the evolution, when the divine secret hidden in the germ shall be perfectly unfolded. With a tear for the dark past, turn we then to the dazzling future, and, veiling our eyes, press forward. The long and weary winter of the race is ended. Its summer has begun. Humanity has burst the chrysalis. The heavens are before it."

· XXVII ·

I NEVER COULD TELL JUST WHY, BUT SUNDAY AFTERNOON during my old life had been a time when I was peculiarly subject to melancholy, when the color unaccountably faded out of all the aspects of life, and everything appeared pathetically uninteresting. The hours, which in general were wont to bear me easily on their wings, lost the power of flight, and toward the close of the day, drooping quite to earth, had fairly to be dragged along by main strength. Perhaps it was partly owing to the established association of ideas that, despite the utter change in my circumstances, I fell into a state of profound depression on the afternoon of this my first Sunday in the twentieth century.

It was not, however, on the present occasion a depression without specific cause, the mere vague melancholy I have spoken of, but a sentiment suggested and certainly quite justified by my position. The sermon of Mr. Barton, with its constant implication of the vast moral gap between the century to which I belonged and that in which I found myself, had had an effect strongly to accentuate my sense of loneliness in it. Considerately and philosophically as he had spoken, his words could scarcely have failed to leave upon my mind a strong impression of the mingled pity, curiosity, and aversion which I, as a representative of an abhorred epoch, must excite in all around me.

The extraordinary kindness with which I had been treated by Doctor Leete and his family, and especially the goodness of Edith, had hitherto prevented my fully realizing that their real sentiment toward me must necessarily be that of the whole generation to which they belonged. The recognition of this, as regarded Doctor Leete and his amiable wife, however painful, I might have endured, but the conviction that Edith must share their feeling was more than I could bear.

The crushing effect with which this belated perception of a fact so obvious came to me opened my eyes fully to something which perhaps the reader has already suspected—I loved Edith.

Was it strange that I did? The affecting occasion on which our intimacy had begun, when her hands had drawn me out of the whirlpool of madness; the fact that her sympathy was the vital breath which had set me up in this new life and enabled me to support it; my habit of looking to her as the mediator between me and the world around in a sense that even her father was not— these were circumstances that had predetermined a result which her remarkable loveliness of person and disposition would alone have accounted for. It was quite inevitable that she should have come to seem to me, in a sense quite different from the usual experience of lovers, the only woman in this world. Now that I had become suddenly sensible of the fatuity of the hopes I had begun to cherish, I suffered not merely what another lover might, but in addition a desolate loneliness, an utter forlornness, such as no other lover, however unhappy, could have felt.

My hosts evidently saw that I was depressed in spirits, and did their best to divert me. Edith especially, I could see, was distressed for me, but according to the usual perversity of lovers, having once been so mad as to dream of receiving something more from her, there was no longer any virtue for me in a kindness that I knew was only sympathy.

Toward nightfall, after secluding myself in my room most of the afternoon, I went into the garden to walk about. The day was overcast, with an autumnal flavor in the warm, still air. Finding myself near the excavation, I entered the subterranean chamber and sat down there. "This," I muttered to myself, "is the only home I have. Let me stay here, and not go forth any more." Seeking aid from the familiar surroundings, I endeavored to find a sad sort of consolation in reviving the past and summoning up the forms and faces that were about me in my former life. It was in vain. There was no longer any life in them. For nearly one hundred years the stars had been looking down on Edith Bartlett's grave, and the graves of all my generation.

The past was dead, crushed beneath a century's weight, and from the present I was shut out. There was no place for me anywhere. I was neither dead nor properly alive.

"Forgive me for following you."

I looked up. Edith stood in the door of the subterranean room, regarding me smilingly, but with eyes full of sympathetic distress.

"Send me away if I am intruding on you," she said, "but we saw that you were out of spirits, and you know you promised to let me know if that were so. You have not kept your word."

I rose and came to the door, trying to smile, but making, I fancy, rather sorry work of it, for the sight of her loveliness brought home to me the more poignantly the cause of my wretchedness.

"I was feeling a little lonely, that is all," I said. "Has it never occurred to you that my position is so much more utterly alone than any human being's ever was before that a new word is really needed to describe it?"

"Oh, you must not talk that way—you must not let yourself feel that way—you must not!" she exclaimed, with moistened eyes. "Are we not your friends? It is your own fault if you will not let us be. You need not be lonely."

"You are good to me beyond my power of understanding," I said, "but don't you suppose that I know it is pity merely, sweet pity, but pity only? I should be a fool not to know that I cannot seem to you as other men of your own generation do, but as some strange uncanny being, a stranded creature of an unknown sea, whose forlornness touches your compassion despite its grotesqueness. I have been so foolish, you were so kind, as to almost forget that this must needs be so, and to fancy I might in time become naturalized, as we used to say, in this age, so as to feel like one of you and to seem to you like the other men about you. But Mr. Barton's sermon taught me how vain such a fancy is, how great the gulf between us must seem to you."

"Oh that miserable sermon!" she exclaimed, fairly crying now in her sympathy, "I wanted you not to hear it. What does he know of you? He has read in old musty books about your times, that is all. What do you care about him, to let yourself be vexed by anything he said? Isn't it anything to you, that we who know you feel differently? Don't you care more about what we think of you than what he does who never saw you? Oh, Mr. West! You don't know, you can't think, how it makes me feel to see you so forlorn. I can't have it so. What can I say to you? How can I convince you how different our feeling for you is from what you think?"

As before, in that other crisis of my fate when she had come to me, she extended her hands toward me in a gesture of helpfulness, and, as then, I caught and held them in my own; her bosom heaved with strong emotion, and little tremors in the fingers which I clasped emphasized the depth of her feeling. In her face, pity contended in a sort of divine spite against the obstacles which reduced it to impotence. Womanly compassion surely never wore a guise more lovely.

Such beauty and such goodness quite melted me, and it seemed that the only fitting response I could make was to tell her just the truth. Of course I had not a spark of hope, but on the other hand I had no fear that she would be angry. She was too pitiful for that. So I said presently, "It is very ungrateful in me not to be satisfied with such kindness as you have shown me, and are showing me now. But are you so blind as not to see why they are not enough to make me happy? Don't you see that it is because I have been mad enough to love you?"

At my last words she blushed deeply and her eyes fell before mine, but she made no effort to withdraw her hands from my clasp. For some moments she stood so, panting a little. Then blushing deeper than ever, but with a dazzling smile, she looked up.

"Are you sure it is not you who are blind?" she said.

That was all, but it was enough, for it told me that, unaccountable, incredible as it was, this radiant daughter of a golden age had bestowed upon me not alone her pity, but her love. Still, I half believed I must be under some blissful hallucination even as I clasped her in my arms. "If I am beside myself," I cried, "let me remain so."

"It is I whom you must think beside myself," she panted, escaping from my arms when I had barely tasted the sweetness of her lips. "Oh! oh! what must you think of me almost to throw myself in the arms of one I have known but a week? I did not mean that you should find it out so soon, but I was so sorry for you I forgot what I was saying. No, no, you must not touch me again till you know who I am. After all, sir, you shall apologize to me very humbly for thinking, as I know you do, that I have been overquick to fall in love with you. After you know who I am, you will be bound to confess that it was nothing less than my duty to fall in love with you at first sight, and that no girl of proper feeling in my place could do otherwise."

As may be supposed, I would have been quite content to waive explanations, but Edith was resolute that there should be no more kisses until she had been vindicated from all suspicion of precipitancy in the bestowal of her affections, and I was fain to follow the lovely enigma into the house. Having come where her mother was, she blushingly whispered something in her ear and ran away, leaving us together.

It then appeared that, strange as my experience had been, I was now first to know what was perhaps its strangest feature. From Mrs. Leete I learned that Edith was the great-granddaughter of no other than my lost love, Edith Bartlett. After mourning me for fourteen years, she had made a marriage of esteem, and left a son who had been Mrs. Leete's father. Mrs. Leete had never seen her grandmother, but had heard much of her,

and, when her daughter was born, gave her the name of
Edith. This fact might have tended to increase the interest which the girl took, as she grew up, in all that concerned her ancestress, and especially the tragic story of
the supposed death of the lover, whose wife she expected to be, in the conflagration of his house. It was a
tale well-calculated to touch the sympathy of a romantic
girl, and the fact that the blood of the unfortunate hero-
ine was in her own veins naturally heightened Edith's
interest in it. A portrait of Edith Bartlett and some of
her papers, including a packet of my own letters, were
among the family heirlooms. The picture represented a
very beautiful young woman about whom it was easy to
imagine all manner of tender and romantic things. My
letters gave Edith some material for forming a distinct
idea of my personality, and both together sufficed to
make the sad old story very real to her. She used to tell
her parents, half-jestingly, that she would never marry
till she found a lover like Julian West, and there were
none such nowadays.

Now all of this, of course, was merely the daydreaming
of a girl whose mind had never been taken up by a
love affair of her own, and would have had no serious
consequences but for the discovery that morning of the
buried vault in her father's garden and the revelation of
the identity of its inmate. For when the apparently life-
less form had been borne into the house, the face in the
locket found upon the breast was instantly recognized
as that of Edith Bartlett, and by that fact, taken in connection with the other circumstances, they knew that I
was no other than Julian West. Even had there been no
thought, as at first there was not, of my resuscitation,
Mrs. Leete said she believed that this event would have
affected her daughter in a critical and lifelong manner.
The presumption of some subtle ordering of destiny, involving her fate with mine, would under all circumstances have possessed an irresistible fascination for
almost any woman.

Whether when I came back to life a few hours afterward, and from the first seemed to turn to her with a

peculiar dependence and to find a special solace in her company, she had been too quick in giving her love at the first sign of mine, I could now, her mother said, judge for myself. If I thought so, I must remember that this, after all, was the twentieth and not the nineteenth century, and love was, no doubt, now quicker in growth, as well as franker in utterance than then.

From Mrs. Leete I went to Edith. When I found her, it was first of all to take her by both hands and stand a long time in rapt contemplation of her face. As I gazed, the memory of that other Edith, which had been affected as with a benumbing shock by the tremendous experience that had parted us, revived, and my heart was dissolved with tender and pitiful emotions, but also very blissful ones. For she who brought to me so poignantly the sense of my loss was to make that loss good. It was as if from her eyes Edith Bartlett looked into mine, and smiled consolation to me. My fate was not alone the strangest, but the most fortunate that ever befell a man. A double miracle had been wrought for me. I had not been stranded upon the shore of this strange world to find myself alone and companionless. My love, whom I had dreamed lost, had been re-embodied for my consolation. When at last, in an ecstasy of gratitude and tenderness, I folded the lovely girl in my arms, the two Ediths were blended in my thought, nor have they ever since been clearly distinguished. I was not long in finding that on Edith's part there was a corresponding confusion of identities. Never, surely, was there between freshly united lovers a stranger talk than ours that afternoon. She seemed more anxious to have me speak of Edith Bartlett than of herself, of how I had loved her than how I loved herself, rewarding my fond words concerning another woman with tears and tender smiles and pressures of the hand.

"You must not love me too much for myself," she said. "I shall be very jealous for her. I shall not let you forget her. I am going to tell you something which you may think strange. Do you not believe that spirits sometimes come back to the world to fulfill some work that lay near their hearts? What if I were to tell you that I have sometimes thought that her spirit lives in me—that Edith Bartlett, not Edith Leete, is my real name. I cannot know it; of course none of us can know who we really are; but I can feel it. Can you wonder that I have such a feeling, seeing how my life was affected by her and by you, even before you came? So you see you need not trouble to love me at all, if only you are true to her. I shall not be likely to be jealous."

Doctor Leete had gone out that afternoon, and I did not have an interview with him till later. He was not, apparently, wholly unprepared for the intelligence I conveyed, and shook my hand heartily.

"Under any ordinary circumstances, Mr. West, I should say that this step had been taken on rather short acquaintance; but these are decidedly not ordinary circumstances. In fairness, perhaps I ought to tell you," he added, smilingly, "that while I cheerfully consent to the proposed arrangement, you must not feel too much indebted to me, as I judge my consent is a mere formality. From the moment the secret of the locket was out, it had to be, I fancy. Why, bless me, if Edith had not been there to redeem her great-grandmother's pledge, I really apprehend that Mrs. Leete's loyalty to me would have suffered a severe strain."

That evening the garden was bathed in moonlight, and till midnight Edith and I wandered to and fro there, trying to grow accustomed to our happiness.

"What should I have done if you had not cared for me?" she exclaimed. "I was afraid you were not going to. What should I have done then, when I felt I was consecrated to you! As soon as you came back to life, I was as sure as if she had told me that I was to be to you what she could not be, but that could only be if you would let me. Oh, how I wanted to tell you that morning, when you felt so terribly strange among us, who I was, but dared not open my lips about that, or let Father or Mother—"

"That must have been what you would not let your

father tell me!" I exclaimed, referring to the conversation I had overheard as I came out of my trance.

"Of course it was." Edith laughed. "Did you only just guess that? Father, being only a man, thought that it would make you feel among friends to tell you who we were. He did not think of me at all. But Mother knew what I meant, and so I had my way. I could never have looked you in the face if you had known who I was. It would have been forcing myself on you quite too boldly. I am afraid you think I did that today, as it was. I am sure I did not mean to, for I know girls were expected to hide their feelings in your day, and I was dreadfully afraid of shocking you. Ah me, how hard it must have been for them to have always had to conceal their love like a fault. Why did they think it such a shame to love any one till they had been given permission? It is so odd to think of waiting for permission to fall in love. Was it because men in those days were angry when girls loved them? That is not the way women would feel, I am sure, or men either, I think, now. I don't understand it at all. That will be one of the curious things about the women of those days that you will have to explain to me. I don't believe Edith Bartlett was so foolish as the others."

After sundry ineffectual attempts at parting, she finally insisted that we must say good night. I was about to imprint upon her lips the positively last kiss, when she said, with an indescribable archness:

"One thing troubles me. Are you sure that you quite forgive Edith Bartlett for marrying anyone else? The books that have come down to us make out lovers of your time more jealous than fond, and that is what makes me ask. It would be a great relief to me if I could feel sure that you were not in the least jealous of my great-grandfather for marrying your sweetheart. May I tell my great-grandmother's picture when I go to my room that you quite forgive her for proving false to you?"

Will the reader believe it, this coquettish quip, whether the speaker herself had any idea of it or not, actually touched and with the touching cured a preposterous ache of something like jealousy which I had been vaguely conscious of ever since Mrs. Leete had told me of Edith Bartlett's marriage. Even while I had been holding Edith Bartlett's great-granddaughter in my arms, I had not, till this moment, so illogical are some of our feelings, distinctly realized that but for that marriage I could not have done so. The absurdity of this frame of mind could only be equaled by the abruptness with which it dissolved as Edith's roguish query cleared the fog from my perceptions. I laughed as I kissed her.

"You may assure her of my entire forgiveness," I said, "although if it had been any man but your great-grandfather whom she married, it would have been a very different matter."

On reaching my chamber that night I did not open the musical telephone that I might be lulled to sleep with soothing tunes, as had become my habit. For once my thoughts made better music than even twentieth-century orchestras discourse, and it held me enchanted till well toward morning, when I fell asleep.

· XXVIII ·

"IT'S A LITTLE AFTER THE TIME YOU TOLD ME TO WAKE you, sir. You did not come out of it as quick as common, sir." The voice was the voice of my man Sawyer. I sat bolt upright in bed and stared around. I was in my underground chamber. The mellow light of the lamp which always burned in the room when I occupied it illuminated the familiar walls and furnishings. By my bedside, with the glass of sherry in his hand which Doctor Pillsbury prescribed on first rousing from a mesmeric sleep, by way of awakening the torpid physical functions, stood Sawyer.

"Better take this right off, sir," he said, as I stared blankly at him. "You look kind of flushed like, sir, and you need it."

I tossed off the liquor and began to realize what had happened to me. It was, of course, very plain. All that about the twentieth century had been a dream. I had but dreamed of that enlightened and carefree race of men and their ingeniously simple institutions, of the glorious new Boston with its domes and pinnacles, its gardens and fountains, and its universal reign of comfort. The amiable family which I had learned to know so well, my genial host and mentor, Doctor Leete, his wife, and their daughter, the second and more beauteous Edith, my betrothed—these, too, had been but figments of a vision.

For a considerable time I remained in the attitude in which this conviction had come over me, sitting up in bed gazing at vacancy, absorbed in recalling the scenes and incidents of my fantastic experience. Sawyer, alarmed at my looks, was meanwhile anxiously inquiring what was the matter with me. Roused at length by his importunities to a recognition of my surroundings, I pulled myself together with an effort and assured the faithful fellow that I was all right. "I have had an extraordinary dream, that's all, Sawyer," I said, "a most-ex-traor-dinary-dream."

I dressed in a mechanical way, feeling lightheaded and oddly uncertain of myself, and sat down to the coffee and rolls which Sawyer was in the habit of providing for my refreshment before I left the house. The morning newspaper lay by the plate. I took it up, and my eye fell on the date, May 31, 1887. I had known, of course, from the moment I opened my eyes that my long and detailed experience in another century had been a dream, and yet it was startling to have it so conclusively demonstrated that the world was but a few hours older than when I had lain down to sleep.

Glancing at the table of contents at the head of the paper, which reviewed the news of the morning, I read the following summary:

FOREIGN AFFAIRS. The impending war between France and Germany. The French Chambers asked for new military credits to meet Germany's increase of her army. Probability that all Europe will be involved in case of war.—Great suffering among the unemployed in London. They demand work. Monster demonstration to be made. The authorities uneasy.—Great strikes in Belgium. The government preparing to repress outbreaks. Shocking facts in regard to the employment of girls in Belgium coal mines.—Wholesale evictions in Ireland.

HOME AFFAIRS. The epidemic of fraud unchecked. Embezzlement of a half a million in New York.—Misappropriation of a trust fund by executors. Orphans left penniless.—Clever system of thefts by a bank teller; $50,000 gone.—The coal barons decide to advance the price of coal and reduce production.—Speculators engineering a great wheat corner at Chicago.—A clique forcing up the price of coffee.—Enormous land-grabs of Western syndicates.—Revelations of shocking corruption among Chicago officials. Systematic bribery.—The trials of the Boodle alderman to go on at New York—Large failures of business houses. Fears of a business crisis.— A large grist of burglaries and larcenies.—A woman murdered in cold blood for her money at New Haven.— A householder shot by a burglar in this city last night.— A man shoots himself in Worcester because he could not get work. A large family left destitute.—An aged couple in New Jersey commit suicide rather than go to the poorhouse.—Pitiable destitution among the women wage workers in the great cities.—Startling growth of illiteracy in Massachusetts.—More insane asylums wanted.—Decoration Day addresses. Professor Brown's oration on the moral grandeur of nineteenth-century civilization.

It was indeed the nineteenth century to which I had awakened; there could be no kind of doubt about that. Its complete microcosm this summary of the day's news had presented, even to that last unmistakable touch of fatuous self-complacency. Coming after such a damning indictment of the age as that one day's chronicle of worldwide bloodshed, greed, and tyranny, was a bit of cynicism worthy of Mephistopheles, and yet of all whose eyes it had met this morning I was, perhaps, the only one who perceived the cynicism and but yesterday I should have perceived it no more than the others. That strange dream it was which had made all the difference. For I know not how long, I forgot my surroundings after this, and was again in fancy moving in that vivid dream world, in that glorious city, with its homes of simple comfort and its gorgeous public places. Around me were again faces unmarred by arrogance or servility, by envy or greed, by anxious care or feverish ambition, and stately forms of men and women who had never known fear of a fellow man or depended on his favor, but always, in the words of that sermon which still rang in my ears, had "stood up straight before God."

With a profound sigh and a sense of irreparable loss, not the less poignant that it was a loss of what had never really been, I roused at last from my reverie, and soon after left the house.

A dozen times between my door and Washington Street I had to stop and pull myself together, such power had been in that vision of the Boston of the future to make the real Boston strange. The squalor and malodorousness of the town struck me, from the moment I stood upon the street, as facts I had never before observed. But yesterday, moreover, it had seemed quite a matter of course that some of my fellow-citizens should wear silks, and others rags, that some should look well-fed, and others hungry. Now on the contrary the glaring disparities in the dress and condition of the men and women who brushed each other on the sidewalks shocked me at every step, and yet more the entire indifference which the prosperous showed to the plight of the unfortunate. Were these human beings, who could behold the wretchedness of their fellows without so much as a change of countenance? And yet, all the while, I knew well that it was I who had changed, and not my contemporaries. I had dreamed of a city whose people fared all alike as children of one family and were one another's keepers in all things.

Another feature of the real Boston, which assumed the extraordinary effect of strangeness that marks familiar things seen in a new light, was the prevalence of advertising. There had been no personal advertising in the Boston of the twentieth century, because there was no need of any, but here the walls of the buildings, the windows, the broadsides of the newspapers in every hand, the very pavements, everything in fact, save the sky, were covered with the appeals of individuals who sought, under innumerable pretexts, to attract the contributions of others to their support. However the wording might vary, the tenor of all these appeals was the same:

"Help John Jones. Never mind the rest. They are frauds. I, John Jones, am the right one. Buy of me. Employ me. Visit me. Hear me, John Jones. Look at me. Make no mistake. John Jones is the man and nobody else. Let the rest starve, but for God's sake remember John Jones!"

Whether the pathos or the moral repulsiveness of the spectacle most impressed me, so suddenly become a stranger in my own city, I know not. Wretched men, I was moved to cry, who, because they will not learn to be helpers of one another, are doomed to be beggers of one another from the least to the greatest! This horrible babel of shameless self-assertion and mutual depreciation, this stunning clamor of conflicting boasts, appeals, and adjurations, this stupendous system of brazen beggary, what was it all but the necessity of a society in which the opportunity to serve the world according to his gifts, instead of being secured to every man as the first object of social organization, had to be fought for!

I reached Washington Street at the busiest point, and there I stood and laughed aloud, to the scandal of the passers-by. For my life I could not have helped it, with such a mad humor was I moved at sight of the interminable rows of stores on either side, up and down the street so far as I could see—scores of them, to make the spectacle more utterly preposterous, within a stone's throw devoted to selling the same sort of goods. Stores! stores! stores! miles of stores! ten thousand stores to distribute the goods needed by this one city, which in my dream had been supplied with all things from a single warehouse, as they were ordered through one great store in every quarter, where the buyer, without waste of time or labor, found under one roof the world's assortment in whatever line he desired. There the labor of distribution had been so slight as to add but a scarcely perceptible fraction to the cost of commodities to the user. The cost of production was virtually all he paid. But here the mere distribution of goods, their handling alone, added a fourth, a third, a half and more, to the cost. All these ten thousand plants must be paid for, their rent, their staffs of superintendence, their platoons of salesmen, their ten thousand sets of accountants, jobbers, and business dependents, with all they spent in advertising themselves and fighting one another, and the consumers must do the paying. What a famous process for beggaring a nation!

Were these serious men I saw about me, or children, who did their business on such a plan? Could they be reasoning beings, who did not see the folly which, when the product is made and ready for use, wastes so much of it in getting it to the user? If people eat with a spoon that leaks half its contents between bowl and lip, are they not likely to go hungry?

I had passed through Washington Street thousands of times before and viewed the ways of those who sold merchandise, but my curiosity concerning them was as if I had never gone by their way before. I took wondering note of the show windows of the stores, filled with goods arranged with a wealth of pains and artistic device to attract the eye. I saw the throngs of ladies looking in, and the proprietors eagerly watching the effect of the bait. I went within and noted the hawk-eyed floor-walker watching for business, overlooking the clerks, keeping them up to their task of inducing the customers to buy, buy, buy, for money if they had it, for credit if they had it not, to buy what they wanted not, more than they wanted, what they could not afford. At times I momentarily lost the clue and was confused by the sight. Why this effort to induce people to buy? Surely that had nothing to do with the legitimate business of distributing products to those who needed them. Surely it was the sheerest waste to force upon people what they did not want, but what might be useful to another. The nation was so much the poorer for every such achievement. What were those clerks thinking of? Then I would remember that they were not acting as distributors like those in the store I had visited in the dream Boston. They were not serving the public interest, but their immediate personal interest, and it was nothing to them what the ultimate effect of their course on the general prosperity might be, if but they increased their own hoard, for these goods were their own, and the more they sold the more they got for them, the greater their gain. The more wasteful the people were, the more articles they did not want which they could be induced to buy, the better for these sellers. To encourage prodigality was the express aim of the ten thousand stores of Boston.

Nor were these storekeepers and clerks a whit worse men than any others in Boston. They must earn a living and support their families, and how were they to find a trade to do it by which did not necessitate placing their individual interests before those of others and that of all? They could not be asked to starve while they waited for an order of things such as I had seen in my dream, in which the interests of each and that of all were identical. But, God in heaven! what wonder, under such a system as this about me—what wonder that the city was so shabby, and the people so meanly dressed, and so many of them ragged and hungry!

Some time after this it was that I drifted over into South Boston and found myself among the manufacturing establishments. I had been in this quarter of the city a hundred times before, just as I had been on Washington Street, but here, as well as there, I now first perceived the true significance of what I witnessed. Formerly I had taken pride in the fact that, by actual count, Boston had some four thousand independent manufacturing establishments; but in this very multiplicity and independence I recognized now the secret of the insignificant total product of their industry.

If Washington Street had been like a lane in Bedlam, this was a spectacle as much more melancholy as production is a more vital function than distribution. For not only were these four thousand establishments not working in concert, and for that reason alone operating at prodigious disadvantage, but, as if this did not involve a sufficiently disastrous loss of power, they were using their utmost skill to frustrate one another's effort, praying by night and working by day for the destruction of one another's enterprises.

The roar and rattle of wheels and hammers resounding from every side was not the hum of a peaceful industry, but the clangor of swords wielded by foemen. These mills and shops were so many forts, each under its own flag, its guns trained on the mills and shops about it, and its sappers busy below, undermining them.

Within each one of these forts the strictest organization of industry was insisted on; the separate gangs worked under a single central authority. No interference and no duplicating of work were permitted. Each had his allotted task, and none were idle. By what hiatus in the logical faculty, by what lost link of reasoning, account, then, for the failure to recognize the necessity of applying the same principle to the organization of the national industries as a whole, to see that if lack of organization could impair the efficiency of a shop, it must have effects as much more disastrous in disabling the industries of the nation at large as the latter are vaster in volume and more complex in the relationship of their parts.

People would be prompt enough to ridicule an army in which there were neither companies, battalions, regiments, brigades, divisions, nor army corps—no unit of organization, in fact, larger than the corporal's squad, with no officer higher than a corporal, and all the corporals equal in authority. And yet just such an army were the manufacturing industries of nineteenth-century Boston, an army of four thousand independent squads led by four thousand independent corporals, each with a separate plan of campaign.

Knots of idle men were to be seen here and there on every side, some idle because they could find no work at any price, others because they could not get what they thought a fair price.

I accosted some of the latter, and they told me their grievances. It was very little comfort I could give them. "I am sorry for you," I said. "You get little enough, certainly, and yet the wonder to me is, not that industries conducted as these are do not pay you living wages, but that they are able to pay you any wages at all."

Making my way back again after this to the peninsular city, toward three o'clock I stood on State Street, staring, as if I had never seen them before, at the banks and brokers' offices, and other financial institutions, of which there had been in the State Street of my vision no vestige. Businessmen, confidential clerks, and errand boys were thronging in and out of the banks, for it wanted but a few minutes of the closing hour. Opposite me was the bank where I did business, and presently I crossed the street, and, going in with the crowd, stood in a recess of the wall looking on at the army of clerks handling money, and the cues of depositors at the tellers' windows. An old gentleman whom I knew, a director of the bank, passing me and observing my contemplative attitude, stopped a moment.

"Interesting sight, isn't it, Mr. West," he said. "Wonderful piece of mechanism; I find it so myself. I like sometimes to stand and look on at it just as you are doing. It's a poem, sir, a poem, that's what I call it. Did you ever think, Mr. West, that the bank is the heart of the business system? From it and to it, in endless flux and reflux, the life blood goes. It is flowing in now. It will flow out again in the morning." And pleased with his little conceit, the old man passed on smiling.

Yesterday I should have considered the simile apt enough, but since then I had visited a world incomparably more affluent than this, in which money was unknown and without conceivable use. I had learned that it had a use in the world around me only because the work of producing the nation's livelihood, instead of being regarded as the most strictly public and common of all concerns, and as such conducted by the nation, was abandoned to the haphazard efforts of individuals. This original mistake necessitated endless exchanges to bring about any sort of general distribution of products. These exchanges money effected—how equitably, might be seen in a walk from the tenement-house district to the Back Bay—at the cost of an army of men taken from productive labor to manage it, with constant ruinous breakdowns of its machinery, and a generally debauching influence on mankind which had justified its description, from ancient time, as the "root of all evil."

Alas for the poor old bank director with his poem! He had mistaken the throbbing of an abscess for the beating of the heart. What he called "a wonderful piece of mechanism" was an imperfect device to remedy an unnecessary defect, the clumsy crutch of a self-made cripple.

After the banks had closed I wandered aimlessly about the business quarter for an hour or two, and later sat awhile on one of the benches of the Common, finding an interest merely in watching the throngs that passed, such as one has in studying the populace of a foreign city, so strange since yesterday had my fellow citizens and their ways become to me. For thirty years I had lived among them, and yet I seemed to have never noted before how drawn and anxious were their faces, of the rich as of the poor, the refined, acute faces of the educated as well as the dull masks of the ignorant. And well it might be so, for I saw now, as never before I had seen so plainly, that each as he walked constantly turned to catch the whispers of a specter at his ear, the specter of Uncertainty. "Do your work never so well," the specter was whispering—"rise early and toil till late, rob cunningly or serve faithfully, you shall never know security. Rich you may be now and still come to poverty at last. Leave never so much wealth to your children, you cannot buy the assurance that your son may not be the servant of your servant, or that your daughter will not have to sell herself for bread."

A man passing by thrust an advertising card in my hand, which set forth the merits of some new scheme of life insurance. The incident reminded me of the only device, pathetic in its admission of the universal need it so poorly supplied, which offered these tired and hunted men and women even a partial protection from uncertainty. By this means, those already well-to-do, I remembered, might purchase a precarious confidence that after their death their loved ones would not, for a while at least, be trampled under the feet of men. But this was all, and this was only for those who could pay well for it. What idea was possible to these wretched dwellers in the land of Ishmael, where every man's hand was against each and the hand of each against every other, of true life insurance as I had seen it among the people of that dreamland, each of whom, by virtue merely of his membership in the national family, was guaranteed against need of any sort, by a policy underwritten by one hundred million fellow countrymen.

Some time after this it was that I recall a glimpse of myself standing on the steps of a building on Tremont Street, looking at a military parade. A regiment was passing. It was the first sight in that dreary day which had inspired me with any other emotions than wondering pity and amazement. Here at last were order and reason, an exhibition of what intelligent cooperation can accomplish. The people who stood looking on with kindling faces—could it be that the sight had for them no more than but a spectacular interest? Could they fail to see that it was their perfect concert of action, their organization under one control, which made these men the tremendous engine they were, able to vanquish a mob ten times as numerous? Seeing this so plainly, could they fail to compare the scientific manner in which the nation went to war with the unscientific manner in which it went to work? Would they not query since what time the killing of men had been a task so much more important than feeding and clothing them, that a trained army should be deemed alone adequate to the former, while the latter was left to a mob?

It was now toward nightfall, and the streets were thronged with the workers from the stores, the shops, and mills. Carried along with the stronger part of the current, I found myself, as it began to grow dark, in the midst of a scene of squalor and human degradation such as only the South Cove tenement district could present. I had seen the mad wasting of human labor; here I saw in direst shape the want that waste had bred.

From the black doorways and windows of the rookeries on every side came gusts of fetid air. The streets and alleys reeked with the effluvia of a slave ship's between-decks. As I passed I had glimpses within of pale babies gasping out their lives amid sultry stenches, of hopeless-faced women deformed by hardship, retaining of womanhood no trait save weakness, while from the windows leered girls with brows of brass. Like the starving bands of mongrel curs that infest the streets of Moslem towns, swarms of half-clad brutalized children filled the air with shrieks and curses as they fought and tumbled among the garbage that littered the courtyards.

There was nothing in all this that was new to me. Often had I passed through this part of the city and witnessed its sights with feelings of disgust mingled with a certain philosophical wonder at the extremities mortals will endure and still cling to life. But not alone as regarded the economical follies of this age, but equally as touched its moral abominations, scales had fallen from my eyes since that vision of another century. No more did I look upon the woeful dwellers in this Inferno with a callous curiosity as creatures scarcely human. I saw in them my brothers and sisters, my parents, my children, flesh of my flesh, blood of my blood. The festering mass of human wretchedness about me offended not now my senses merely, but pierced my heart like a knife, so that I could not repress my sighs and groans. I not only saw but felt in my body all that I saw.

Presently, too, as I observed the wretched beings about me more closely, I perceived that they were all quite dead. Their bodies were so many living sepulchers.

On each brutal brow was plainly written the *hic jacet* of a soul dead within.

As I looked, horrorstruck, from one death's head to another, I was affected by a singular hallucination. Like a wavering translucent spirit face superimposed upon each of these brutish masks I saw the ideal, the possible face that would have been the actual if mind and soul had lived. It was not till I was aware of these ghostly faces, and of the reproach that could not be gainsaid which was in their eyes, that the full piteousness of the ruin that had been wrought was revealed to me. I was moved with contrition as with a strong agony, for I had been one of those who had endured that these things should be. I had been one of those who, well knowing that they were, had not desired to hear or be compelled to think much of them, but had gone on as if they were not, seeking my own pleasure and profit. Therefore now I found upon my garments the blood of this great multitude of strangled souls of my brothers. The voice of their blood cried out against me from the ground. Every stone of the reeking pavements, every brick of the pestilential rookeries, found a tongue and called after me as I fled: "What hast thou done with thy brother Abel?"

I have no clear recollection of anything after this till I found myself standing on the carved stone steps of the magnificent home of my betrothed in Commonwealth Avenue. Amid the tumult of my thoughts that day, I had scarcely once thought of her, but now obeying some unconscious impulse my feet had found the familiar way to her door. I was told that the family were at dinner, but word was sent out that I should join them at table. Besides the family, I found several guests present, all known to me. The table glittered with plate and costly china. The ladies were sumptuously dressed and wore the jewels of queens. The scene was one of costly elegance and lavish luxury. The company was in excellent spirits, and there was plentiful laughter and a running fire of jests.

To me it was as if, in wandering through the place of doom, my blood turned to tears by its sights, and my spirit attuned to sorrow, pity, and despair, I had happened in some glade upon a merry party of roisterers. I sat in silence until Edith began to rally me upon my somber looks. What ailed me? The others presently joined in the playful assault, and I became a target for quips and jests. Where had I been, and what had I seen to make such a dull fellow of me?

"I have been in Golgotha," at last I answered. "I have seen Humanity hanging on a cross! Do none of you know what sights the sun and stars look down on in this city, that you can think and talk of anything else? Do you not know that close to your doors a great multitude of men and women, flesh of your flesh, live lives that are one agony from birth to death? Listen! Their dwellings are so near that if you hush your laughter you will hear their grievous voices, the piteous crying of the little ones that suckle poverty, the hoarse curses of men sodden in misery, turned halfway back to brutes, the chaffering of an army of women selling themselves for bread. With what have you stopped your ears that you do not hear these doleful sounds? For me, I can hear nothing else."

Silence followed my words. A passion of pity had shaken me as I spoke, but when I looked around upon the company, I saw that, far from being stirred as I was, their faces expressed a cold and hard astonishment, mingled in Edith's with extreme mortification, in her father's with anger. The ladies were exchanging scandalized looks, while one of the gentlemen had put up his eyeglass and was studying me with an air of scientific curiosity. When I saw that things which were to me so intolerable moved them not at all, that words that melted my heart to speak had only offended them with the speaker, I was at first stunned and then overcome with a desperate sickness and faintness at the heart. What hope was there for the wretched, for the world, if thoughtful men and tender women were not moved by things like these! Then I bethought myself that it must be because I had not spoken aright. No doubt I had put the case badly. They were angry because they thought I was berating them, when God knew I was merely thinking of the horror of the fact without any attempt to assign the responsibility for it.

I restrained my passion, and tried to speak calmly and logically that I might correct this impression. I told them that I had not meant to accuse them, as if they, or the rich in general, were responsible for the misery of the world. True indeed it was that the superfluity which they wasted would, otherwise bestowed, relieve much bitter suffering. These costly viands, these rich wines, these gorgeous fabrics and glistening jewels represented the ransom of many lives. They were verily not without the guiltiness of those who waste in a land stricken with famine. Nevertheless, all the waste of all the rich, were it saved, would go but a little way to cure the poverty of the world. There was so little to divide that even if the rich went share-and-share with the poor, there would be but a common fare of crusts, albeit made very sweet then by brotherly love.

The folly of men, not their hard-heartedness, was the great cause of the world's poverty. It was not the crime of man, nor of any class of men, that made the race so miserable, but a hideous, ghastly mistake, a colossal world-darkening blunder. And then I showed them how four-fifths of the labor of men was utterly wasted by the mutual warfare, the lack of organization and concert among the workers. Seeking to make the matter very plain, I instanced the case of arid lands where the soil yielded the means of life only by careful use of the watercourses for irrigation. I showed how in such countries it was counted the most important function of the government to see that the water was not wasted by the selfishness or ignorance of individuals, since otherwise there would be famine. To this end its use was strictly regulated and systematized, and individuals of their mere caprice were not permitted to dam it or divert it, or in any way to tamper with it.

The labor of men, I explained, was the fertilizing stream which alone rendered earth habitable. It was but a scanty stream at best, and its use required to be regulated by a system which expended every drop to the best advantage, if the world were to be supported in abundance. But how far from any system was the actual practice! Every man wasted the precious fluid as he wished, animated only by the equal motives of saving his own crop and spoiling his neighbor's, that his might sell the better. What with greed and what with spite some fields were flooded while others were parched, and half the water ran wholly to waste. In such a land, though a few by strength or cunning might win the means of luxury, the lot of the great mass must be poverty, and of the weak and ignorant bitter want and perennial famine.

Let but the famine-stricken nation assume the function it had neglected, and regulate for the common good the course of the life-giving stream, and the earth would bloom like one garden, and none of its children lack any good thing. I described the physical felicity, mental enlightenment, and moral elevation which would then attend the lives of all men. With fervency I spoke of that new world, blessed with plenty, purified by justice and sweetened by brotherly kindness, the world of which I had indeed but dreamed, but which might so easily be made real. But when I had expected now surely the faces around me to light up with emotions akin to mine, they grew even more dark, angry, and scornful. Instead of enthusiasm, the ladies showed only aversion and dread, while the men interrupted me with shouts of reprobation and contempt. "Madman!" "Pestilent fellow!" "Fanatic!" "Enemy of society!" were some of their cries, and the one who had before taken his eyeglass to me exclaimed, "He says we are to have no more poor. Ha! ha!"

"Put the fellow out!" exclaimed the father of my betrothed, and at the signal the men sprang from their chairs and advanced upon me.

It seemed to me that my heart would burst with the anguish of finding that what was to me so plain and so all-important was to them meaningless, and that I was powerless to make it other. So hot had been my heart that I had thought to melt an iceberg with its glow, only to find at last the overmastering chill seizing my own vitals. It was not enmity that I felt toward them as they thronged me, but pity only, for them and for the world.

Although despairing, I could not give over. Still I strove with them. Tears poured from my eyes. In my vehemence I became inarticulate. I panted, I sobbed, I groaned, and immediately afterward found myself sitting upright in bed in my room in Doctor Leete's house, and the morning sun shining through the open window into my eyes. I was gasping. The tears were streaming down my face, and I quivered in every nerve.

As with an escaped convict who dreams that he had been recaptured and brought back to his dark and reeking dungeon, and opens his eyes to see the heaven's vault spread above him, so it was with me, as I realized that my return to the nineteenth century had been the dream, and my presence in the twentieth was the reality.

The cruel sights which I had witnessed in my vision, and could so well confirm from the experience of my former life, though they had, alas! once been, and must in the retrospect to the end of time move the compassionate to tears, were, God be thanked, forever gone by. Long ago oppressor and oppressed, prophet and scorner, had been dust. For generations, rich and poor had been forgotten words.

But in that moment, while yet I mused with unspeakable thankfulness upon the greatness of the world's salvation and my privilege in beholding it, there suddenly pierced me like a knife a pang of shame, remorse, and wondering self-reproach, that bowed my head upon my breast and made me wish the grave had hid me with my fellows from the sun. For I had been a man of that former time. What had I done to help on the deliverance whereat I now presumed to rejoice? I who had lived in those cruel, insensate days, what had I done to bring them to an end? I had been every whit as indifferent to the wretchedness of my brothers, as cynically incredulous of better things, as besotted a worshipper of Chaos and Old Night, as any of my fellows. So far as my personal influence went, it had been exerted rather to hinder than to help forward the enfranchisement of the race which was even then preparing. What right had I to hail a salvation which reproached me, to rejoice in a day whose dawning I had mocked?

"Better for you, better for you," a voice within me rang, "had this evil dream been the reality, and this fair reality the dream; better your part pleading for crucified humanity with a scoffing generation, than here, drinking of wells you digged not, and eating of trees whose husbandmen you stoned." And my spirit answered, "Better, truly."

When at length I raised my bowed head and looked forth from the window, Edith, fresh as the morning, had come into the garden and was gathering flowers. I hastened to descend to her. Kneeling before her, with my face in the dust, I confessed with tears how little was my worth to breathe the air of this golden century, and how infinitely less to wear upon my breast its consummate flower. Fortunate is he who, with a case so desperate as mine, finds a judge so merciful.

POSTSCRIPT

THE RATE OF THE WORLD'S PROGRESS

To the Editor of the Boston Transcript: The *Transcript* of March 30, 1888, contained a review of *Looking Backward,* in response to which I beg to be allowed a word. The description to which the book is devoted, of the radically new social and industrial institutions and arrangements supposed to be enjoyed by the people of the United States in the twentieth century, is not objected to as depicting a degree of human felicity and moral development necessarily unattainable by the race, provided time enough had been allowed for its evolution from the present chaotic state of society. In failing to allow this, the reviewer thinks that the author has made an absurd mistake, which seriously detracts from the value of the book as a work of realistic imagination. Instead of placing the realization of the ideal social state a scant fifty years ahead, it is suggested that he should have made his figure seventy-five centuries. There is certainly a large discrepancy between seventy-five centuries and fifty years, and if the reviewer is correct in his estimate of the probable rate of human progress, the outlook of the world is decidedly discouraging. But is he right? I think not.

Looking Backward, although in form a fanciful romance, is intended, in all seriousness, as a forecast, in accordance with the principles of evolution, of the next stage in the industrial and social development of humanity, especially in this country; and no part of it is believed by the author to be better supported by the indications of probability than the implied prediction that the dawn of the new era is already near at hand, and that the full day will swiftly follow. Does this seem at first thought incredible, in view of the vastness of the changes presupposed? What is the teaching of history, but that great national transformations, while ages in unnoticed preparation, when once inaugurated, are accomplished with a rapidity and resistless momentum proportioned to their magnitude, not limited by it?

In 1759, when Quebec fell, the might of England in America seemed irresistible, and the vassalage of the colonies assured. Nevertheless, thirty years later, the first President of the American Republic was inaugurated. In 1849, after Novara, Italian prospects appeared as hopeless as at any time since the Middle Ages; yet only fifteen years after, Victor Emmanuel was crowned King of United Italy. In 1864, the fulfillment of the thousand-year dream of German unity was apparently as far off as ever. Seven years later it had been realized, and William had assumed at Versailles the Crown of Barbarossa. In 1832, the original Antislavery Society was formed in Boston by a few so-called visionaries. Thirty-eight years later, in 1870, the society disbanded, its program fully carried out.

These precedents do not, of course, prove that any such industrial and social transformation as is outlined in *Looking Backward* is impending; but they do show that, when the moral and economical conditions for it are ripe, it may be expected to go forward with great rapidity. On no other stage are the scenes shifted with a swiftness so like magic as on the great stage of history when once the hour strikes. The question is not, then, how extensive the scene-shifting must be to set the stage for the new fraternal civilization, but whether there are any special indications that a social transformation is at hand. The causes that have been bringing it ever nearer have been at work from immemorial time. To the stream of tendency setting toward an ultimate realization of a form of society, while vastly more efficient for material prosperity, should also satisfy and not outrage the moral instincts, every sigh of poverty, every tear of pity, every humane impulse, every generous enthusiasm, every true religious feeling, every act by which men have given effect to their mutual sympathy by drawing more closely together for any purpose, have contributed from the beginnings of civilization. That this long stream of influence, ever widening and deepening, is at last about to sweep away the barriers it has so long sapped, is at least one obvious interpretation of the present universal ferment of men's minds as to the imperfections of present social arrangements. Not only are the toilers of the world engaged in something like a worldwide insurrection, but true and humane men and women, of every degree, are in a mood of exasperation, verging on absolute revolt, against social conditions that reduce life to a brutal struggle for existence, mock every dictate of ethics and religion, and render well-nigh futile the efforts of philanthropy.

As an iceberg, floating southward from the frozen North, is gradually undermined by warmer seas, and, become at last unstable, churns the sea to yeast for miles around by the mighty rockings that portend its overturn, so the barbaric industrial and social system, which has come down to us from savage antiquity, undermined by the modern human spirit, riddled by the criticism of economic science, is shaking the world with convulsions that presage its collapse.

All thoughtful men agree that the present aspect of society is portentous of great changes. The only question is, whether they will be for the better or the worse. Those who believe in man's essential nobleness lean to the former view, those who believe in his essential baseness to the latter. For my part, I hold to the former opinion. *Looking Backward* was written in the belief that the Golden Age lies before us and not behind us, and is not far away. Our children will surely see it, and we, too, who are already men and women, if we deserve it by our faith and by our works.

—EDWARD BELLAMY.

AFTERWORD

I used to pound oakum and bust concrete for a plumber who had been a German soldier in World War II, Ed Heinz, nice guy. When I was sad, he would cheer me up by saying, in his heavily accented English, "Tell me a story—it doesn't have to be true."

One day over coffee and doughnuts with all the other workmen, electricians and drywallers and carpenters and glaziers, sunning themselves on the open floor of a half-finished building, Ed said casually, as if to the air, "Say what you will about old Hitler—I won't argue politics with you. But one thing I can tell you: you weren't afraid to walk the streets at night."

Another time, as we sweated in a crawl space soldering old pipes amongst the mud and maggots, Ed reminisced, "My wife used to be an expert at forming lead pipes. She won a national competition and almost got to shake Adolph Hitler's hand."

Utopias are never utopias for everyone. One might envision streets exactly that safe in Bellamy's utopia, and national trade competitions just like the one that Mrs. Heinz aced. How does such a Wonder World turn dark?

Clearly, old Hitler honored his country's laborers. The celebration of labor as a noble enterprise characterizes all ends of the political spectra. Bellamy's mouthpiece, Mr. Leete, is at pains to demonstrate that there is no low nor high among workers. If a bricklayer does her best at that job, she is as esteemed as a surgeon or an architect. Well, Ayn Rand says the same thing. In *Atlas Shrugged*, the supercapitalist hero, John Galt, on seeing the concentration and efficiency of a counterman at a roadside diner, takes the fellow under his wing and installs him as a manager in his new society.

Their political views seem opposite, but both Bellamy and Rand excoriate the Reds. For Rand, Communists are all rotters, full of arrogance, self-love, and larceny, but Bellamy just sees them, like the rest of us atavistic presocialist humans, as clumsy and deluded. (He opines that they've been hoodwinked and bankrolled by fat cats to prejudice the people against reform.) So Rand requires an Atlas shrug to reorder society, a vicious upheaval that will correctly transmogrify self-interest into the guiding principle of all social relations, but Bellamy sees us all just coming to our senses, breathing a collective sigh, and setting things right for everybody.

"Regulation" is all, for Bellamy, with the government as the regulator.

I want to say, how could Bellamy have been so blind and stupid as to consider humans, against all the evidence of history and the senses, to be either rational or perfectible? What myopia is this that so afflicts our utopians? Look at Pol Pot or Jim Jones or Sendero Luminoso's Chairman Gonzalo. Or Mussolini or Lenin. They tried to impose principles on us. *Principles*, for pity's sake! And what did we get? Efficient railways—and killing fields.

Hell, take Saint Paul, for that matter. One blinding insight on the road to Damascus, a flurry of organizing and systematizing, ramified and refined by generations of scholastics—and the result, as Gibbons pointed out in the most unpopular passage of *Decline and Fall*, was many times more bloody murders of Christians by Christians than the Romans ever committed. With every orthodoxy comes a heterodoxy—and so suppression and mayhem.

"God will know his own," the papal prelate told his general during the thirteenth-century campaign against the heretics of southern France, who were mixed up among the faithful and hard to distinguish from them. "Kill them all."

So fell the Albigensians, the Jews, and Jerusalem's

Saracens, blood up to the horse bridles of the holy Crusaders, and then, a little later, the Indians, all for a principle. And if you think such bloody consequences are disproportionate to the innocuousness of Bellamy's straightforward precepts, consider the innocence of *their* starting point: "Love your neighbor."

Moral purity and rationality always morph into fascism because one size, with us humans, never fits all. It's of a piece with our human variability—congenital cantankerousness, an essential characteristic of the species, and, I contend, a healthful, even salvific, one at that. Variability, our Darwinists point out, is a survival trait in a radically variable world. Hence the superiority of sex over mitosis.

Take art. Art is unprincipled. Art is *de trop*. Art is a patina that remains when the dust and the divan have vanished. It is fundamentally ungovernable, in my view. Bellamy himself was an artist, surely. The structure of *Looking Backward* is wonderfully artful. He achieves an alienation from his own society by placing himself and his readers in the future, lending an air of objectivity to the book's ruminations about Bellamy's actual time. That trick alone, and it is grandly played, is worth the price of admission.

At the book's exact center Bellamy places a neat self-reflection: focusing on Dickens and Tennyson (while implying—Bellamy), he discusses the social power of literature. Then, to excellent dramatic effect, he places at the penultimate moment a total reversal, a dream within a dream, fooling us all for a dozen pages—well, fooling *me,* anyway—fattening us for the kill, to bring home more forcefully the beauty of the new age as against the horror of the old.

Bellamy's art won him a big audience. But, as an artist, he is certainly the exception. Better artists than Bellamy have suffered obscurity and extinction. In Bellamy's utopia, he specifically points out, the measure of artistic value is popularity. When regulation is all, as it is in Bellamy's thinking, that is a simple corollary. Produce the most of what there's the most demand for, whether it's thermal underwear or oil paintings. He contends that a general increase in the level of education would make a more discerning public, but I am unconvinced. The general level of education has never yet stopped people in posttribal societies from preferring the banal and the slick and the maudlin. In Bellamy's utopia there would be lots of black velvet Elvises, and their creators would get subsidies.

Again, my point is that there is an irreducible something to us human beings that absolutely resists regulation. We are quirky. We are off-centered. We are downright contrary. And those of us who are most so are our artists. Bellamy's utopia is, at best, soporific. It could produce no real art.

I tried a utopian scam at seven. A lonely little boy, I envisioned my front porch as a literary Mecca with pals lounging beside me on the glider and perched at the banister reading *Action* and *Archie* and *World's Finest* comics. Sign on, I told everybody, trundling up and down the block on my red Schwinn with two throaty balloons roaring at the rear spokes, and you get a free Superman cape that will enable you to fly. Along with everyone else, incredibly, I believed.

Had I been as smart as Edward Bellamy, I would have put the date of delivery beyond the span of my little life. God bless the perfect future. The First Coming is never enough. I had to suffer the disbandment of my club when the capes failed to show at the appointed hour. Bellamy's social activist clubs, on the other hand, proliferated. No catastrophic balloon payments and no sunset date, when the sunrise is forever before you. Back in 1887, the year 2000 was more than a century away.

I passed through another utopian phase with everybody else in those famous nineteen sixties. I hitchhiked across the continent looking for Shangri-La. (Never mind that it was the wrong continent for that.) I stopped at the Lama Foundation commune in New Mexico, with its huge geodesic dome overlooking a gorgeous near-lunar landscape. Willowy long hairs strummed guitars and spouted nostrums from fourteen or fifteen different spiritual traditions as easily as if they were passing gas. To see them carefully, lovingly milk their goats brought tears of longing to my eyes. Down the road, at a commune called Tree Frog, they had other methods of buoying their spirits, chief among them heroin.

In those days the "Blanket People" wandered the highways wrapped in khaki wool blankets, preaching the gospel of "Lightning Amen," their star-ascended leader—and of marijuana. "Tell me a story," we hippies begged. "It doesn't have to be true." In Seattle I happened on a house where a band of utopian zealots had settled. They handed me a stone that fell open in my hands along a neat split. Inside, it said: "YOU ARE FORGIVEN." They sat all around me with big eyes, waiting for me, at the inspiration of a stone, to have some kind of conversion experience. I wanted to please them, but it was just a trick stone.

Goat milk, heroin, marijuana, split stones—such are the bases of utopianism, and this, too: rational thought. That last is the preferred opiate of your social engineers, your ivory tower revolutionaries. That, and one thing more: blind love.

It took a lot of squinting and smoking for a hippie to retain his utopian ideals in the New Mexico of the sixties and seventies, when they were surrounded by poor Mexican farm families who hated their gringo guts. During the time of my sojourn, a young local who had befriended the bourgeois-parented communards, in an act of tragic class consciousness, killed one of them. I can see a Bellamy laboring over his typewriter in one of those hippie yurts, imagining a future social harmony that the present discord would give rise to.

Like Marx, Bellamy offers an insightful diagnosis of the failures of capitalism but falls down in the prognosis and prescription departments. Bellamy even understands the distortions in the psychology of our store clerks, who are constrained by their calling to lie and manipulate. For Bellamy, the simple act of shopping is a lens into society as a whole. He thought he could fix things with a government-run Wal-Mart. (On the other hand, Internet shopping of today closely corresponds to the ideal that Bellamy projects. All goods are available everywhere, and nobody is tricked to this aisle or that or flattered or wheedled or hard-sold.)

I envy Bellamy his loving optimism. Engels, a few decades earlier, had chronicled the horrors of capitalist industrialization in Manchester and had seen no hope except in violent upheaval. Like the capitalist philosophers whom Bellamy's Reverend Barton mocks for believing "that the antisocial qualities of men, and not their social qualities" are fundamental, Engels saw history as the bloody conflict of the self-interest of the masses of workers against the self-interest of the bosses. That's close to the way I see it—read the papers.

For Bellamy, however—as for Plato and for Pollyanna—ignorance is the only evil. Without great dissension or strife, the transition from the many "trusts" to "The Great Trust" of all the people's government occurs in a single generation, by universal assent. Consider this sentence, astonishing and ridiculous to those of us who actually inhabit the twenty-first century: ". . . the popular sentiment toward great corporations and those identified with them had ceased to be one of bitterness, as they came to realize the necessity as a link, a transitional phase, in the evolution of the true industrial system" (page 38). Well, Marx and the Party "realized" that, too, that capitalism was a necessary step in the progress toward socialist paradise, but "without bitterness"? Of what species can Bellamy have been thinking? Surely not homo sap.

Bottom line: OK, I *adore* Bellamy. I admit it. He cuts to the bone. His vision is radical and incisive: "Buying and selling is essentially antisocial in all its tendencies" (page 57). His morality is vigorous, absolute: "The amount of the effort alone is pertinent to the question of desert" (page 61). How elegant and thoroughgoing is his assessment of charity, full of thunderclap insight and irony: "Did you not rob them when you put them off with crusts . . ." (page 88). Because we are all inheritors of all, as deserving, each of us equally—and as undeserving—as any rich man's child.

I remember once upon a time believing in goodness and purity that way—when I was twelve. I sold straw hats for Jack Kennedy in 1960, for example. Frank Sinatra was crooning songs about ants with "high hopes" who managed to fell rubber trees—that was our America. Vestiges of my high hopes even remained during the Carter years. Here was a guy who kept a list of his campaign promises and checked them off one by one—until he didn't. Who knelt in prayer in the Oval Office and preached to the world about human rights—and he still devotes himself to international good works, Habitat for Humanity, monitoring elections, mediating international disputes, and all. Almost like George Foreman, who ascended from bad-boy fisticuffs to that grill of his, famous and benign. But the fellow also presided over an administration that sold helicopters and guns to Central American governments that used them to slaughter women and children fleeing their noncompliant huts.

I remember encountering my high school world history teacher, a good Catholic, one Sunday outside his church. Mr. McHugh pointed across Lincoln Square at an antiwar banner that hung from a lintel of the Unitarian Church. "They think people can change," he sneered. Original sin was his point.

Finally, I've parted company with the idealists. If they have the courage of their convictions, they end up like Kurtz in Conrad's *Heart of Darkness*, deranged by the squalid fallout of their austere vision; otherwise, like Bellamy and other mere philosophers and litterateurs, ensconced in their armchairs, they cluck and tut and pontificate their way to an illustrious flower-strewn grave—and no consequence.

I'm a Buddhist now. I don't believe in human goodness. I believe in human consciousness. Awareness is our redemption, not goodness. We are incapable of goodness. We are only capable of being aware. For us homo saps, there is no other real good—so I do believe. *Existence is suffering*. That's No. 1 of Uncle Buddha's Four

Truths. Everything is askew. With Miss Clavel, "Something is not right!" but no doctor can ever cure our Madeline. The Great Wheel wobbles, the bearings grind down, we creak and groan and fall apart.

It's the opposite view to that of Bellamy's ilk. Which view, I ask you, is truer to the case? The extravagance of Bellamy's optimism is transparent, for example, in his predictions concerning future attitudes toward inheritance and toward international law. In a society where every person's needs are met simply by virtue of his having been born, accumulation of wealth must be viewed as a burden, not a luxury, because of the difficulty of storing or distributing all the superfluous boodle, he says. No sophist ever reasoned more vacuously. Safes and warehouses and money bins and mansions testify to the contrary, and sufficiency has never been a deterrent to excess. Veblen knew it: conspicuous consumption, class based on waste, potlatch, for pity's sake; like those Kwakiutl chieftains, we make things to destroy them to show that we can. It's not a socially determined quality—it's just *us*.

As to Bellamy's view of the conduct of nations—something Machiavelli had definitively illuminated centuries earlier—it's utter fantasy. For a nation to prefer its own interests, says Bellamy, would cause it to be isolated and punished in the postcapitalist world. "The law," says Dr. Leete, our man of the future, "requires that each nation shall deal with the others, in all respects, on exactly the same footing" (pages 92–93). As if "the law" somehow existed all on its own, independently of the powers and passions of mortal men, and enforced itself once things were properly "regulated." As if might didn't make right and well-financed propaganda didn't predominate over the paupers' truth.

Read the papers. Every article every day confirms Machiavelli and proves poor Bellamy the fool.

Which view is truer to the case . . . ?

"Looking back," sermonizes Reverend Barton, with regard to the labor unrest of the 1880s, "we cannot wonder at their desperation, for certainly humanity was never confronted with a fate more sordid and hideous than would have been the era of corporate tyranny which they anticipated" (page 35).

In other words, *this* era, *our* era, the real one.

But I love Bellamy. I love him. How can you not? When Reverend Barton sermonizes: "The long and weary winter of the race is ended. Its summer has begun. Humanity has burst the chrysalis. The heavens are before it" (page 191), I leap to my feet. The book falls from my hands. Tears fill my eyes. *Looking Backward* tells a story that soars and glisters.

If only it were the least little bit true!

—Eliot Fintushel

SELECTED
BIBLIOGRAPHY

Abrash, Merritt. "*Looking Backward:* Marxism Americanized." *Extrapolation,* vol. 30, no. 3, Fall 1989.

Bellamy, Edward. *The Duke of Stockbridge.* 1879; 1900. Cambridge, MA: Harvard University, 1962.

———. *Equality.* 1897. New York: Greenwood, 1969.

Bowman, Sylvia. *The Year 2000: A Critical Biography of Edward Bellamy.* New York: Bookman, 1958.

———, *et al.,* eds. *Edward Bellamy Abroad: An American Prophet's Influence.* New York: Twayne, 1962.

Franklin, H. Bruce. *Future Perfect: American Science Fiction of the Nineteenth Century.* Revised edition. New York: Oxford University, 1978.

Gardner, Martin. "Looking Backward at Edward Bellamy's Utopia." *The New Criterion,* vol. 19, no 1, September 1, 2000.

Griffith, Nancy. *Edward Bellamy: A Bibliography.* Metuchen, NJ: Scarecrow, 1986.

Halewood, W. H. "Catching up with Edward Bellamy." *University of Toronto Quarterly,* vol. 63, no. 3, Spring 1994.

Hammond, Jeffrey. "Swept Away by One Breath." *Texas Studies in Literature and Language,* vol. 32, no. 2, Summer 1990.

Lens, Sidney. *Radicalism in America.* New York: Crowell, 1966.

Levitas, Ruth. "Utopian Fictions and Political Theories: Domestic Labor in the Work of Edward Bellamy, Charlotte Perkins Gilman, and William Morris." In: Val Gough and Jill Rudd, eds. *A Very Different Story.* Liverpool, England: Liverpool University, 1998.

Morgan, Arthur E. *The Philosophy of Edward Bellamy.* Whitefish, MT: Kessinger, 2008.

Morris, William. "Looking Backward." *The Commonweal,* vol. 5, no. 180, June 27, 1989.

———. *News from Nowhere.* 1891. Asa Briggs, ed. New York: Penguin, 1989.

Patai, Daphne, ed. *Looking Backward: 1988–1888: Essays on Edward Bellamy.* Amherst: University of Massachusetts, 1988.

Peyser, Thomas. *Utopia & Cosmopolis: Globalization in the Era of American Literary Realism.* Durham, NC: Duke University, 1998.

Pfaelzer, Jean. "Nineteenth-Century American Utopianism." *American Transcendental Quarterly,* n. s. 3, March 1989.

Roemer, Kenneth. "The Literary Domestication of Utopia: There's No *Looking Backward* without Uncle Tom and Uncle True." *American Transcendental Quarterly,* n. s. 3, March 1989.

Scheik, William. "The Other Bellamy." *Texas Studies in Language and Literature,* vol. 32, no. 2, Summer 1990.

Widdicomb, Richard. "Dynamite in Disguise: A Deconstructive Reading of Bellamy's Utopian Novels." *American Transcendental Quarterly,* n. s. 3, March 1989.

———. *Edward Bellamy: An Annotated Bibliography of Secondary Criticism.* New York: Garland, 1988.

BIG BROTHER IS WATCHING

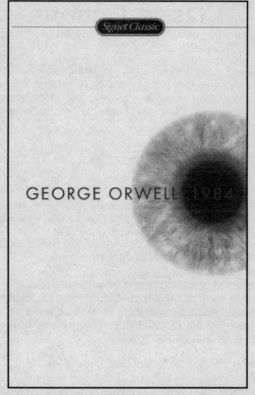

GEORGE ORWELL 1984

**A prophetic, nightmarish vision of a
"Negative Utopia" that's timelier
than ever—and its warnings
more powerful.**

Classic Fiction

LORD JIM
Joseph Conrad
Tortured by his conscience, an arrogant Englishman flees civilization for a distant jungle trading post. Here, alone in a world which few white men visit, a world where he is worshiped by natives, he begins to discover who he really is.

THE SECRET AGENT
Joseph Conrad
This extraordinary novel is one of Conrad's supreme masterpieces and one of the unquestioned classics of the English novel. It tells a chillingly prophetic tale of terrorism and intrigue, and is a precursor to the espionage thrillers of Graham Greene and John le Carré.

DEATH IN VENICE & Other Stories
Thomas Mann
A wonderful new translation of Mann's masterpiece, this is the tragic story of a foolish, forbidden love, the imagined perfection of youth, and the ruin brought about by an obsessive devotion to "the ideal." This volume includes seven other short stories by Mann.

THE RED BADGE OF COURAGE & Four Stories
Stephen Crane
One of the best known war stories of all time, it captures all the emotions of a young man encountering for the first time the horrors of battle. Originally published in 1895, it was immediately acclaimed by Civil War veterans for its vivid and authentic portrayal. This collection also includes four of Crane's best-known stories.